The Religious Right is Wrong

The Ethics of Religion and the Gay Community

DR. F. LEE BARHAM

Bridgeview Publishing
9 0 South Street, Suite 8
adelphia, PA 19147

Acknowledgements

Thanks to Michael Lindlau for his patience, Rabbi Joel Greenberg, Fr. Robert Haller, Ph.D., O.P., Fr. John Bickel, M.Div., MS., OFM, Comv., Bishop John Shelby Spong, Prof. Jeff Markovitz, Ruth Zalesky, Fr. William Auth, O.S.F.S., Rev. Edward Napier and my parents, Floyd and Laura Barham who laid the groundwork for my religious beliefs.

Table of Contents

Article 18

Universal Declaration of Human Rights

Everyone has the right to freedom of thought, conscience and religion; this right includes freedom to change his religion or belief, and freedom, either alone or in community with others and in public or private, to manifest his religion or belief in teaching, practice, worship and observance.`

Ed Dobson,

former VP of Moral Majority, Inc.:

I haven't changed in the sense that I believe sexuality is a gift from God to be expressed exclusively within the commitment of heterosexual marriage and that all other expressions of that are outside the boundaries of God's creative intent as revealed in the Scripture. However, I do not believe that gives you a license to hate people, including homosexuals, and I think part of the struggle for people is that it's easy, it's easy to beat up what you don't understand. I have sat and listened to story after story after story from gay people of their journey and have cried with them and tried to listen to the awful pain they go through. [It] hasn't changed what I believe about the practice of homosexuality, but it has reminded me that 'Whom you would change you must first love.' Martin Luther King, Jr. said that. And in general, Christians have not been very good about loving gay people. Oh, they'll tell you they hate the sin but they love the sinner, but I don't see much love for the sinner.

William Sloane Coffin:

About Leonard Matlovich: a gay
Vietnam War veteran.

He served for 12 years in the US Air Force, received exemplary ratings, won a Bronze Star and Purple Heart. After revealing his homosexual orientation, he was dishonorably discharged. His tombstone reads: "Here lies a man who was given a medal for killing two men, and a dishonorable discharge for loving one.

Bishop John Shelby Spong

Author

I think that we have in recent years entered a "New Dark Age" in the Western world. It is marked by the rise of religious systems that seek to build security by encouraging prejudice against a designated Victim…the homosexual has become the religious hysteria of our day. This kind of behavior is always a response to fear and to a rapidly changing world. Security-providing religion, which always requires a victim, is like a drug that carries us over the rough places of life. It is certainly not the wave of the Christian future.

Preface

$\mathcal{T}$he purpose of this book is to educate, enlighten, challenge and, in some cases, change the attitudes of certain Christians about their closely held but erroneous belief system regarding the Bible and the gay community. While the content is about fundamentalists, or the conservative Christian movement, they are not the primary target of my writing. By the very nature of their belief system, fundamentalists cannot consider an alternate view of the Bible, because the basis of their faith is, and always has been, that the Bible as an infallible, inerrant, and unchanging guide in their quest for salvation and eternal life. For these Christians, the Bible is to be read and accepted at face value. They believe it is pure truth, as presented, word-for-word. I doubt fundamentalists will or can participate in the discussions presented in this book. In fact, I believe they will condemn this work. However, I believe there are many Christians, in and out of the gay community, who can and will appreciate a "gay reading" of the Holy Scriptures.

Toward this goal, some in the gay community must learn to surrender their engrained prejudices of unworthiness directed toward themselves and their brothers and sisters in the gay community. The would-be gay Christian must learn to ignore the various hurtful, sinful titles given them by the conservative religious-right. Just as they have the right to interpret the Bible and its mysteries, so does the gay community. It is this "suffering" and struggling group for whom this material is written. I trust the "arrow" finds its "mark."

Mark Twain

Loyalty to a petrified opinion never yet broke a chain or freed a human soul

Introduction

G rowing up gay in the religious South of the 1940s, I experienced firsthand the stigma that fundamentalist Christianity imposed on homosexuals. I became aware of "feelings" for members of the same sex when I was about seven. As time passed, my feelings grew stronger and stronger until as a teenager I knew beyond a shadow of a doubt, I was different, even though I didn't know the words to describe this difference. Although I tried to live a life that was in keeping with my childhood faith, it was difficult, because I was taught that my sexual orientation was sinful and scorned both by Christians and by Christ. Over time, my sexual orientation and my religion clashed, until, as a mature adult, I concluded that the religious prohibitions against homosexuality were not the true teachings of a loving Christ.

In this book, I share some of the information that led me to reshape my views of Christ, Christianity, and the world of the religious-right as it affects the American gay community in the 21st century.

Although acceptance of the gay community and their lifestyle has increased among Americans in the past fifty years, gays are still stigmatized as much, if not more, than before by those with a fundamentalist Christian background or leaning. Religious fundamentalism, or orthodoxy, is a part of many, if not most religions. It's a feature of orthodoxy to be convinced one is right, that one is following the truth. A corollary is the belief that it's one's duty to make sure everyone else does the same by instituting laws (religious and secular) that will force them to comply.

First, let me begin by defining some terms. Orthodox or evangelical religious leaders and their followers, of all religions, are known as fundamentalists. In general, fundamentalists believe their scripture is holy, divinely inspired, ordained by their god, and are to be accepted at face value, word for word. In this book, I will limit my comments to fundamentalists who are Christian, sometimes called the religious-right, a religiously motivated political group in the United States.[1]

Terms like "Christian right" and "religious-right" are often used interchangeably, although they are not synonymous. "Religious-right" includes Christians, Muslims, Orthodox Jews, and others. They sometimes cooperate in national and international projects through the World Congress of Families and United Nations NGO gatherings. "Christian right" on the other hand refers only to the Christian segment of the religious-right.

The term "Christian right" comprises approximately 15% of the voting public in the United States. This group usually votes for candidates who are members of the

---

1   http://www.theocracywatch.org/introduction2.htm

Republican Party. John C. Green of the Pew Forum on Religion and Public Life said Jerry Falwell used the label "religious-right" to describe himself, until the phrase developed negative connotations, such as hard-edged politics or intolerance. As a result of this connotation, few people applied the term to describe themselves. Gary Schneeberger, vice president of media and public relations for Focus on the Family, once said that the term "religious-right" had been traditionally used in a pejorative way to suggest extremism. The phrase "socially conservative evangelicals," while not very exciting, was the preferred way to describe the group.

Evangelical leaders, like Tony Perkins of the Family Research Council, have called attention to the problem of equating the term "religious-right" with evangelicals. Although evangelicals constitute the core constituency of the Christian right, not all evangelicals fit the description. The problem of description is further complicated by the fact that "religious conservative" may refer to groups like the Mennonites and the Amish, who are theologically conservative but not involved in politics.[2]

Conservative political groups, motivated by religion, are often referred to as the religious-right. Just as some Jews want to establish a religious state in Israel and some Muslims want to establish a world-wide religious state based on the Quran, some Christian fundamentalists want to establish a theocracy in the United States, that is, a government subject to the authority of religion.

In America, most members of the religious-right are politically conservative and often belong to groups like the Republican Party and/or the Tea Party, although they may belong to other political groups as well.

Generally speaking, most Americans have a "live and let live" philosophy, and they are willing to share with others the American dream of equality for all, provided no harm is done to anyone. Not so with the members of the religious-right. Their actions suggest that they want all Americans, of all faiths or no faith, to live by rules and laws that support only their own fundamentalist beliefs. People with these ultra-conservatives beliefs are sometimes called Dominionists. According to WordIQ.com, Dominionism is "a trend in Protestant Christian evangelicalism and fundamentalism that encourages not just active political participation in civic society but also attempts to take over and dominate the political process." Dominionists often deride other conservative religions, such as Islam, and are extremely biased toward their own brand of Christianity. They believe theirs is the one true religion whether or not others are willing to accept such a pronouncement. I call this attitude of dominance a tyranny!

The faith of most Christians, or other religious people, is not reasoned but taught, learned, and accepted on trust from a caring family member or friend, or an admired minister, priest, rabbi, or mullah. Most people are born into a religion, and each person has his or her own biases. Most Christians were born into a Christian family. They didn't first explore other faiths before choosing Christianity.

While many believers may attempt to understand their faith, many others accept it as a truth that needs only to be obeyed, not understood. Few fundamentalists seem to

---

2   http://www.answers.com/topic/Christian-right#ixzzldy0Bmhi

question their religious beliefs. This, I would argue, leads to a blind acceptance of their espoused religion without truly knowing Christ and his teachings through the Bible, or understanding how God wants us to interact with Him. Many believers fail to recognize that the Bible they read was, and is, interpreted and translated by people who have their own biases. This applies to the publishers of the Bible as well as its readers.

Some traditional beliefs become matters of faith, even if the Bible has nothing to say about them. For example, although the New Testament doesn't mention whether or not Christ was married, fundamentalists castigate anyone who raises the possibility that He might have had a wife, no doubt because the idea that Christ might have had carnal thoughts and feelings or engaged in carnal acts like other men offends them. Perhaps, for them, sex is too sullied for God to have participated. Yet these same people will tell you that Christ was God and man. To ignore his humanity seems a contradiction to me.

As a young Jewish male of his era, Christ was probably under great societal (and probably parental) pressure to take a wife. If he did marry, he no doubt had sex. To fundamentalists, even thinking such a thought is anathema, but I ask—would having sex have made him any less God? Apparently, fundamentalists think it would. Perhaps they believe Christ, the man, was above being a "man." If God, as man, could be born, walk, weep, speak, sleep, eat and die, why couldn't he have been human in all areas of life? Fundamentalists tell us such thoughts are evil, to which I say that attitudes like these show that fundamentalists use emotion to support their faith, which leads them to dislike, disdain, and even hate other Christians who don't share their views.

Blind faith in fundamentalism permits religious extremists to demonize gay people, and this in turn allows them to lash out at the gay community in religious, social, and political ways that are harmful to all Americans. Fundamentalists do this because they say the Bible tells them so. I believe the religious-right is wrong!

CHAPTER I

Fundamentalism: a brief history

...there is always the likelihood that any theology that claims to be universal is not more than theology from the particular perspective of those who are in power.

JUSTO GONZALES: *OUT OF EVERY TRIBE AND NATION*

a few times in my life, I have thought it would have been good for me to have been born into fundamentalist family where my father was a minister. Perhaps, through such an experience, I might understand how Christians are taught to hate the gay community. Additional insight would have also come from directly knowing something about the history and intent of fundamentalism.

Fundamentalism has existed in one form or another since ancient times. Invariably, it seems to emerge from the extreme swings of the pendulum concerning religious beliefs. Various civilizations have often seen one religious movement altered or replaced with another faith or blending of a foreign faith with an extant belief system. Some of these changes have been promulgated by wars, art, travel, political changes, philosophical movements, science, prophets, ministers, rabbis, mullahs, popes, and politicians. Invariably, the Christian fundamentalist movement is an attempt to return to a more familiar, simple and easily understood belief system. Protestant reformers such as Martin Luther, John Calvin, and others looked backward to older Christian traditions to anchor their reforms. Richard Marius's book, *Martin Luther, the Christian Between God and Death,* details how Luther, filled with hate that aggravated his already disturbed mental state, pulled away from Catholicism. He recreated the religious conservatism which became Protestantism (protestors). Luther's conservatism was, however, less conservative than the Church of Rome during his era.

The Puritans are often spoken of in semi-reverent tones as the founders of America. Their arrival in the New World was not to create an America like the one we know today. They were leaving England because they could no longer tolerate the religious structure (bishops, priests, etc.) they had known in the Anglican Church. While they embraced the official King James Version of the Bible they wanted nothing to do with the Anglican rituals that harkened back to the Catholic Church. The Puritans wanted to worship God in the ways and methods they *thought* the early Church had utilized. They had little or no knowledge of the many forms of early Christian beliefs and methods of worship, e.g., Gnosticism. Freedom of belief, for all people, was not their goal in the new world. They wanted everyone to be Puritan. In a sense they wanted and had a theocracy. There are those who still believe America needs to be a theocracy – a conservative, Christian theocracy.

....

Christians have made an *idol* out of the Bible.

ELIZABETH STUART, *JUST GOOD FRIENDS*

....

I find it ironic that the religious-right frequently relies on the King James Version of the Bible to support their denouncement of the gay community. Historians have proven that King James was, beyond a doubt, a gay man, and a *flaming-gay* at that. Author Rick Norton has written how King James was actually mocked after his coronation, "Rex fuit Elizabeth: nunc est regina Jacobus." Literally translated "As Elizabeth was King: Now James is Queen.

"King James (1603-1625) had a lover in the person of George Villiers, the Duke of Buckingham, who is buried in the Henry VII Chapel of Westminster Abbey near the body of his lover, King James. The duke was killed by a soldier who had been under his command. The soldier believed the duke was the "anti-Christ" and had to die. The duke's tombstone/plaque reads, "THE Enigma of the World." After all, the duke was a man who rose to the highest rank in the royal court despite his widely alleged affair.[3] (See Norton in the Bibliography.)

More than 200 years after King James' death, Dwight Moody, a prominent evangelist, founded the Moody Bible Institute (1886) in Chicago to preserve conservative Biblical teachings. By 1930 there were some fifty fundamentalist Bible colleges in the United States. Another twenty-six were added during the Depression years. The founding of Bible colleges was not the only way in which the fundamentalists tried to protect their religious turf and belief system. They created broadcasting companies,

---

3   http://en.wikipedia.org/wiki/George_Villiers,_1st_Duke_of_Buckingham

founded publishing houses to help spread the word, and created a world of religious conservatism.

Generally speaking, long-term, geographically conservative areas had less intense or later occurring fundamentalist movements. This was especially true in America's South, which had been conservative in its religious beliefs since the founding of our country. The North had long held a more liberal social, political, and religious outlook on life. It was the Border States, Virginia in particular, which had the most active fundamentalist movements in the mid-20th century. These movements centered on Jerry Falwell (in the Lynchburg area), Pat Robertson (in Virginia Beach), Jim and Tammy Faye Bakker (in Charlotte, North Carolina) and James Dobson (now of Colorado Springs). It was James Dobson, through Karl Rove (political adviser), who had blessed President George W. Bush's appointment of Harriet Miers' nomination to the Supreme Court. President Bush needed Dobson's blessing, "given as a qualification to any public office." This public pronouncement was reported in an article, 'Faith Based Hypocrisy,' in the *Washington Post* on October 7, 2005, page A23. Southern California had its share of fundamentalist activity and is still generally known as a very conservative area. Jerry Falwell may best be known for his Moral Majority which had four purposes. The organization was:

1. **Pro-life**: meaning antiabortion. The organization wanted to over Roe v. Wade
2. **Pro-family**: meaning anti-gay marriage and antigay rights of any kind.
3. **Pro-moral**: being against immorality and promoted the use of "moral" people to elect other moral people to legislative and administrative offices to help institutionalize the aims of the Moral Majority.
4. **Pro-American**: a code word for making America Christian again through Christian politics.

Each center of religious activity had, in various ways, attempted to isolate itself from the threatening secular world so often described as: atheistic, a cesspool, Satan filled, nihilistic, degrading, enslaving etc. Minnesota Representative Michele Bachmann is the latest politician to promote the thought that homosexuality enslaves its members. For decades, the movement saw the promulgation of centers of education espousing their own conservative religious beliefs.

In May 1994, religious representatives from Colorado, Arkansas, California, Florida, Hawaii, Kansas, Kentucky, Michigan, Missouri, New Mexico, New York, Ohio, Oregon, Rhode Island, Texan, Virginia, and Washington gathered in Colorado Springs to plan a culture war against a large group of American citizens known as the gay community. Had it not been for a leak to the *Washington Times* newspaper, (May 19, 1994, section: A, Nation, edition 2, p. A3), the world may not have known of this secret plan. Reporter Valerie Richardson described the secret meeting at the Glen Eyrie Conference Center in Colorado:

Leaders of anti-homosexual-rights groups across the nation wrapped up two days of top-secret meetings here yesterday aimed at strengthening their movement before the critical November elections. In the first national meeting of its kind, representatives from about 40 state organizations gathered at the birthplace of Amendment 2,[4] the only statewide anti-homosexual-rights measure to be approved by voters to discuss strategies for repeating its success.

A recording of the event found its way into a private collection. The ultimate owner, Skip Porteus, donated the tapes, an extensive library of gay-related ephemera, and other fundamentalist anti-gay material to Tuft's University Library for online cataloging. These materials had been in the collection of the Institute of First Amendment Studies and are cataloged in Tuft's library. [5] In a simple, but effective move, the leaders of the religious-right who attended the meeting changed their focus from national politics to local politics. Frederick Clarkson wrote in the Nov/Dec 1991 issue of *The Freedom Writer*, "The Christian Coalition intends to take over the Republican Party from the inside, and elect thousands of right-wing Christians to state and local office, as well as the Congress, through a massive and disciplined bloc of voters." The religious-right had found the missing ingredient necessary to galvanize their constituents—hate. An important social issue like homosexuality was just the thing needed to incite their members' movement and ensure their continued political and financial existence. It was "militant homosexuals" or the "gay agenda" they fronted as their *raison d'être*. Nancy Ammerman chronicled these aspects of fundamentalism in her article, "North American Protestant Fundamentalism" that was later included in the book *Fundamentalism's Observed* (1991).

The 1950s saw the arrival of television which not only brought Entertainment into an ever increasing number of American homes but also extended the reach of the fundamentalists' movement. Oral Roberts was a leading televangelist of the 1970s. He later founded a college and medical center to promote conservative religious beliefs and combine God's and man's healing abilities. Part of the plan-of-care for patients in his hospital was the religious gift of daily prayers.

Many of the early fundamentalists were itinerate, tent evangelists who often conducted week long revivals. Evangelists Billy Graham and Rex Humbard joined the ranks of the televangelists who slowly replaced the ubiquitous roaming revivalist preachers. Many of these televangelists became household names. Among them, Billy Graham became an adviser to American Presidents

While modern fundamentalists were not always friendly to other Christians who did not embrace their conservative movement, these modern conservatives were not as ruthless as those of the fourteenth century. At that time, Christians dragged Jews to baptismal founts demanding that they accept the conservative Catholic, Christian faith

---

4   Later struck down as unconstitutional by Colorado's courts.

5   http://nils.lib.tufts.edu/

or face death. Cathar Christians[6] and Muslims also met their deaths, because of their differences with conservative religious beliefs.

Changing times can and do cause some people to look backward and long for a time past when things were more comfortable or had more meaning. This looking back was exemplified by the reformers of the middle ages. Martin Luther, John Calvin, and others looked back to more ancient Christian traditions to find meaning that helped each, in their own way, establish a new equilibrium in their personal belief system. As Luther was consolidating his attitudes about a need for change within the Catholic Church, he was tormented by his hate and rage against the Pope, the Turks, Jews, women, etc. Richard Marius, in his book, *Martin Luther, the Christian between God and Death,* details Luther's pain at the loss of his previous beliefs that led to his new Protestantism. Not unlike other reformers and conservatives, their love of God is offset by hatred for those who did not share their religious beliefs. Not unlike modern radical Islamists, some religious reformers like John Calvin and Huldrych Zwingli (the Luther of Switzerland) were prepared to kill dissidents. For these fundamentalists, logic or reasoning had little, if anything, to do with their religious beliefs.

Luther was the first major Protestant religious leader to push reasoning out of religion. In doing so, he was the first to secularize Christianity, according to author Richard Marius. It seems Luther believed that an emphasis on individual faith would make *truth* more subjective. This kind of understanding has created a belief system more in keeping with modern Western mentality. Simply stated, Luther wanted to shun the godless world while Calvin and Zwingli believed that Christians should engage in the political and social life of the times.

Calvin saw no reason to discriminate between science and religion. According to Alister McGrath, *A Life of John Calvin* (1988), the Bible, was not to be taken literally but as a vehicle to convey truth in terms that human beings could grasp and understand. This is not the current attitude of many twenty first century fundamentalists who believe the Bible should be read and understood literally. This conflict can be seen in the concept of the Holy Trinity which is never mentioned in the Bible.

The concept of the Trinity was a slowly evolving concept that reached its culmination in the creedal statement of Nicea and Chaldcedon. The roots of the concept are found in the New Testament, especially Johanine theology. It was fourth century Greek Orthodox theologians who first conceived the notion of the Holy Trinity.

> …Father, Son and Spirit are not objective facts but simply terms we use'
> to express the way in which the 'unnamable and unspeakable' divine
> nature adapts itself to the limitations of our human minds.

These are the words of Gregory of Nyssa in "Not Three Gods" as noted in Karen Armstrong's book, *A History of God* (1993). Modern fundamentalists accept the Holy

---

6   Sect with dualistic and Gnostic elements in the Languedoc region of France in the 11th century and flourished in the 12th and 13th centuries. They did not believe in one all-encompassing god.

Trinity as a fact and make that understanding a major part of their religious belief system.

At the turn of the twentieth century, America had arrived at the so called Progressive Age in which citizens tried to grapple with the problems of the industrial age and urban living. While all was not well within the various Protestant denominations, they did cooperate in such things as foreign missionary work, promoting prohibition of alcohol, and improving education, especially religious education. Protestants produced a *Social Gospel* as a way of returning to the perceived old ways of the Hebrew prophets, Jesus, and the New Testament, i.e., visit the sick, visit prisons, feed and clothe the poor, etc. They even went so far as to set up institutions that would provide these services on church grounds, much like today's city missions. The Salvation Army is a good example of the movement.

In 1910, the Presbyterians of Princeton produced the five fundamental dogmas essential to their faith:

1. The inerrancy of the Holy Bible,
2. The virgin birth of Christ,
3. Christ's death on the cross as atonement for sins,
4. The bodily resurrection of Christ,
5. His miracles as reality.

The literal interpretation of the Bible was a primary tenet of the Presbyterian belief system and a world goal of many conservatives in the early Twentieth Century. They also promoted the concept of the inerrancy of the Holy Scriptures. Regarding this matter, I would like to quote from Robin Meyers' book, *Why the Religious-right is Wrong,* p. 143,

> …as one of my seminary professors pointed out, that not a single person whose words ultimately became part of the Bible had any idea that he or she was writing a part of the Bible. What's more, none of them wrote in English, meaning that the various translations (and mistranslations) that we now possess cannot possibly be the literal word of God…That means we must 'interpret' the Bible, and that is fraught with danger. The only thing more dangerous is not interpreting it—carefully, critically, honestly.

William Bell Riley, founder of several schools including a seminary, and A.C. Dixon convened a Philadelphia conference in 1919 to address issues near and dear to the hearts of religious conservatives. Thousands of conservative Christians attended the meeting and established the World's Christian Fundamentals Association. It was an interdenominational organization founded by the Reverend Riley of the First Baptist Church, Minneapolis, Minnesota. It was created to launch a new Protestantism based upon premillennial interpretations of biblical prophecy. The organization soon turned its focus more towards their opposition to evolution. However, their overall goal was to promote a conservative religious front against the political and religious liberals (evolutionists) of the day. Author, Marsden, in *Fundamentalism and American Culture*, quoted Riley as proclaiming that his was a long-term goal and said, "It is a war from which there is no discharge."[7]

In 1920, Curtis Lee Law,* while attending the annual Northern Baptist Convention, declared and defined a fundamentalist as someone ready to,

> …do battle to regain territory lost to Antichrist and to do battle royal for
> the fundamentals of the faith.

His quote was printed in the *Watchtower Examiner* and widely distributed to fellow fundamentalists.

The fundamentalist and Presbyterian theologian J. Gresham Machen argued in his book, *Christianity and Liberation*,

> …[that] liberals were pagans and anyone denying the virgin birth of
> Christ denied Christianity itself.

Another conservative person, the psychologist James H. Leuba of Bryn Mawr College, went on to write in *Belief in God and Immorality*,

> …statistics had proven that a college education endangered religious
> belief.

When read as literature, the Bible can be seen as one of the most unusual works of literary art in history, but to teach it in secular schools, as religious authority, would be incompatible with the integrity of an educator's role.

According to Jerome Segal (p.24),

> The Bible is almost never read as literature. Almost all reading of it is
> through the lens of religion whether or not one reads it as Scripture.

Those who read the Bible as literature will find their understanding of it will differ significantly than a reading of it as a religious text. One comes to Biblical texts with certain central religious beliefs and certain purposes that make sense only in context of our beliefs (biases). Inerrancy is one of those mind sets no matter the fact that the Bible contains contradictions.

The point in question is one statement that is contradictory to many Christian's belief about God's exclusive divinity. In Genesis, Chapter 6, we read about the "sons of God" or divine beings. These beings find human females attractive and together

---

7   http://www.christianethicstoday.com/issue/018

they give birth to half human and half divine creatures. Aren't these statements contradictory to our general thoughts about the Bible and its inerrancy? Are these divine beings not also divine or God like? Are they not immortal? Is the Bible polytheistic? We should keep in mind that the name for *God* is really a derivative from many ancient tribal deities also called god.

What would the fundamentalist's belief system have us believe about God and morality as seen in the Old Testament? The Bible does not tell us that God is well motivated, just, or the source of morality. In fact the Bible suggests that God had regrets about making mankind who became evil (not very god like). He tells us he would never do (regrets?) a certain thing again (destroy the earth by flooding). Moses convinced God to change his plans over and over in the Exodus story. Abraham asked God to be just at the moment he is about to be unjust by destroying all the people of Sodom—apparently the few good citizens as well. These facts don't seem to challenge many fundamentalist's claim of biblical inerrancy. They function outside an "educated" or informed reading of the sacred texts.

The theory of Darwinism had an important impact on the conservative belief system of many American Christians. Their loss of face in the Scopes' "monkey trial" bruised them considerably. The then tarnished image of the conservative Christian was largely due to the inept skills of the plaintiff's attorney, William Jennings Bryan. The Scopes' trial had failed to leave the liberals mortally wounded—the avowed goal of the conservative plaintiff. The liberals persevered. Maynard Shipley wrote in *The War of Modern Science,*

> …if the fundamentalists managed to seize power in the denominations
> and impose their strictures on the people by law, Americans would lose
> the best part of their culture and be dragged back to the Dark Ages.

Once again, the fundamentalists felt threatened. Their faith sprang from deep seated fear that could not be comforted by purely rational argument alone. Fundamentalist conservatism still coexisted with liberalism but in great contention. This produced anxiety, and when attacked, the conservatives lashed out with extremely bitter aggressiveness, often while smiling and speaking in quiet tones (often through clenched teeth) saying, "We love the sinner but hate the sin." Some conservatives retreated to further refine and defend their faith.

Robin Meyers (p. 23), has this to say,

> Fundamentalists of all stripes love a bully pulpit but hate a round table
> [discussion]. Why share power when you are right and everyone else is
> wrong? Who needs dialogue when your monologue is sacrosanct? Why
> let false prophets [non-fundamentalists] into the room when you can
> bolt the door and preach to the choir?

Among the more conservative fundamentalists are the Pentecostals. They are a renewalist, Christian religious movement that places great emphasis on a personal experience of God through baptism of the Holy Spirit and speaking in tongues. This religious phenomenon is a regular part of their religious service and a few other conservative Christian Churches. These Christians believe God, acting through the Holy Spirit, plays a direct role in all aspects of their everyday life.

The Pentecostals returned to a core of values that had been described as the "psyche in which the unending struggle for a sense of purpose and significance goes on." They tried to access a primal spirituality that lay beneath the creedal formulations of their tradition, yearning for ecstasy and transcendence, as a way of escaping the spiritual absence of the brave, new, and wickedly modern world.

The first Christians were the twelve apostles. Some experts identify the apostles as the earliest Christian conservatives. We do not, however, hear of them being baptized of water as Christ had done, but, on the day of Pentecost, they received a baptism of the Holy Spirit and began to speak in tongues. In the early 20th century, Methodist minister, Charles Parham began teaching that modern Christians could speak in tongues, like the ancient disciples, if they were baptized with, or filled with, the Holy Spirit.

Today's Pentecostal churches rarely have ministers with advanced degrees or conduct uniform, worship rituals. They often believe that Pentecostal ministers have the power to cast out demons and devils and can heal various afflictions. I have heard some Pentecostal Christians say, "A service without the spirit bringing down tongues and causing the speaking in tongues would be missing something in their worship of God." Some Christians have called this unintelligible speech Christian *babble*. The sounds are said to be like crooning, keening or jabber.

While some religious conservatives and fundamentalists cling to this form of worship, Paul had something to say about speaking in tongues. His words, as seen below, are a disputed translation by some scholars.

I Corinthian 14:5,

> I would that ye all spake with tongues, but rather that ye prophesied:
> for greater [is] he that prophesieth than he that speaketh with tongues,
> except he interpret, that the church may receive edifying.

Paul wants church members to spend their time in spreading Christ's teaching, not speaking in unknown tongues.

"Ecstatic speech or 'speaking-in-tongues' was so greatly prized by some Christians in ancient Corinth that the apostle Paul said this in one of his letters to the Church:

I Corinthians: 14:19,

Yet in the church I had rather speak five words with my understanding, that [by my voice] I might teach others also, than ten thousand words in an [unknown] tongue.

I Corinthians: 14:27,

If any man speak in an [unknown] tongue,
[let it be] by two, or at the most [by] three, and
[that] by course; and let one interpret.

I Corinthians: 14:28,

But if there be no interpreter, let him keep silence in the church; and let him speak to himself, and to God.

Those drawn to the Pentecostal churches, where speaking in tongues is common, seem to be interested in structure such as the inerrancy of the Bible, strong rules about NOT drinking alcohol, NOT using tobacco and NO premarital sex and observing strict social rules. In Africa, where, the movement is strong, there is often a strong background of belief in the spirit world (animist) where malevolent spirits (in America, the devil) abound and are ready to produce evil in the lives of humans. These cultural / religious taboos are quite in keeping with people who need structure as a part of past lives devastated by poverty, addictions and poor health.

The Pentecostals and other conservatives seemed to withdraw into their collective shells in the 1930s. They created their own institutions where they felt safe and secure from the sinful and profane communities which surrounded them.

They shut themselves off as did the ancient Hebrews from their idolatrous neighbors. Anger fermented as Christian fundamentalism became a religion of rage and distrust. Conservative ministers spoke angrily from their pulpits and radio programs about the heathen beliefs of non-conservative Christians. The Reverend Pat Robinson of the Christian Broadcasting Network (700 Club) made a public announcement following a sizeable earthquake along the eastern seaboard in August, 2011, as being caused by metrosexuals—men acting "partially gay," getting facials and manicures.

Some say the conservatives' anger grew from fear, but fear of what? Conservatives felt that if they did not fight back against a number of liberal ideas there might not be another generation of believers to carry on their conservative religious beliefs [Christ will let Christianity die out].

In the middle of the twentieth century, Conservative Christians began sending their children to church schools, which in turn began to coalesce, creating associations with the impact of a political pact to lobby governments for laws favorable to their conservative religious beliefs. It often appeared that the conservatives wanted to clone, not babies, but their personal religious beliefs at the expense of other's personal beliefs.

In the 1970s, The Internal Revenue Service (IRS) threatened to cancel the tax exempt status of some conservative, religious colleges because their institutional rules were counter to those of public policy. The Supreme Court supported the IRS's move against Goldsborough Christian Schools in North

Carolina, which had refused to admit African-Americans, and Bob Jones

University, which banned interracial dating on its campus, claiming the Bible forbade interracial relationships. Racial discrimination and hatred had become an acceptable conservative Christian value.

> The idea that religion and politics don't mix was invented by the Devil to keep Christians from running their own country.
>
> **JERRY FALWELL,**

Secular humanism became the target of conservative movements in the late twentieth Century. Secular humanism is based on a philosophy that embraces human reason, ethics, and justice, in the search for human fulfillment. It specifically rejects religious dogma but holds a viewpoint that ideology—be it religious or political—must be thoroughly examined by the individual and not simply accepted or rejected on faith. The name *secular humanism* is still tossed about in the twenty-first century by conservatives who carry on their battle for religious fundamentalism.

The Pro-Family Forum defined and published their definition of secular humanism in The publication, *Is Humanism Molesting Your Child?* The article listed the following elements entailed in the definition.
Secular Humanism:

- Denies the deity of God, the inspiration of the Bible and the divinity of Jesus Christ.
- Denies the existence of the soul, life after death, salvation and heaven, damnation and hell.
- -Denies the Biblical account of Creation.
- -Believes that there are no absolutes, no right, no wrong—that moral values are self-determined and situational. Do your own thing, "as long as it does not harm anyone else."
- Believes in the removal of distinctive roles of male and female.
- Believes in sexual freedom between consenting individuals, regardless of age, including premarital sex, homosexuality, lesbianism and incest.

- Believes in the right to abortion, euthanasia, and suicide.
- Believes in the equal distribution of America's wealth to reduce poverty and bring about equality.
- Believes in control of the environment, control of energy and its limitation.
- Believes in the removal of American patriotism, and the free enterprise system, disarmament and the creation of one-world socialistic government.

It is interesting to note that the care of the poor and the environment was seen as evil by some of the earliest members of the fundamentalist movement. They argued that the "end" was near and time should not be spent on anything other than getting sinners to Christ—saving souls.

In 1980, the Council for Democracy and Secular Humanism produced their own definition of secular humanism.[8] It expounds on the subject to include:

1. Free inquiry
2. Separation of church and state
3. The ideas of freedom
4. Ethics based on critical intelligence
5. Moral education
6. Religious skepticism
7. Reason
8. Science and technology
9. Evolution and
10. Education

Tim LaHaye wrote in, *The Battle for the Family*, human secularism was "…anti-God, anti-moral, anti-self-restraint and anti-American." He went on to say that, "secular humanism was promoted by a small cadre of liberals that controlled the government, public schools and the television net- works, in order to destroy Christianity and the American Family."

In the *Return of the Puritans*, according to the fundamentalist author, Pat Brooks,

> …the secular humanists formed a huge conspiratorial network which was fast approaching its goal of bringing in a new world order, a vast world government that would reduce the world to slavery.

The fundamentalists seemed to believe that America was God's country and its God was a Christian God. They did not, however, share the same set of values that were so fanatically *back to the "good ole days"* of the Puritans. They did, however, long for

---

8   http://www.secularhumanism.org

the fervor of the earlier hellfire and brimstone tent revivals so prevalent in earlier conservative communities. The modern fundamentalists were more interested in having the *right* governance in church and state, believing that such a goal would "…compel other men to walk in the right way." John Eidsmore stated in *God and Caesar* that "The Founding Fathers certainly did not want a pure, direct democracy in which the majority can do as it pleases." The idea that a government would implement laws apart from God's laws was anathema to these staunch conservatives.

Hal Lindsey whom we know from his book, *The Late Great Planet Earth,* seemed to join the conservative movement at the end of the 1970s. In 1980, he published *Countdown to Arma*geddon, in which he wrote,

> …we must actively take on the responsibility of being a citizen and member of God's family…we must elect officials who will…reflect the Bible's morality in government. [and] shape domestic [and]…foreign policies to protect…our way of life.

Televangelist, Pat Robertson wrote in *American Date with Destiny,*

> The American revolutionaries had wanted nothing to do with mass rule; they wanted to establish a republic in which the will of the majority and all egalitarian tendencies would be controlled by Biblical law.

This protection took the form of televangelism. Some ministers saw television as a way of delivering God's message to many more sinners and worshippers than they could ever reach from their pulpits. Television-religion began to proliferate and, in its heyday, produced over a billion dollars in annual revenue for the industry, while employing over a thousand people, according to Susan Harding who reported on the Praise The Lord Ministries scandal. Jerry Falwell said that in the 1970s about 40 percent of Americans owning television sets listened to his televised sermons. The Reverend D. James Kennedy of Ft. Lauderdale, Florida's, Coral Ridge Church was another prominent televangelist who had been a staunch supporter of all that was conservative and fundamental. This minister was guided by a list of *Beliefs.*

One of which is listed here:

> **Belief**: There should be no separation of church and state. That doctrine exists only in the minds of liberals…It is not in the Con- stitution, First Amendment, the Bill of Rights or anywhere else for that matter. It appears only as a passing comment in a personal letter from Thomas Jefferson that carries no constitutional weight. The wall of repression erected against religious values through the deliberate misrepresentation of Jefferson's words, however, has led to a plague of relativism and moral decay that has eroded civic responsibility and moral decency in the country for the past 100 years.

On October 7, 1801, the Baptist Association, of Danbury Connecticut, sent a letter to the newly elected President, Thomas Jefferson, in which they voiced concerns that there was not enough protection of religious liberty in their State's constitution. They were concerned that there could be a state- established religion (State religion was one reason so many people left Europe for the new world). The Danbury Baptists noted that:

> Our sentiments are uniformly on the side of religious liberty—religion is at all times and places a matter between God and individuals—that no man ought to suffer in name, person or effects on account of his religious opinions—that the legitimate power of civil government extends no further than to punish the man who works ill to his neighbor…

The Danbury Baptists were a religious minority in Connecticut and concerned that some religious majority might

> …reproach their chief magistrate…because he will not, dare not assume the prerogatives of Jehovah and make laws to govern the Kingdom of Christ, thus establishing a state religion at the cost of the liberties of religious minorities.

President Jefferson responded to the Baptist in a letter dated January 1, 1802, in which he concurs with the religious group's views on religious liberty and the separation of civil government from church affairs.

Jefferson wrote:

> …I contemplate with sovereign reverence that act of the whole American people which declared that their legislature should make no law respecting an establishment of religion, or prohibiting the free exercise thereof,' thus building a wall of separation between Church & State.

In the 20th century, secular humanism continued to threaten and raised its ugly head against conservatives for decades. The movement was offered by conservatives as the blame for many of America's problems. While sex was generally a subject not often discussed by the fundamentalists, there grew a perceived problem about the softening of masculinity in American men. Tom and Beverly LaHaye discussed their concerns regarding men's impotence in their book, *The Act of Marriage*. They said, modern men were,

> …less certain of their manhood than formerly. Men were sexually troubled and concerned about their wives' sexual satisfaction.

The alleged reason for all these male problems was the new self-assertion of women, which was made possible by secular humanism running rampant in the country. "Men," they said, "were becoming feminized and castrated."

Homosexuality's perceived growth in America was as feared as the alleged feminization of America's men and was blamed for America's moral decline. During one of his televised programs, the well-known televangelist, James Robinson said, "… [homosexuality] is almost too repulsive to imagine or describe." Fundamentalist writers seemed to overlook the fact that it might be possible that conservative Christians may be responsible for the sad state of sexual affairs they protested. It is as though they deplored the very traits they wanted Christian men to espouse. They promoted Christian values such as: forgiveness, mercy, tenderness, etc., which many men considered to be feminine characteristics. The conservatives wanted tough, virile, militant, and aggressive Christian men, not "soft" Christ-like men. Conservatives wanted warriors, Christian soldiers.

In 1978, there was significant friction within a more moderate religious organization known as the Christian Voice. This was an advocacy group which promoted conservative Christian standards. The group employed hundreds of political organizers, including Susan Hirschman, Chief of Staff to former House Majority Leader Tom DeLay. Congressman Tom Hagadorn chaired the organization for several years. Tim LaHaye, co-author of the *Left Behind* series had also been active in the organization. Many of the techniques used by twentieth century political campaigns to garner votes were developed by Christian Voice. However, its early leading members: Paul Weyrich, Terry Dolan, Richard Viguerie (all Catholic) and Howard Phillips desired a more vocal and conservative organization than Christian Voice was prepared to become. These four leaders severed their ties with Christian Voice and recruited Jerry Falwell to found the group known as the Moral Majority. This organization came into existence for several reasons, but it too promoted a stronger and more virile Christian manhood.

…the impious presumption of legislators and rulers, civil as well as ecclesiastical who, being themselves but fallible and uninspired men, have assumed dominion over the faith of others, setting up their own opinions and modes of thinking as the only true and infallible, and as such endeavoring to impose them on others, hath established and maintained false religions over the greatest part of the world and through all time.

THOMAS JEFFERSON, *THE VIRGINIA ACT FOR ESTABLISHING RELIGIOUS FREEDOM, 1786*
HTTP://RELIGIOUSFREEDOM.LIB.VIRGINIA.EDU/SACRED/VAACT.HTML

The Moral Majority organization became quite active in political circles enjoining their members to register to vote and elect political leaders who would promote a conservative religious agenda.

Thoughts of science and sex have continued to preoccupy fundamentalists. Many tried to have the theory of evolution removed from secular institutions' curriculum and textbooks. They either want(ed) so-called Creation Theory or Intelligent Design theory taught in its place or as a coequal in some circumstances. While some conservatives can (could) comprehend that some insects, animals and fishes evolved, they cling to the belief that God created man as he is, and continues to be, since the time of man's creation in the Garden of Eden. Believers want their children to hear this information in public schools as well as in churches and Sunday schools. While the Intelligent Design Theory does not mention God, a God is certainly and quite clearly to be found between the lines of all literature used to describe the theory. Opponents argue it is nothing more than Creationism in disguise.

Sex, from the time of the middle ages, has been a rather taboo subject for many Christians. However, the apostle Paul had much to say about the subject in his writings. Sex is barely recognized by fundamentalists as a natural drive. Many Christians see it as a drive polluted by the sin of Adam and Eve, i.e., the eating of forbidden fruit and not sex that caused them to be cast out of Eden.

While sex is necessary for humankind to be *fruitful and multiply,* it is often considered dirty, sinful and avoidable. "Male and female created he them," (Genesis 1:27), the word *nequebah (ה ב ק כ)*, is translated "female," but actually means "the thing to be *screwed,* bored or perforated."[9] This word reflects the level of respect given by ancient Hebrews to women. Contemporaneously speaking, "*boring*" is perhaps a little less "dirty" when performed within a heterosexual marriage.

Many Americans get their prudish feelings about sex from their Puritan forefathers. Some later Protestant sects gave up sexual relations altogether. It was the Victorians and the Victorian era that created some of the strongest and most characteristic fundamentalist religious traits.

Allegedly, Queen Victoria once told a bride-to-be that when it came to sex, "…shut your eyes and think of England [your duty]."

For fundamentalists, sex outside of marriage was and is anathema. They proclaimed sex had to be reserved for marriage alone. Many conservative Christian parents wanted to keep sex education out of public schools, arguing that sex education promoted promiscuity, not abstinence. Many insist that sex education should be taught at home. Yet, very few Christian virgins go into marriage with significant information about sex, because many parents are too embarrassed to discuss the subject with their children. The religious-right now laments that there are too few virgins and too few people who *save* themselves for marriage.

---

9   Strong Lexicon Concordance H5344

Some conservatives will say that secular humanism has led to promiscuity among America's youth. This may be true; however, too few parents admit to having the time, or desire, to limit what their children see in movies, on television or in the virtual world. All are sources of heavily promoted sexual subject matter used to sell everything from toothpaste to cars. With neglect by parents being partially responsible for early sexual experimentation, several recent studies have revealed, that among surveyed groups, sexual relations begin around twelve years of age and as many as seventy percent of teenagers, age sixteen, have had at least one sexual experience. Despite this statistic, many Christian parents do not want their children, either boys or girls, to learn about birth control at school. These parents seem to chant the mantra of Nancy Reagan, "Just say no." Is it any wonder the birth rate of "illegitimate" children is escalating among the very young in America? For whatever reason, America's youth do not say no and too many don't know about birth control. Many religious mothers and fathers are to be held responsible for their contribution to this state of affairs—promiscuity and unwanted pregnancies.

In 2007, The Food and Drug Administration (FDA) approved the use of a vaccine which would help prevent a certain viral infection that is associated with cervical cancer—a cancer that carries a rather high death rate. The vaccine held great promise for preventing cancer in a significant number of America's female population. However, the inoculation is worthless if a female has the virus prior to the vaccination. Therefore, the FDA suggested that the vaccination be given to young females before they become sexually active, since the major route of transmission of the virus was through sexual contact. Once a woman became infected with the virus, it would not produce any difficulty for years. However, it could be transmitted during these quiescent periods.

....

Jerry Falwell is now in a better place, side by side with the angels-and homosexuals, people with HIV and feminists, who, he has surely learned, have as much right to eternal happiness and salvation as he does.

BOB BERENS, *TIME MAGAZINE, JUNE 11, 2007*
(REGARDING JERRY FALWELL'S DEATH)

....

There was an attempt by Texas health officials to provide vaccinations for the appropriate age groups within its jurisdiction. The state's pediatricians, in government and private practice, encouraged parents to take advantage of the vaccine. What many should have seen as an act of Christian charity was seen by others as an unwelcomed move against conservative Christian values. The conservatives fought the public health policy and the administration of the vaccine. Some conservative parents believed their in-law-to-be would be a virgin at the time of his or her marriage to the parent's child.

Given this belief, there was no threat of passing the virus between the newly married couple and therefore no reason for the vaccination.

Others may have opposed the vaccinations because sex was a central issue in the need for the vaccine, and some parents refused to face the thought of their daughters having sex. Some simply felt uncomfortable discussing the inoculations with their twelve year old daughters, because premarital sex was the basis for the vaccination. Many or most of these children had never had a discussion about sex with their parents or at school.

A Kentucky legal case (Dempsey S485) rejected mandatory vaccinations because "parents and healthcare providers may have difficulty explaining to 11-year-olds why they needed a vaccination against a sexually transmitted disease." As a result of these fears and ignorance, many young girls would never have the protection from cervical cancer they might have had, if they had received parental permission to receive the vaccination.

Karen Armstrong's, *The Battle for God: A History of Fundamentalism*, stated,

> ...theologies and ideologies [of conservatism] are rooted in fear. The desire to define doctrines, erect barriers, establish borders, and segregate the faithful in a sacred enclave where the law is stringently observed springs from that terror of extinction which has made all fundamentalists, at one time or another, believe that the secularists were about to wipe them out...we can see the [fear of] nihilism that informs the fundamentalists' program.

Fundamentalists say they accept the Bible as being literal, and apparently accept the consequences of the stories and circumstances as they play out in the Holy Book. Most Christians accept the concept that Christ is an all-powerful, omniscient power. He took on human form and lived an everyday life as a method of spreading his word, demonstrating his endless love, dying for the redemption of our sins, and thus attracting converts to what has become the Christianity we know today. This simplistic understanding overlooks contradictions.

There are many examples of contradictions in the Bible. Fundamentalists conveniently avoid these either out of ignorance or personal biases. To follow this thought, look at some of Jesus' activities in the Bible. In Mark 5: 13, we see Christ had exorcised a demon and sent it (them) into a herd of swine that ran off a cliff, into a lake, where they perished. One could ask why a loving God would chose to act this way to help the possessed man. The man obviously needed help that only God could provide—he freed the man of his demons! That was good! Why, however, destroy someone's property or source of livelihood (raising pigs)? A point of interest is the fact that if the man was a pig owner, he was not Jewish. This raises the question, was Jesus being hateful to a non-Jew.

There are a few historians who would argue this story did not take place In Israel but in one of the islands in the western Mediterranean (near Spain) to where some Jews from Israel had moved and given up kosher ways. Some raised pigs. Jesus allegedly went to the island to bring the self-exiled Jews back to Israel, but He was rebuked and this story tells us how he dealt with his failed mission.

William Barclay wrote in *The Daily Study Bible: The Gospel of Mark and The Gospel of Luke* (p. 106 / p. 115) that Christ sent the demons into the swine so the demon-besieged man, as well as onlookers, would know that the demons had left the possessed man. Some commentators have added the idea that the incident was partly for publicity, i.e., Christ's might. This explanation seems rather weak when God could have done so many other things that would not have destroyed the swine owner's livelihood. To Jews, swine were anathema, and therefore, their destruction was of no concern to them, because Jews thought pigs were worse than worthless and unclean. This answer is difficult to understand because in Genesis, we read that all animals, swine included, were created as "good."

Genesis: 1: 25,

> And God made the beast of the earth after his kind, and cattle after their
> kind, and everything that creepeth upon the earth after his kind: and God
> saw that [it was] good.

Swine were made by God and named by Adam. God said they were good. Why destroy them? Perhaps, it was ignorance about perceived uncleanliness and diseases which are manageable today.

Pigs didn't normally roam loose like wild animals in ancient Israel. A herd would probably have been owned by some non-Jew (Christian or pagan) and probably constituted a significant source of food and income for the owner.

Bible readers are happy to know that the man who was the victim of the devil was freed of his demons, but overlook the lost assets constituted by the pig's demise. Is the true parable of the story not that Christ can deliver man from his demons but that something bad should happen to pig owners and / or pigs. Did Christ make a show of his abilities at the expense of the swine's owner?

Most fundamentalists would agree that Christ could have destroyed the demons without destroying someone's living. The question is why didn't he? We may never know, but this scenario, uncleanliness, has been cited by some radicals as a reason to kill gay people. The reasoning goes like this: Gayness is caused by a devil that exists within a gay person. Since humans cannot cast out that demon it must be eliminated or killed within the body that it occupies. Therefore, just as Christ had to destroy the swine to rid the world of the victim's former demon so does man kill the gay person to rid the world of a gay-devil-possession. So killed, the demon cannot go on to afflict another person. We often hear the fundamentalist community raise their voice against the gay community because of its alleged threat to "family values." Biblical verses are also used to support conservative claims against "gay families." We also hear quoted the "honor your mother and father" phrase along with admonitions to observe all the Ten Commandments. Christ says in:

Matthew 10: 35,

> For I am come to set a man at variance against his father, and the daughter against her mother, and the daughter-in-law against her mother-in-law.

Christ himself is voicing his own rejection of so called "family" values since he is more important than family and family ties. Fundamentalists cling to this type of societal structure known as the family, which God himself sees as a hindrance to Christian fellowship and charity.

Christ has commanded us to care for our fellow man and never to call them, or refer to them, disparagingly. Yet he says in:

Mathew 23: 33,

> [Ye] serpents, [ye] generation of vipers, how can ye escape the damnation of hell?

No doubt the reference to snakes is related to the disdain held for these animals as the manifestation of the devil in the Garden of Eden. Nevertheless, is this evil speaking not a contradiction?

After Adam and Eve had eaten of the forbidden tree, we read in,

Genesis 3: 8,

> And they heard the voice of the LORD God walking in the garden in the cool of the day: and Adam and his wife hid themselves from the presence of the LORD God amongst the trees of the garden.

This part of Genesis reveals that God *walked* in the garden. This verse certainly suggests that God (the Father) had anthropomorphized or had human form (a belief in the Church of Jesus Christ of Latter-day Saints[10]). Also note that God apparently liked the cool of the day. This is another suggestion of God's human nature. If we were to extrapolate to other corollaries of the human body, we could ask did he have eyes to see, ears to hear, a mouth to speak and eat, and genitalia. Such suggestions are anathema to most conservatives, yet these same Christians insist that the Bible is to be taken literally and infallibly.

---

10   http://whatmormonsbelieve.org/Mormon_doctrine.html

The above contradictory examples are just a few of the many to be found in the Bible. We can continue to question and argue about the infallibility of the Scriptures yet, regardless of how the question is ultimately answered, if ever answered, the *literal* authority of the Bible is compromised by its own inconsistencies. Yet the conservatives and fundamentalists cling to their argument of literality. If one tries to argue scripture with many fundamentalists, they appear to revert to the actions of the early Gnostic Church in which its members believed they had the true knowledge about God, and only "true" believers were able to see or know the "knowledge" found in Scripture. Doctor Bart D. Ehrman, University of North Carolina, (p.60) wrote this about anyone who argued against the Gnostics:

> …were told these truths were not available to just anybody. Only those who had the spark of the divine within could receive them…These others could not know the truth because they were not from above. This made it exceedingly difficult to argue with Gnostics. If you claimed they were wrong, they could simply point out that you didn't "know." If you interpreted a passage of Scripture to counter their claims, they could smugly assure you that you misunderstood the passages. If you claimed that their interpretation violated that natural meaning of the text, they could say that the real meaning lies beneath the surface, there only for those with eyes to see.

What then is the reason behind accepting the literality of the Bible that so fascinates the fundamentalists? I, and many others, believe the literality argument supports attempts of the religious-right to establish a *new order* in America, somewhat like the theocracies found in several middle-eastern countries, but one based on the Christian Bible. In fact, several authors have likened such a *new order* to that of the Fascists governments in Europe in the 1940s. Some like to refer to this new order as Christian Fascism. The noted author, Robin Meyers (p. 35) has written,

> America is going fascist, and it's doing so with the help of religious zealots whose real passion is for the politics of privilege not the radically disturbing presence of Jesus. This will sound alarmist to some, but the truth is that no country ever thinks it is going fascist until it wakes up one day to that indisputable reality. Then the people will say, "How did this happen?" And the answer is "one day at a time, and with the blessing of the church.

Mel White, in *Religion Gone Bad*, has succinctly delineated the component parts which define a Fascist organization. He closely follows those previously set out by Laurence W. Britt in "Fascism Anyone?" which appeared in the *Free Inquiry Magazine*, vol.23, No.2. Britt was a former Xerox executive who was interested in Fascism. The following are his fourteen characteristics of Fascism with my sub-notes:

1. **Powerful and Continuing Nationalism**
   Madison Avenue-like slogans are prominent
2. **Disdain for Recognition of Human Rights**
   Fearful of gay and human secularism rights
3. **Identifying of Enemy groups as a Unifying Cause**
   Gays are causing the downfall of the American family and values
4. **Supremacy of the Military**
   Military spending trumps other social needs and excludes gays
5. **Rampant Sexism**
   Male domination, anti-Prolife and anti-gay
6. **Mass Media Control**
   Start your own radio station/ program
7. **Obsession with National Security**
   Fear tactics
8. **Intertwine religion and government**
   Elect "God fearing Americans" to all governmental bodies
9. **Protect Corporate Power**
   Corporate Political Pacts fund political campaigns
10. **Suppress labor and labor unions**
    These are the electorate
11. **Disdain for intellectuals and the arts**
    Fundamentalists refuse to consider research of the Bible
12. **Rampant Cronyism and Corruption**
    Select groups make the rules and protect each other.
13. **Obsession with Crime and Punishment**
    Forgo civil protections in the name of patriotism
14. **Fraudulent Elections**
    Get the "right" politicians elected.

Fundamentalists seemed pleased to have had a fellow Christian, in the person of James G. Watt, Secretary of Interior, in Reagan's White House. He told Congress not to worry about our forests because of God's imminent return. Watt was quoted by Bill Moyer in *Armageddon and the Environment,* December 6, 2004 as saying, "After the last tree is felled, Christ will come back." This politician, toeing the fundamentalist's line, was not elected but appointed by Reagan.

At the time of the writing of Moyer's book, the Public Broadcasting System (PBS) was telecasting a miniseries entitled *The Inquisition.* The series chronicled the *History of the Inquisition After 600 Years.* The story line was lifted from actual records written by the inquisitors and stored in Vatican vaults for hundreds of years. The program alleged the medieval Roman Catholic Church, which had State powers to condemn and imprison, wanted to:

—protect the Church from loss of political and religious power and

> —help mankind save its soul. The Catholic Church believed they
> alone were the only way to salvation. Therefore, the Church
> had a duty to do all possible to fulfill its role of salvation.

Unfortunately, if one confessed their sin of heresy, they could be burned at the stake anyway.

As I watched the series, I noted similarities between the Roman Catholic Church of the middle ages and the Fundamentalist Movement of the 20th and 21st Centuries. Fundamentalists suggested they, and they alone, were the guardians of true Christianity and (save but by the power of the modern state) wanted to do all they could to bring about a new order of Christian Fascism. Author Reverend Mel White warned the general Christian community "…not to underestimate the method, intent and means of this movement in reaching its goal. America must exercise Christian vigilance."

The simple and often overlooked commandment "You shall love your neighbor as yourself" is radical in that it presumes we love ourselves—a lot.

Love is the most central issue in Christianity. We are to love one another as God loved us. Nothing drives a "true" believer crazier than the idea that God loves heathens, infidels, idiots, and gay people as much as God loves devout Republicans and fundamentalists.

We read in:

Galatians 3: 26 - 28,

> In Christ…there is neither male nor female.

One might argue the meaning of these verses, but they may certainly mean that God loves us no matter what our gender (or predetermined life style) and with the full knowledge *He* knows of the desires *He* gave us such as: hunger, thirst, love, orientation and sex. Christ was about upsetting ancient Hebrew norms. Among them was the accepted rule of how men and women should interact. In the 14th chapter of Mark, we see a woman (party crasher) who unexpectedly approached a gathering where Jesus was among a group of men. The woman anointed Christ's head with a luxury item (oil) known as nard, imported from India. The men protested the act and waste of the expensive oil. Secondly, we note that the woman was uninvited, and thirdly, she touched a man not known to be a relative, an act condemned by Jewish law.

Christ refused to rebuke her for any of her social, religious, cultural transgressions, or the use of the expensive oil. Each of these acts, anathema to a regular Jewish male, was praised by Christ, a Jew determined to overthrow established norms.

In general, ancient Hebrew women were considered to be unclean, especially so during the time of menstruation. If a woman was to touch a stranger, she placed the man in a position of being ceremonially unclean. Nevertheless, Christ was not bothered by Jewish laws which bound these ancient peoples inside their defining prejudices. If Jesus can ignore the uncleanliness of such an ancient woman can he not ignore the *alleged* uncleanliness of what ancient Hebrew priests and writers held for the gay community of today? *He* could but doesn't because, *He* made gay people. Nowhere does he say gay people are unclean. This concept is a one born of ignorance and personal biases.

During the writing of this book, I happened upon a television program produced by Crosstv.com. A very articulate spokesman promoted the idea that the Bible was *the* authoritative word of God. As such, it could be used as proof for various religious claims. From my view point, the word authoritative was used too loosely by the commentator.

I perceive an *authority* as some reference source, or person whose pronouncements or opinions were accepted and respected by a huge majority of the population, even the world. For example, Mother Teresa was an authority on the care of the socioeconomically deprived people of India. I believe educated and informed people of the world could agree on that statement. The proof of her authority was observable and quantifiable. Can we say the same of the Bible?

Presumably, only Christians accept the Bible as the authoritative word of God. Billions of non-Christians do not. The Bible has only the authority that our Christian faith brings to the subject. We give authority to the Bible because of what we believe it says and stands for. Our faith is a kind of bias.

Franciscan Father Richard Rohr, founder of the Center for Action and Contemplation, Albuquerque, NM, conducts conferences regarding cultural changes in the church. One speaker, Brian McLaren, a Protestant pastor, gave this speech at one of the Center's meetings: "The Historical Jesus: What You Focus on Determines What You Miss."[11] This speech seemed apropos to what many fundamentalists focus on and, as a result of their narrow mindedness, what they overlook.

The Reverend Timothy Keller, pastor of Redeemer Presbyterian Church in New York City, oversees a flock of five thousand members. His is a mega- church. This minister has often said in his sermons, "Doubt is the cornerstone of faith." He encourages not only self-examination but inquiry into the Christian faith, its tenants and why we do or don't believe in Christ.

Lisa Miller wrote in *Newsweek Magazine,* December 31, 2008, p 89, an article concerning American's religious beliefs. Her conclusion: "What's dangerous about the world today is not belief in God—or secularism or unbelief—but author Gomes writing in *The Scandalous Gospel of Jesus.*

Gomes took a folksy but eloquent poke at people who were sure they had the *right* answers about the Christian faith. He believed the solution to divisiveness in our faith and churches was a "certain amount of modesty" in our beliefs.

Non-Christians give little or no authority to the Bible because the book is outside the realm of their belief system. Many such people doubt that it was an inspired book. Even Thomas, the doubting apostle, required and received physical proof of Christ's resurrection by placing his finger into Christ's wounds. Modern Christians read the

---

11   http://ncronline.org/news/how-you-get-there

story, but for them, there is no actual *proof* of the wounds; only their faith leads them to believe the incident occurred. As much as the fundamentalists would like to use the Bible as "proof of the proof," that is not acceptable. Only pride can lead people to believe that their beliefs are more valid than mine, or other's beliefs. For fundamentalists, God's proof is not on paper; it is in faith—the faith of each individual.

I personally like the approach taken by Lisa Miller in the November 23rd issue of *Newsweek Magazine* (p. 24),

> There is no definitive religious interpretation. There are only narrow and broad-minded interpreters.

Fundamentalists often say that members of the gay community are sick, deprived, unnatural, and "warped" people capable of changing their "life style" at will. Perhaps these religious people should read,

Ecclesiastes 1: 15,

> That which is crooked cannot be made straight…

While some religiously conservative Americans hint at wanting a theocracy, they should know that such cannot survive in America's modernity where a key feature is the shifting away from emphasis for the privileges of the establishment (institutions, governments and politicians). Individual freedoms are now front and center. The world is less accepting of temporal power being invested in those who claim that their decisions about worldly life carries divine authority from a source beyond our physical sphere.

Heaven and earth are separate provinces. They should remain that way. All too often, when the two near a merger, bad thing happen. We have seen worldly corruption makes its way into religious establishments and when that happens religious authorities lose their credibility, a scenario all too often played out on American TV.

Reverend Doctor Mel White

GAY AUTHOR: *RELIGION GONE BAD,*
THE HIDDEN DANGERS OF THE CHRISTIAN RIGHT

I have a personal way of deciding who is an evangelical Christian and who is a fundamentalist. An evangelical loves and accepts me in spite of what the Bible says or doesn't say about homosexuality. A fundamentalist cannot.

The religious factions that are growing throughout our land are not using their religious clout with wisdom . . . I'm frankly sick and tired of the political preachers across this country telling me as a citizen that if I want to be a moral person, I must believe in 'A,' 'B,' and 'C,' and 'D.' Just who do they think they are? . . . I will fight them every step of the Way if they try to dictate their moral convictions to all Americans in the name of 'conservatism.'

FORMER US SENATOR (R) BARRY GOLDWATER

CHAPTER II

Religion-Addiction

What is it about the religious-right that makes so many of them such fervent defenders of their religion and belief system? Why do they feel they are absolutely correct about their religious stand against so many facets of modern life, often referred to as liberal ideologies, which must be stamped out, curtailed, or controlled? In particular, I am referring to their anti-feminine, anti-gay, anti-American Civil Liberties Union, anti-reproductive rights campaigns, as well as their need for "protection" of family values, freedom of religion, separation (and in some instances, joining) of church and State, etc.

If one steps back and examines their doctrine, it becomes obvious that the religious-right is fearful of something. This fear needs to be scrutinized, not just in religious terms, but through the eyes of the secular world, and modern medicine. Medicine is a broad field and therefore, my mention of medicine needs further clarification. I suggest we examine the almost palpable fear of the religious-right through the eyes of addiction medicine.

Addiction medicine is a subset of the field of psychiatry and psychology that concerns itself with conditions such as alcoholism, drug addiction, sexual addictions, and behavioral addictions.

How can one equate fear of religion with alcoholism or other addictions?

My answer is, you can't, but such fear (fundamentalism), whiskey and crack cocaine do share some common traits in that they can lead to overt signs and symptoms of addiction.

Let's examine the qualities of an addiction:

- External powers (addictive agents) can disrupt major role obligations, i.e., job, family, etc.
- An addiction is ongoing without external interference.
- Addiction provides relief of internal pain and denials.
- Withdrawal of the addicting external agent can cause physical and psychological pain.
- An addiction requires ever escalating exposure to the addictive agent in order to maintain past levels of psychological wellbeing.
- The ultimate endpoint of addiction is crashing if left untreated.

Most of the world is aware of the dangers of excessive use of alcohol, cocaine, heroin, etc., and need no further explanation. The idea that religion can become an addiction may come as a surprise to some readers, but the idea is not new or earth shaking. While any religious belief systems (Buddhism, Islam, Hinduism, Judaism, etc.) can become addictive, I want to limit my discussion to Christian fundamentalism. I do not want to imply that all fundamentalists, or their leaders, are religion-addicts, but some are. I do not want to imply that religion, in and of itself, is bad.

Modern Americans are experiencing an epidemic of obesity, and one of its associated dangerous conditions is diabetes. The most common cause of obesity is overeating and in some cases food addiction. While food addiction can be a problem, society as a whole does not criticize food or eating as being bad, only their excesses are a thing of concern. Over eating is of concern for its health implications and for covering up a food-addict's underlying psychological pain.

Working at one's chosen job can be a way to express one's humanity and promote the common good. Work may be fulfilling, if it helps people develop their values. Yet, one's job and work can become compulsive and a vehicle for avoiding life's problems, poor relationships, and family turmoil. Work, and the workplace, can become an addiction when the worker attains more pleasure, satisfaction, recognition, and psychological support at work than they receive at home, from friends, or even religious institutions.

Retired workaholics are often left without a core set of values by which to measure their personal worth and life's meaning. Many retired employees experience the pain of withdrawal when work's succor is removed, and the former employee is left to his or her ill adapted coping devices.

A measure of this phenomenon, called workaholism, was seen in a Boston college study which found that twenty-six percent of American workers take no vacations and forty percent of American workers had no plans to take a vacation in 2006, according to another poll taken by The May Conference Board.

Drugs, food, sex, and work can be addictive. So too can religion. Medical science has produced a growing body of evidence indicating that the human brain responds to certain behavioral process just as it does to addictive substances. A brain-produced chemical, dopamine, is the substance most often studied in addiction and is believed to be responsible for the high associated with addictive substances and behaviors such as gambling, risk-taking behaviors, certain political activities, and certain financial games. The amount of pleasure derived from these behaviors varies, depending on the person and how the activity may relieve suppressed personal, psychological pain, suffering, threats to self-esteem, or other vague thoughts that produce psychic distress. In *Science 2*, Vol. 294, p. 980-982, Constance Holden wrote, "Behavioral Addictions: Do They Exist?"

> Scientists have traditionally confined their use of the term addiction to substances that clearly foster physical dependence. That's changing, however. New knowledge suggests that, as far as the brain is concerned, a reward's a reward, regardless of whether it comes from a chemical or an experience. And where there's a reward—as in gambling, eating, sex, or shopping—there's the risk of getting trapped in a compulsion.

Dr. Robert N. Minor, author of, *When Religion is an Addiction*, (p.34) has written that addictive behavior is a process, one that can become an overt addiction, as when the process becomes the center of one's life and /or one of the most important reasons for living. I am not inferring that all people leading a religious life, or living life as a religious vocation, are addicted. However, any process can become addictive, if the process becomes the major escape for whatever psychological pain leads to the use of the chosen process for psychic pain relief.

Dr. Minor goes on to say,

> Instead of changing their boring, demeaning or psychologically or physically deadly working conditions or the corporate dominated society that sets them, the person becomes dependent for escape in what may be otherwise healthy activities. Instead of dealing with the issues of a difficult marriage or other relationships, loneliness or meaninglessness, the person becomes dependent for relief by participating in or becoming a fan of repetitive activities that provide "entertainment" or escape.

Escape may produce a psychological high but the high is one that the addict relies upon for self-assurance and self-gratification. Unfortunately, the mood-altering fix or high doesn't last long. Soon, the psyche needs another fix of greater intensity than the last causative agent. The proverbial vicious cycle begins.

In Alcoholics Anonymous, one of the first things a member has to do is to admit that they are an alcoholic—an addict. A process-addict would also have to admit that they too have an addiction if they are to recover, but their frequent denials of this fact are as common as an unrepentant alcoholic's denial of their problem. As with an alcoholic, process-addiction leads to self-deception and the lie that they are okay and in control. Untreated addicts, of all stripes, hide their inner feelings from themselves and others. Author, Dr. Abraham J. Twerski, writes in *Addictive Thinking*:

> Virtually all of an addict's defense mechanisms are unconscious, and
> their function is to protect the addict from some intolerable, unacceptable
> and catastrophic awareness.

This hiding of self is to prevent others from seeing the addict's true problem, and even the addict may not be completely aware of the deception. The addict is attempting to preserve his or her personal integrity, damaged though it may be. The addicted person is content to tell us how we should feel; not how we actually feel, e.g., we should feel good about raising children no matter how exhausting, time consuming, or expensive the task.

The super-religious are compelled to spread the word of God and to convince others, both believers and nonbelievers, to agree with their world view of religion. This is their goal, and to them the end justifies almost any means. The forward to Leo Booth's book, *When God is a Drug*, was written by John Bradshaw, a noted psychotherapist, who writes,

> The denial of religion-addicts is the most delusional denial of all
> addictions. Delusion [here] means 'sincere denial'.

Over time, the social vision of religion-addicts begins to dim. They begin to see people as pawns, but they fail to see how their own addiction may harm others. The addict learns to manipulate people who often acquiesce to the addict for many reasons. In the end, others are often accused of being the addict's problem, e.g., the boss is unrelenting, their wife is nagging, fate is against me, barking dogs, or even an angry God. However, sooner or later, the addiction becomes acceptable to the addict. They often believe the addiction is normal and sees those without the addiction as being abnormal.

Left untreated, addicts soon find themselves isolated and feeling lonely, even in a crowded room. Ultimately, they lose friends, relationships, jobs, reputation, and even their own future. Along the way, people known as enablers, usually people quite close to the addict, make it possible for the addict to avoid confronting their problem. If enablers did cause the addict to see his / her problem, the act might cause physical violence being perpetrated by the addict upon those who attempted to remove the addict's veil of denial. In such cases, the would-be exposer is often blamed for the problems suffered by the addict.

The aforementioned writer, John Bradshaw, is an ex-monk, counselor, and a former addict who knows quite well how enablers promulgate addictions. Enablers are believed to suffer from one or more major factors affecting the addict, low self-esteem being a primary factor. This will be discussed later.

In the 1960s the "Jesus Movement" saw its devotees preaching that people should get high on Jesus, not drugs. Followers of the movement claim to have found emotional similarities between religion and their drug experiences. Jesus became the replacement for the high of hallucinogenic drugs. Simultaneously, some LSD users proclaimed their high to be, per se, a religious experience. It should come as no surprise that people who were addicted to substances or behavioral processes could substitute a drug high for the high of being righteous, a condition called "cross over addiction." The phrase we know as *being born again* may actually be a substitution of one addiction for another. A cross over addiction to religion-addiction can carry a level of dependency equal to that of the previous addictive force or substance. The substituted addiction will remain successful as long as religion continues to provide a fulfilling high that is at least equal to the abandoned addiction. However, the replacement high of being "good," "righteous," and "on the side of God" is not permanent. These new highs need ever increasing amounts of reinforcement and perhaps new enablers. Many of these new believers soon become religion's "back sliders."

In the case of the religious-right, the emotional high of feeling righteous can be a relief from annoying psychological consequences of fundamentalist doctrines regarding evil that are central to the movement. Unfortunately, most of what many people believe about evil and hell is really a paraphrased notion derived from Dante's, *The Divine Comedy*, written between 1308 and 1321 AD.

The poem is divided into three sections: Inferno or Hell, Purgatory, and Paradise. In the poem, a character, Vergil, travels through the afterlife and describes certain environments and specific punishments provided for specific types of sins and sinners. Many of Dante's descriptions of Hell have inadvertently been incorporated into modern Christian's belief system.

The belief that the world is sinful, that all people are sinful, and that an individual is totally sinful and undeserving of God's grace can be so degrading to a sense of self-worth that depression may soon follow an acceptance of the concept. Once these ideas are personally accepted, the doctrine that paves the way to salvation is one, we are told, which is only available through conservative Christianity.

A necessity for maintenance of a person's religion-addiction is teachings by the religious-right that people are base, evil, and spiritually lost.

The addict learns that he/she deserves eternal damnation and horrible punishments from God. No wonder they feel conflicted when they also hear God described as a loving father. In psychological terms, this dualistic model of love may lead some people to expect God's love to come with some kind of punishment. The concept that we are sinful can be psychologically disturbing and is not often dwelt upon outside Church. Most Christians, especially church leaders, would prefer to dwell on being saved from the fruits of their evil lives, not being punished or harboring certain evils within themselves.

Another contributing factor to religion-addiction is the Christian thought that human beings are created in God's image. However, the religious-right would have the last word in this assumption by telling the religion-addict that human beings are not really made in God's image, instead they are evil, depraved, contemptuous, filled with sin and broken beyond repair. If such information becomes internalized, the believer has no place to turn except to the religious-right who also offers the only fix for a broken and sinful life. This salvation, however, carries a caveat of eternal vigilance against the ever-present temptations of the world, you can never feel, or be, safe. Satan and hell waits around every corner.

A classic example of unworthiness can be found in the writings of St. Augustine, a fourth century Father of the Roman Catholic Church. As a child, St. Augustine was physically and mentally abused by his father. Princeton University Professor of Pastoral Theology, Donald Capps, detailed in *The Childs Song: The Religious Abuse of Children*, how St. Augustine was a severely beaten child. Presumably, the young Augustine felt his punishment was deserved. He must have been bad, otherwise he would not have been so severely punished (abused).

After internalizing this kind intimation and assuming his own depravity, Augustine would later write about his innate evil and the evil of all children. Capps noted that Augustine even rejected his only son as one "born out of sin." Presumably, he meant fornication. Augustine was the Catholic leader who would proclaim that sin was passed from parents to children via sexual intercourse or "concupiscence."[12] This thought ultimately led to the concept of "original sin" which can only be washed away by baptism, and according to certain Christian beliefs, is a requisite for salvation.

Some theologians argue that original sin exists but has nothing to do with sex. The sin passed from Adam to today's human race was the sin of ignoring God's insistence that Adam and Eve not eat of the tree of knowledge that grew in the Garden of Eden. It could be argued that St. Augustine's late-life abhorrence of sex was simply the continuation his earlier Manichean religious beliefs. He incorporated these teachings about the sinfulness of sex, into his new Christian belief system. Saint Augustine appealed to the Pauline-apocalyptic understanding about forgiveness of sin, but he developed the idea of original sin via procreation. This was not a new concept to St. Augustine. He borrowed the idea from second century theologian Tertullian, who first developed the notion that sin is transmitted from generation to generation through "original sin."

Medieval theologians and 16th-century Protestant reformers, primarily Martin Luther and John Calvin, promoted the concept of original sin. Later, more liberal Protestant theologians would develop a more optimistic view of human nature that was incompatible with the idea of original sin.

Augustine, using language of the fourth century, described himself as a sexual addict who later went "cold turkey" in regard to his sex life. He lamented about the harm his sexual escapades had wrought. About his sexual addiction, he wrote in his *Confessions* (author's ordering):

[1]   My invisible enemy trod me down and seduced me because I was easy to beseduced.

[2]   …the madness of raging lust exercised its supreme dominion over me.

[3]   …out of "slavery" to "the habit of satisfying an insatiable lust…" [which he was afraid to live without.]

[4]   I drew my shackles along with me, terrified to have them "knocked off."

[5]   a friend says he was "amazed at my enslavement" to sex.

---

12   Augustine: *De bono Coniugali*

St. Augustine led a colorful life. He spent much of his youth with prostitutes. Later he would say of these women, "If you expel prostitution from society, you will unsettle everything on account of lusts" (Richards, p. 118).

Hence, the Catholic Church was willing to live rather comfortably side by side with these "sinners." This thinking was similar to that of St. Thomas Aquinas who wrote, "If you do away with harlots, the world will be convulsed with lust." [13]

Patrick Carnes, in *Sexual Anorexia: Overcoming Sexual Self-Hatred,* wrote about what remained after sexual addicts went cold turkey.

> …an unrelenting obsession with and fear of their sexuality, which is reinforced by the tremendous damage caused by their previous sexual behavior. It is almost as if they have been so traumatized by what they have done that sex in any guise becomes the abuser, the enemy.

After what Patrick Carnes called Augustine's sexual anorexic period, the church father began to project his sexual addiction on to other human beings, declaring that no man could live a virtuous life through his own virtue, because all men were inherently evil. Interestingly, it appeared that St. Augustine believed that innate evil prevented us from avoiding sexual sin through parental sex, which gave birth to all mankind, and original sin. This concept of sinful flesh was part of the ancient Manichean religion which held sway over Augustine's life for eight years before he became a Christian convert.

While most fundamentalists do not reference a Catholic like St. Augustine in their religious beliefs, the church father certainly created the background in early Christianity which spread its (and his) influence into modern, conservative religious ideology.

Experts, in addiction medicine, tell us that fear of abandonment is a constant cornerstone in all addictions ranging from: sexual addiction, drug addiction, alcohol addiction, and even behavioral or process addictions.

Psychologist and psychiatrists tell us that childhood corporal punishment can lead to unsettling adult psyches and deep seated fears of abandonment. Even in the twenty first century, feelings of unworthiness, shame, and emotional hurt are still being imbedded in the minds of young children by way of corporal punishment. Too many parents would prefer the rod to spoiling the child. Author Alice Miller in, *For Your Own Good*, has written,

> For some years now, there has been proof that the devastating effects of the traumatization of children take their inevitable toll on society—a fact that we are still forbidden to recognize. This knowledge concerns every one of us and—if disseminated widely enough—should lead to fundamental changes in society; above all, to a halt in the blind escalation of violence.

---

13   The Suma Theologica of St. Thomas Aquinas, ST II-II, q. 10, a. 11

If society ever seriously considered childhood corporal punishment and its long-term consequences, children and parents would have to confront too much personal and psychological pain for the task to be completed. Similarly, for many religion-addicts, it is more comfortable for them to believe that they deserve hell, but find salvation, without dwelling on the negative aspects of their sins. The religious-right has coerced many Americans into believing that the fundamentalists' concept of humanity's deplorable state is the true view of modern Christianity. Add to this misery some religious or political rhetoric that heaps upon the religion-addict reinforcement of their alleged unworthiness. Religion-addicts will delight in knowing he/she deserves more punishment and needs more salvation. Addicts need a religious fix to ward off their feelings of deep-seated depravity. This fix will protect them from confronting childhood hurts and inner feelings of unworthiness buried deep within their innermost self.

Many specialists working in the field of addiction medicine tell us that low self-esteem is at the heart of most addictions. Many medical specialists believe that enablers (co-dependents) and addicts share this common trait of low self-esteem or inadequacy. These often unconscious feelings may be reinforced if the addict's chosen religion repeatedly leads them to believe in their unworthiness as a failed, sinful human being. There is a favorite American hymn known to non-Christians as well as believers called *Amazing Grace*. A line of the song reads,

Amazing grace how sweet the sound that saved a wretch like me…

The lyrics stress wretchedness, fear, being lost, and blindness. A fundamentalist can internalize these messages of absolute unworthiness as absolute truth, and when they find salvation, feel relieved and righteous about it. The relief of "knowing" that salvation has been granted to a sinner can lead to its own "high," thus producing a subconscious reward for the religion-addict. This feel-good aspect of religion may account for the success of some megachurches that rely on auditory and visual excitement similar to those of a Broadway musical.

Reinforcing these feelings of unworthiness is the story of Christ's crucifixion. Mel Gibson's movie, *The Passion of Christ,* was released in 2004. It caused quite a social and religious stir because of the overly dramatic and brutal scenes of Christ's scourging. Rockland County, New York, Medical Examiner, Doctor Frederick T. Zugibe, is a world renowned medical forensics expert that has worked on the Shroud of Turin Committee, and is one of the few people who has conducted research on the subject of crucifixion. Doctor Zugibe attests that NO man would have survived a beating such as that portrayed in Gibson's movie. If, through some miracle, a man survived such a beating, he would not have had energy to carry his own cross even a few feet.

Needless to say, the scourging scene was overdramatized. However, if accepted as fact, religion-addicts might more easily accept their inner feelings about being an unworthy sinner thus warranting the torture of Christ's rejection and hell. For some, Christianity holds that the man, Jesus, thought to be perfect, had to undergo horrific suffering because religion-addicts and their fellow men were and are unspeakably sin-ful. Christ's suffering becomes the addict's personal fault.

If an addict accepts, either consciously or unconsciously, that they are evil, they must ask, "What then is my sin?" Rarely is there a conscious answer to this question without aid of professional, psychological intervention. A sinner's unconscious pain can be so soothed with religious salvation that it becomes the fix for the intolerable pain buried deep within the addict's psyche—the disquieting sin(s). Any doubting, of the fix of salvation, leaves the addict without emotional and psychological relief, causing them to face their psychic pain alone.

When logic should lead religion-addicts away from certain ministers or leaders of the religious-right, religion-addicts often move closer. Some of these apparently above-sin leaders have been caught in overt sexual sins, often making public pleas for forgiveness. Prior to their sin being made public, some leaders called for the murder of certain foreigners. Some have proclaimed that God's wrath has been visited on the United States through AIDS or tornadoes because of America's collective sins. Some have said that US soldiers were being killed in Iraq because of the American sin of homosexuality.

Religion-addicts need to feel that these repentant religious leaders, in spite of their fall from grace, can still offer sinners a way to salvation. The addict needs to hear them speak of salvation for sinners, for such is the bedrock of many addict's belief system. To abandon these often outspoken religious leaders would be to admit that the addict has been either duped or is a fool—something the addict's psyche cannot handle. To separate themselves from these prophets of damnation would cause addicts to confront the unconfrontable, the sinner's own unworthiness or shame.

Religious people do not set out to become a religion-addict. Most religious people simply want something added to their lives that will help them feel better about them-selves and their fellow man or their wish to find their place in the universe or answer such questions as, "Why am I here" or "What is my purpose?" However, addiction can imperceptibly takeover a person's belief system, and when it does, any previous reli-gious action or feeling thought to have been abnormal, may now seem quite normal and factual. This fact is especially strong in so called religious cults where followers are taught what to believe and what not to believe and to never question the cult's ideology. Cultists are made to believe that questioning of their religious (cultic) belief system is in itself a sign that external forces of evil are working against them and the cult. Cultists rarely admit they belong to a cult. Instead they belong to—insert a name—religious group or organization. To seriously question the group's ideology could lead to evic-tion from the group, leaving many former members with crushing psychological prob-lems of unworthiness, loneliness and sinfulness—they are left alone to confront the uncomfortable.

Those followers who remain in the addiction of religious life are constantly reminded that they have an increasing need for more prayer, more Bible reading, more confes-sions, more charitable work, more tithing, more time at church, more time at prayer meetings, giving more witnessing, etc., if the believer's doubts are to be assuaged.

These group members are almost never assisted by medical professionals when confronting the problems that besiege the addicted member.

An addictive practice of the religion-addict can be Bible reading, the bedrock of the faith of the religious-right. Religion-addicts have difficulty confronting logic in and about their religion. They often use the Bible to stop logical or intellectual religious inquiry—even their own. Addicts are known for saying, "It says so in the Bible" or "It is forbidden by the Ten Commandments," and "The Old Testament says…" The all-important phrase, "**IT** is the revealed word of God" can be a real argument stopper.

Once someone has said, "I know…," there is little one can do to move that person forward, because the mind is closed or has prejudged the issue.

Blind obedience to the *word* may in itself be a sign of religion-addiction. The acceptance of the absolute, authoritative nature of the scriptures can be a salve to the bruised psyche of a religion-addict whose mind is then freed of threatening external and internal stimuli that might disturb successfully repressed psychological hurts and shame. Any attempt to objectively interpret scripture could lead addicts into conflict and doubt about their deeply held religious beliefs. Doubt often causes cracks in the believer's narrow belief system and loss of psychological cover for the repressed psychological problems that led to their religion-addiction in the first place.

Biblical rules, like the Ten Commandments, have long been items that the religious-right thought should be melded with our governmental and political life. Those suffering from religion-addiction are quite comfortable in foisting such rules and religious ideologies on people living in religious or secular groups whose ideologies may differ from those of the addict. Addicts often project their own feelings of unworthiness (and need for religious rules) onto others and in so doing gain a measure of relief from their own deep seated fears. These addicts may feel that trying to pass laws that infringe on other people's freedoms (Sunday blue laws, prohibiting alcohol usage, deny a woman an abortion, prohibiting gay marriage) is just and not the addict's problem or fault— "the addicts are just doing God's work."

It is the addict's sense of perfection that permits them to ignore what others would call egotism or arrogance—some would say religious pride. These individuals are often used as tools in the quiver of politicians seeking support from the religious-right in their fight against liberals.

Rarely can religion-addicts say, "I *believe* the Bible means this…" instead they emphatically declare, "The Bible *says* this." The former allows for discussion and possible negative outcomes in relationship to the speaker's beliefs. The latter is dogmatic and closed to differing interpretations.

The addict cannot question their closely held beliefs, otherwise the protection of their addiction fails, and once again, the addict is confronting the unconfrontable. Maintenance of the addict's presumed intellectual powers guarantees that nothing will negate their righteous high.

According to therapist Craig Nakken (p 41), all addicts, not just religion-addicts, are prone to add ritual to their addiction. Ritual brings comfort, predictability, excitement, and connection with the familiar. The addict knows that if he acts, in a certain way, he can expect certain psychological rewards—the fix.

This fix may be especially rewarding for religion-addicts who lose faith in people or even God, but find their fix in rituals normally used in worshiping God. For a few religion-addicts, evangelical services which include hand waving, dancing in the spirit, speaking in tongues, rhythmic music, shouting, etc., can evoke a psychological release and an emotional fix. Even the style and delivery of a minister's sermon may produce a fix for some addicts' psychological discomfort. Some addicts may and do accept style-over-substance as something meaningful in their life.

In general, religion-addicts attempt to avoid reality and responsibility, often through unconscious denial, in their march toward perfectionism.

Those so afflicted often attempt to earn their way into heaven or, minimally, gain a small portion of God's favor. Despite continuing psychological damage, addicts continue to pursue their illusive goals.

This striving has nothing to do with God; it is service to self. According to Arterburn and Felton (p.20),

> Toxic faith is also a counterfeit for the spiritual growth that can occur through a genuine relationship with God. The toxic faithful find a replacement for God. How they look [their religious façade] becomes more important than who God is. Acts of religion replace steps of growth. A facade is substituted for a heart longing to know God. The facade forms a barrier between the believer and God, leaving the believer to survive with only a destructive addiction to religion.

It is not uncommon for religion-addicts to come from a family where parents are overly rigid. Rigidity can also be found in the religion-addict who is often extremely intolerant of differing religious opinions. Rather than being able to see other's religious point of view, the addict vehemently rejects them and strongly resists changing his or her own point of view or belief system. Self-obsession causes addicts to believe they are right and incapable of committing serious errors in religious doctrine. Their belief is the true (one) and only acceptable belief.

An almost permanent and deeply buried sense of overwhelming disappointment frequently lies at the root of the addict's affliction. The merger of disappointment with the psyche becomes a type of unconscious historical event that becomes psychologically important when it leaves its owner feeling worthless or having low self-esteem. The earlier mention of corporal punishment, or other kinds of abuse, can lead a child, and later the adult, to feel unloved and have a sense of detachment and loss. This poisoning of the psyche often paves the way to religion-addiction.

A religion-addict's feeling of unworthiness is often swept away by the attention they direct to a newly found religion or congregation. The addict's willingness to self-sacrifice for the church is applauded by fellow church members, often unaware of their role in the subservient person's addiction. Church work, and its appreciation by others, helps generate self-esteem and feelings of worthiness of God. The sense of relief gained by church centered work often leads the addict to become more immersed in church work to the exclusion of other activities.

The religion-addict often becomes totally at peace only when in the company of other like-minded believers. When a problem arises, the addict often avoids reality by seeking solace from fellow members who are almost guaranteed to assure the addict that everything will work out alright, in spite of the fact that the addict's lingering abdominal pain may actually indicate an appendectomy is needed, or that being fired happened because of missed time on the job while the addict was doing church work. Addicts becomes as much at ease with other religion-addicts as an alcoholic entering a bar. Religion-addicts often have a mistaken belief that the more they give of themselves or their assets, the more they will receive from God.

> Their giving is more like a materialistic investment than a spiritual act of worship. Such believers hope their affluence will increase as they give more to a ministry.

> Arterburn p.16

This is not unlike the so-called "Prosperity Religious Movement." Anne Schaefer and Diane Fassel's book, *The Addictive Organization, p*rimarily concerns itself with corporate organizations or so called "big business," but the tenets espoused in the book are quite applicable to some churches.

> …For people to trust one another in areas of uncertainty where outcomes are not yet known, they need to respect the competence of others. In some companies [churches], the system is trusted more than the individual. Indeed the system [church] is often designed to protect against individual actions. (p. 20)

Institutions, including churches, may in themselves be addicts (and addictive). A church may exhibit all the traits of addiction. Some churches attract religion-addicts who in turn support the addiction of the church. Church member and the church may act as co-dependents.

Traditional organizations and churches share concerns about their bureaucratic procedures and processes as well as rigid adherence to them. This observance may lead to loss of sight of the mission of the organization (or church) and the essence of its stated purpose. In many fundamentalist churches, there is a single leader or minister of note. It is not uncommon for a church to exhibit the quirks of its leader, as it is for a CEO to impress his personality upon his company. Neuroses, addictions, behavioral problems, and charisma of the leader can, and often do, meld with the organization, producing either great successes or great problems. The Jonestown Massacre of

Guyana is modern history's worst example of member, leader, and church involvement in religion-addiction. As Schaef and Fassel (p. 46) have written,

> We know that being caught in an addictive system, or any dysfunctional organizational [church] system, limits seeing, hearing, and knowing.

It is said that society as well as organizational entities (churches) can be an addictive system. Each body can behave like an individual addict in the way they function and the processes they establish. Some experts argue that the theory of an addictive personality clouds the argument. The problem is not that there are people with addictive personalities, but that there exists a process of addiction underlying an addictive system which surrounds and influences all of us. Substance and behavioral addictions usually have meaning beyond the personal.

> Our society needs addictions, and fosters addictions because the best-adjusted person in society is the person who is not dead and not alive, just numb, or functions like a voodoo zombie.

Anonymous

When you are "alive," you are constantly challenging many of the processes of society: nuclear threats, racism, polluted water, environmental pollution, the arms race and carcinogenic foods, etc. The dead, however, are not able to do society's work. It is therefore in society's interest to espouse things that take the edge off life's problems and get us going with our psychological fixes and keep us numbed out and zombie-like, yet working for the larger society.

Besides a society's allowing businesses to establish a social norm where it is acceptable to cheat, steal, and lie, the use of addictions of all types separates us from our spiritual awareness. To the extent that religious systems are involved in the same processes as addicts, they support our remaining in their addictive system. Whenever we choose religion and exclude or minimize spirituality, we are opting for the structure, control, and rules of a potentially addictive system. Reliance on religion, via religion-addiction, may distract us from the search we can only do from the depths of our own inner being.

Sex is a topic rarely mentioned, in a positive way, in church. Congregations are free to recognize nature's natural drives such as: hunger, sleep, love, itching and scratching, fight or flight, the urge to void or defecate, to bear down in labor and delivery, but sex is almost a taboo subject in most churches except for admonitions against it.

Thirst is among the first God-given senses; it protects us from dying of dehydration. If we sense thirst, we are naturally attracted to water to quench our thirst. We may use soft drinks or other liquids to quench our thirst, but such drinks are secondary to water. If the reasoning of fundamentalists is to be followed, the consumption of anything other than water to quench our thirst would be sinful, since water, not soft drinks, is the desired object of thirst. The consumption of soft drinks for quenching a thirst, instead of water, is equal to having sex for pleasure and not procreation. Today, we know that soft drinks as well as sex can be addictive, but each has its place in modern society.

Sex may become an addiction for heterosexuals as well as homosexuals. However, being a homosexual is not an addiction. While gay people have always known they didn't choose to be gay, science is finding more and more evidence that they are correct. Recent science has found similar evidence about bisexuality. Despite the argument by some fundamentalists, religion cannot negate innate sexual orientation. Nevertheless, many gay people seek to escape feelings of unworthiness foisted upon them by the religious-right and escape feelings of psychic pain of shame by involving themselves in religious works. Some of these people become religion-addicts. When this happens, the religious-right claims a victory for God (and themselves). This is a tragedy.

Because a church, of any denomination, can function as an addictive organization, especially in the way it handles issues like sexuality, it often attracts ministers and members with sexual problems. The structure of some church systems involves a dualism concerning sex. On the one hand sex and sexual matters are repressed, and, on the other hand, marital sex is good for some, only if there is the possibility of conception. Some churches obsess about licit and illicit sex, which can lead to an inordinate amount of interest in all things sexual. As long as the church remains focused on the dualism of sex, it and its members are constantly swinging between the shame and "no never" of sexual repression and the intrigue or obsessions about sex. This may in part explain the behavior of some recently disgraced nationally known fundamentalist ministers and priests.

Churches of all denominations have members who fall into one of two groupings: poor or wealthy. Each group probably has a selective hearing of a given sermon. Some churches preach from one end of the spectrum of wealth or lack thereof. In that church, the poor man hears sermons that say, "We suffer and are without in this life but will have a reward in the next life." The wealthy man may hear a sermon that is interpreted as, "Riches in this life are a sign of God's love for us now."

Neither group bothers to examine the present reality. Likewise, religious and other addicts, along with their enablers, always trust in the hope that things are going to get better tomorrow: the alcoholic will stop drinking, or the family will get out of debt. A constant, passive dwelling on the future keeps everyone stuck in the present with their problem unchanged. The promise of some future success is itself a fix that gives temporal relief from psychic pain in the "here and now."

Fundamentalist ministers often start their own churches. Some create megachurches, many of which can be seen on television. Some ministers become religious advisors to presidents and are sought out by political figures, primarily because of the political weight these ministers have with large numbers of voters.

Unfortunately, there are few measures of how well a minister or church is doing spiritually or religiously. True, churches often announce they have members numbering in the thousands. Accounting records of member donations are somewhat public, e.g., a gross income of $23,000,000. Some church literature reveals that a church has: a cafeteria, a nursery, a day care center, a health club, a swimming pool, a home meal program, a book and / or TV publication program, bus drivers for church buses, church guards (with guns), development fund drives, a choir with "X" number of voices, a ten rank organ or full orchestra, produces lavish pageantry rivaling Broadway, a church camp, or a particular minister serves on a national religious association board. They produce reports regarding: growth in church membership, baptisms per month, funerals per year, and hospital visits or prison visits. I wonder is these churches know how to measure their spiritual objectives—souls saved?

Knowing there can be religion-addiction in churches, their leaders and church members, should we care about church membership, donations or good deeds as the desired measure of the spiritual worth of a person or group? Probably not. There seems to be no good measure of the church's greatest mission. Unfortunately, there are no survey reports from heaven or an accounting of souls saved. Nevertheless, claims of fundamentalists having a monopoly on absolute truth and the path to salvation seem boastful and prideful at best. They cannot offer the most important thing sought by church members—certainty.

Ephesians 2:8-9,

> For grace are you saved through faith; and that not of yourselves; it is the gift of God; not of works, lest any man should boast.

Hopefully, this brief look at religion-addiction will help the reader understand the fundamentalists' hatred of the gay community (often covered with smiles and pro-nouncements of "love of the sinner") as being as much a protection of the addict's bruised and wounded psyche as it is pro-religion.

The religious cover-up of many conservative religious people's deep-seated and unconscious feelings of unworthiness, shame and depravity is necessary for the addicted person's wellbeing. That cover-up may produce psychic relief manifested as a high of religious-righteousness. Remember that addict's claim to absolute knowledge of the Bible's meaning is often an (unconscious) expression of the addict's fear of being unable to control their internal devils and otherwise protect against self-introspection.

As author Twerski has noted,

> One of the features of addictive thinking is the addict's perception of always being right. Many of the other traits prevalent in addictive thinking—denial, projection, rationalization, omnipotence—are brought into play to bolster the insistence that the person has always been right...I cannot stress enough the importance of realizing that addicts are taken in by their distorted thinking and that they are its victims. It we fail to under- stand this, we may feel frustrated or angry in dealing with the addict.

How then can the gay community win against the prejudices of the fundamentalists and religion-addict? I suggest we take the advice of Doctor Minor (p. 148),

> Stay on task. If you're seeking safe schools for all children, keep that the center of your discussion. If you want the government not to control women's bodies, say so again and again. If you believe the government has no right to tell consenting adults whom they can and cannot love, don't get caught in side discussions. If you seek equal opportunity for all people regardless of race or ethnicity, keep that the center of your message as that really is the important issue to you. If poison-free neighborhoods are your cause, then keep the message on pollution hurting people…

> Never say…partial birth abortion", "gay rights," "intelligent design," "gay marriage," "the government," etc. Speak clearly in terms of what you believe it really is. Say "a seldom used late term procedure," "equal rights for all," "government interference in women's bodies," "creationist ideology," "marriage equality," "the administration."

Whatever the gay community may do, it should not become an enabler of the religion- addict. Don't argue religion with them; you will lose to their self-denial and closed minds. Speak to your own needs and those of the rest of society. Be not a lone voice crying in the wilderness, but find other like-minded people and advocate together while waiting for the downfall of those who advocate against you.

> The hyper-religious probably is not psychologically enabled to understand the practicality of the idea of not judging, nor do they understand how not judging could possibly be a religious idea. That is, there is something in judging others that relieves them of the pressure of self-criticism that was inflicted on them by other human beings. Not judging becomes the one religious commandment they comfortably overlook.

R. S. Pearson, p.21

There is scripture to support this opinion.

St. Matthew 7: 1,

> Judge not, that ye be not judged.

Let those who seek equality not fall into the trap of the religion-addict In judging our oppressors. To do so only takes our collective eye off the target.

The concept of religion-addiction has been explored in this chapter. This addiction may account for much of the antigay ferment within the fundamentalist movement and the hatred of some conservative Christians for the gay community. For fundamentalists to acknowledge the possibility that God created gay people would be counter to their biases, the Bible's alleged teachings, and their need for absolute certainty in their belief system. The possibility that gay is *good* threatens their psychological status quo and the loss of the fix for their psychological pain. Religion-addicts don't truly hate gay people, they fear the return of psychological pain if they become objective about their beliefs.

In the next chapter, the concept of hypocrisy will be examined in light of conservative Christian concepts.

You've got to be taught to hate and fear.
you've got to be taught from year to year,
it's got to be drummed in your dear little ear
you've got to be carefully taught…

You've got to be taught before it's too late,
before you are six or seven or eight,
to hate all the people your relatives hate,
you've got to be carefully taught!

RODGERS AND HAMMERSTEIN
1958 MOVIE SOUTH PACIFIC SONG:
YOU'VE GOT TO BE CAREFULLY TAUGHT

CHAPTER III

Hypocrisy

For those pedophiles and predators across this country that have harmed or are considering harming a child, let me tell you that you are on notice…Your days in the shadows are over.

Mark Foley, *Time Magazine, September 17, 2007, p. 57*

*H*ypocrisy: to publically decry what one privately clings to.

In this chapter, the concept of hypocrisy in a fundamentalist's world will be briefly explored and examined in regard to the harm it creates in the Christian and gay community.

The year 2006 saw a rash of "gay-outings" for some of America's best known religious and political leaders. Congressman Foley, Florida Republican, was already "out" to some of his friends and associates in Washington, DC; however, his public proclamations against pedophilia and child molestation were sheer hypocrisy. He was head of the Congressional Caucus on Exploited and Missing Children and publically pronounced pedophiles to be, "America's most depraved."

Despite his sponsoring legislation to protect children from predators, he was caught sending suggestive sexual emails to underage males serving, or had served, as pages in the House of Representatives. Foley has since left Congress.

When Congressman Foley resigned, there was an empty seat in the House that needed to be filled. Like a knight in shining armor, in 'rode" Tim Mahoney, Democrat of Florida. Mister Mahoney, a married man, vowed to restore morality to the Congress. However, on October 13, 2008, ABC News reported on Congressman Mahoney's affair with a female staff member. He made an offer to pay her $121,000 hush money and secure her a job with a Nashville, Tennessee, political consulting firm—so much for the sanctity of marriage and the restoration of Washington, DC's morality.

The Reverend Ted Haggard was the founder of a fundamentalist church in Colorado that boasted eleven thousand members. He was also a member of the National Association of Evangelicals, which had thirty million members. As a minister, with a wife and children, he had been an outspoken public figure rallying against gay marriage rights in Colorado.[14]

To some, he appeared to be a God-fearing homophobe, yet, he was forced to resign his ministry and religious leadership roles because he was "outed" by a gay, male prostitute, Mike Jones, with whom the minister had a sexual and drug related relationship for years. Mike had not known his client's identity until he saw Reverend Haggard on television speaking against gays, gay-rights and gay marriage for fellow Coloradoans. Mike said he could not let such hypocrisy go unanswered, so he "outed" Haggard to the press. In April of 2007, Reverend Haggard emerged from a short term reprogramming center for gay men, his wife standing by his side, and pronounced he was cured of homosexuality. Late in 2007, the minister appealed for funds to be used for attending college. He wanted to obtain a master's degree in counseling. His wife wanted to obtain a master's degree in psychology. He, his wife, and two sons would live in a church sponsored half-way house where they would provide counseling services to residents.[15]

Another evangelical, religious leader from Colorado, the Reverend Paul Barnes, resigned his ministry, leaving his long-term marriage in the wake of his disclosure that he had been fighting the demons of homosexuality since childhood.

It would be devastating for the future of Western Civilization to say that homosexual unions [have] The moral equivalent of a heterosexual monogamous Marriage.

TED HAGGARD,
TIME MAGAZINE, SEPTEMBER 17, 2007, P. 57

Like sex, money has been a weakness of many ministers. *Time Magazine* published an article, "Going After the Money Ministries." November 26, 2007, p. 51 & 52. Therein was the revelation that some ministries had focused more on the personal welfare of their founders than the classically held belief of religion and religious charity. One minister, Joyce Meyer, has been criticized for her grand lifestyle, which included a private jet and a $23,000 commode. Ministers Benny Hinn, Eddie Long, Joyce Meyer, Creflo Dollar, and Paula White had received letters of inquiry from the US Senate

---

14   <http://www.abcnews.go.com/print?id=5997043> Oct. 13, 2008

15   http://www.comcast.net/news/national/index.jsp?cat=DOMESTICC&fn=/2007/08/74785

Committee on Finance investigating certain, perhaps questionable financial matters of their ministries. Minister Dollar has two homes and a Rolls Royce. Minister Paula White gave the gift of a Bentley to Minister T. D. Jakes.

Some of these ministries promote a "Prosperity Gospel," in which adherents believe they will garner financial rewards if they give of their money along with good thoughts and acts. Such ministries often feed on religion-addicts. Continued tax exemptions could be on the line for some of these ministries. No matter the outcome, such investigations fuel the perception of hypocrisy in religion. Being expelled from one's church for sexual misconduct is not peculiar to the twenty-first century. Fundamentalists seem to dwell on the sinfulness of sex and those who engage in sex, especially the gay community.

Religious hypocrisy is not confined to civilian life as was demonstrated in *Questionable Conduct: Chaplains, Sexual Abuse and What the Military Knows*, published by *Newsweek*, December 24, 2007, p. 46,

> ...60 military chaplains have been convicted or at least are strongly suspected of committing sexual abuse..." over the last 5 years.

Months earlier, the Governor of New Jersey publically resigned his office, wife standing by his side, saying he was a "gay American."

There were concurrent rumors that alleged the governor was about to be exposed as having allegedly sexually harassed a male state employee. This alleged act was going to lead to a public law suit that would have embarrassed the governor. The employee was an alleged former lover to whom the governor had given a major paid position in state government for which the alleged lover was unqualified. The governor had managed to promote his political aspirations by hiding his true sexual orientation under the rubric of marriage, two to be exact, and children.

The Christian Church's on-going obsession with sex and sexuality and the centrality it has put on controlling and forbidding sexuality in its message of sinfulness, is a suspicious sign that religion-addiction and sexual addiction have been regularly re-enforcing each other. In the middle of ethical challenges as large as war, suffering, diseases, failing relationships, and poverty, right-wing religion is obsessed with controlling sexuality, not just its own but everyone's worldwide.

ROBERT N. MINOR, p. 78

The following headline came across my internet provider's home page on August 28, 2007. This lead story was another example of hypocrisy from another conservative Christian.

Arrest Clouds Idaho Senator's Future

By MATTHEW DALY, Associated Press Writer
8-28-07

WASHINGTON—Idaho Sen. Larry Craig, who has voted against gay marriage and opposes extending special protections to gay and lesbian crime victims, finds his political future in doubt after pleading guilty to misdemeanor charges stemming from complaints of lewd conduct in a men's room.

The Idaho Senator had a past besmirched by allegations of homosexual activity. He had been a staunch supporter of "family values" and "the sanctity of marriage." He had often spoke and voted against gay rights. In early December 2007, Fox News Television revealed alleged homosexual relationships between the Senator and eight American men. Mike Jones, of the Reverend Haggard story, was allegedly one of the men involved.

Following the expose of Senator Craig's men's room adventure, Bryan Fisher, executive director of Idaho's Values Alliance, called for a precinct-by-precinct campaign of erotic cleansing, stating,

> …the party should regard participation in the self-destructive homosexual lifestyle as incompatible with public service on behalf of the GOP.

The New Yorker, September 17, 2007, p. 32

On February 14, 2008, the New York Times, in their online newspaper, posted the outcome of a Senate Ethics Committee report wherein Senator Craig was admonished for his men's room affair and also questioned the Senator's use of $200,000 in campaign funds to pay for his legal bills without appropriate committee approval. As usual, the wife stood by his side as he proclaimed his innocence.

On January 3, 2006, Reverend Lonnie W. Latham, a minister at South Tulsa Baptist Church, was arrested in Oklahoma City for acts of lewdness and soliciting a male undercover policeman for sex. The minister had been an outspoken advocate of anti-gay legislation. He had called for the gay community to reject its sinful ways, while he hid his gay orientation. The reverend has since resigned as pastor of his church and has stepped down from the executive committee of the Southern Baptist Convention, where he was one of four representatives from Oklahoma.

"Thank God for dead soldiers," is a phrase often shouted by Westboro Baptist Church members from Topeka, Kansas, as they demonstrate at funerals of fallen

American soldiers. Church members and their pastor, Fred Phelps, believe God allows American soldiers to die as punishment for America's acceptance of homosexuality. In October, 2007, a Baltimore federal jury awarded eleven million dollars to the father of a fallen marine at whose funeral the reverend and his followers intentionally inflicted mental pain.[16]

The actions of this church and its minister are blatant hatred, not the acts one expects from a Christian organization.

The late twentieth and early twenty-first century saw the Catholic Church having its share of undesirable revelations regarding priests and multiple episodes of pedophilia, which occurred and was permitted to occur, nationwide for half a century. Many of these cases involved underage males.

In some dioceses, the Catholic Church is near bankruptcy not only from having to settle multimillion dollar law suits regarding these crimes of pedophilia, but for years of sweeping the dirty secret of these illegal occurrences under the rug. Church leaders knowingly transferred molesting priests from parish to parish, in order to keep the occurrences from the public and from bringing embarrassment to the Church.

As of the summer of 2011, the archdiocese of Philadelphia had still not settled its role in these acts of pedophilia. In 2012 one church leader became the first American Catholic priest to be sentenced for his crimes.

On June 14, 2007, civil rights leader and minister, Reverend James L. Bevel was scheduled for a bail hearing on charges of incest. The minister had worked closely with the Reverend Doctor Martin Luther King and had been responsible for organizing the 1963 Children's Crusade in Birmingham, Alabama. The alleged crime happened to a relative between her / his thirteenth and seventeenth years of age.[17]

Hypocrisy is not peculiar to America. It is found all over the world. One hotbed of hypocrisy was the Gaza Strip in Israel. For many years, Palestine leader Yasir Arafat had been a declared enemy of Israel and America. Over time, his anti-American rhetoric softened somewhat, but Arafat was known to find America repulsive for its homosexuality. These protestations were another example of "not throwing stones if you live in a glass house." Arafat was married for many years, but his wife and he rarely saw each other. She lived in Paris while he remained in the Gaza Strip. As a Palestinian and Muslim, Arafat was often seen in various places praying as a devotee to his Muslim religion, which had strong prohibitions against homosexuality. On August 12, 2007, the *Israel Today* publication released what had been hush-hush information about the leader's death. The publication reported that Arafat had died of AIDS. The leader's rumored sexual interest in young boys and his personal bodyguard was kept under raps. Those who might be interested in learning more about this story can Google the subject for a wealth of information.[18]

Many Churches were once places of quiet contemplation, prayers, sermons, religious rituals, and "respectful" music in keeping with the actions of the worship service.

---

16   http//www.baltimoresun.com/news/local/bal-westboro1031.0.7191706.story? coll-bal_tab01_layout

17   http://www.comcast.net/news/national/index.jsp?cat=DOMESTIC&fn=/2007/06/09/685293

18   http://www.israeltoday.co.il/default.aspx?tabid=178&nid=13739

Now, even liberals complain that churches have become commercial establishments with book stores, cafeterias, health clubs, swimming pools, nurseries, bingo/social halls, big screen televisions and "rock" bands that stir worshipers with the music's tempo—not the loosely attached words of praise (the awe is secondary to the thunder). Conservative churches, the Southern Baptists in particular, had for years forbade their members from listening to rock-and-roll (the Elvis era) and newer rock music, which enticed people to sexual lust if not to illicit sexual activity. Now, that same music is used as a form of Christian worship.

This new form of worship is often called "emergent" Christianity.

> …[Emergent] Christians are fired up not about wedge- driving culture–war issues, but about spreading non- judgmental love and compassion… in the eyes of the emerging church, Christianity lived out in the respect-table confines of megachurches and suburbia is fading into irrelevance as a new generation comes of age with passion for healing society and a reluctance to shout moralistic dogma…Emergents tend to be more tolerant than establishment evangelicals on issues such as abortion and homosexuality.

USA Today, Monday, November 12, 2007, 15A

Scriptures inform us to love our fellow man, turn the other cheek and not to kill. The Ten Commandments are very specific and direct. However, in mid-2007, America found itself in a lingering war in Iraq. Everyone there seemed to be our enemy. There appeared to be no end in sight for the conflict between the Sunni, Shiites and Americans. In general, it was liberal politicians and the American populous who wanted America to withdraw from this war. However, it was President Bush and conservative Christians who supported our continued presence in Iraq and Afghanistan. The major reason expressed by these supporters was fear, fear that Muslim fundamentalism (jihadists) would come to America. As a result of these wars, American mosques were seen by some Christians as sanctuaries for infidels who would devour our nation's Christian faith.

It is one thing to war against a theocracy in another country and another to want a theocracy in America, but that happened during the Republican presidential primaries in the United States in 2012. Former Senator Rick Santorum traveled about our country abhorring the stated policy of President J.F. Kennedy's wanting separation between church and state. Apparently, he felt the same way as the framers of the constitution. Santorum, on the other hand, wanted his conservative Catholic Christianity front and center in all Americans' life. He wanted Congress to join him in outlawing contraception, same sex marriages, and abortions (even pregnancies occurring from rape). The senator said that these pregnancies "…should be viewed as a gift from God."

Christian faith tells us to love one another, and conservative ministers extol the values embodied within family structures. Yet, every day, somewhere in America, some boy or girl is being ostracized from their family and friends because their gay lifestyle has been willingly or unwillingly disclosed. Having people like Senator Santorum tell America that these boys and girls are despicable doesn't help.

Life for some of these boys and girls is so threatened that the gay student must seek education in special schools created and run exclusively for gay pupils.[19] Students, not so lucky to find such a school, may have to suffer both physically and mentally their being born gay. Many live amid students who do not understand their own social and religious beliefs much less the status of those they taunt. Often, suicide is the only way out for some of these tormented, gay students.

Many gay teenagers are forced to leave their homes when parents suddenly develop homophobia on learning their children are gay. Many children are literally thrown out of their homes along with what few possessions they might have. Now homeless, these teenagers are forced to live on the streets, or if they are lucky, they might find housing in one of the twenty-five safe-houses for gay homeless scattered across America. The May 17, 2007, issue of the *New York Times,* Section A, page 18, reports that as many as twenty percent of all homeless people, under the age of twenty-one, are gay. Carl Siciliano, founder and executive director of the Ali Forney Center, is addressing the growing problem of homeless gay, lesbian, bisexual, and transgender youth in New York City. A large number these people are without homes on a daily basis—yet only 250 beds of 3,800 in shelters are set aside for youth.[20]

The greatest fear for a gay student is to have their peers embarrass them by yelling or screaming "queer", "fag", "homo" or "fairy" at them in public. In some areas of our country, the taunts become deadly acts, as the Matthew Shepard occurrence in Wyoming clearly demonstrates. Matthew, a gay student, was horrendously killed and left hanging on a remote country fence. His death was considered a hate crime. His killers said they were fearful of Matthew's gayness and its contagion.

America's gay youth undergo significant challenges, as they pass through their teen years. Sometimes, the stresses get to be unbearable, and some gay teens consider suicide their only escape from the mental torment which bears down on them.

A 2005 Massachusetts Department of Education survey of 3,500 high school students, in partnership with the Centers for Disease Control and Prevention, found almost 11 percent have seriously considered suicide. That percentage is almost four times as high for 10 to 24-year-olds who identify themselves as gay, lesbian, or bisexual.[21]

The Trevor Project operates the only nationwide helpline for around-the- clock crisis and suicide prevention for gay and questioning youth. Charles Robbins, executive director of The Trevor Project said, "Add on the challenges of sexual orientation, or gender identity, and we get 15,000 calls a year."

---

19 *Time Magazine,* "A Separate Peace?" http://www.theology.edu/ugarbib.htm, October 24, 2011, p. 42

20 National Public Radio (text and audio) (11/20)

21 <http://www.cnn.com/2008/SHOWBIZ/07/02/trevor.project/> 7-2-08

I've never seen a man in my life I wanted to marry…. And I'm gonna be blunt and plain, if one ever looks at me like that, I'm going to kill him and tell God he died…

TELEVANGELIST JIMMY SWAGGART'S *SERMON*,
CITED BY DAVID BATSTONE, HTTP://WWW.SOJO.NET

Many of these young people may come from homes where the father was homophobic. Netta Weinstein and other researchers have found that homophobia may psychologically protect the individual who harbors these feelings. They prevent the owner from considering their own possible homosexual leanings.[22]

Texas is home to a large numbers of conservative Christians. The state is known as the buckle of the Bible belt. Former President George W. Bush, a born-again Christian, makes his home in Texas. As such, one might expect the state to be full of Christian love toward all men of all creeds and colors. However, the police records in Texas reveal otherwise:

— 1993, Nicholas Ray West, a gay Southern Baptist man, was murdered in Tyler, Texas, because he was gay. Nicholas was picked up from a Tyler, Texas street at gunpoint, by a group of Texas men. They drove Nicholas twenty miles out into the country where they forced him to remove his pants and then proceeded to shoot him nine times. This group of men, living in the Bible belt, had heard all the derogatory adjectives mentioned below. Once Nicholas' gayness had been demonized by Texas ministers and other Texas citizens, it became acceptable, in the rogue group's collective eye, to destroy this man for being gay.

— 1994, January, Michael Benishek, a gay man, was found murdered in San Antonio.

— 1994 February, Tommy Musick, a gay man, killed by an 18-year-old homophobe.

— 1994, March, Joe Trevino, a gay man, killed in El Paso, Texas, by men who had previously killed another gay man in El Paso.

— 1994, April, John A. Burwell, a gay man killed in the area of San Antonio, Texas, by a 16-year-old boy.

---

22   http://psycnet.apa.org/journals/psp/102/4/

— 1994, June, Paul Quintanilla, a gay man killed in the Dallas area and then had his genitals and throat slashed.

— 1998 A North Carolina minister published an open letter regarding Aaron McKinney's trial read, "Gays are under the death penalty. His blood is guilty before God (Leviticus 20:13). If a person kills a gay, the gay blood is upon the gay and not upon the hands of the person doing the killing. The acts of gays are abominable to God. His word is there and we can't change it."

— July 1999 Tyler and Matthew Williams a gay couple. Winfield Mowder and Gary Matson in their California home. Matthew told his mother he had murdered the men because, "I had to obey God's law rather than man's law. I didn't want to do this, but I felt I was supposed to. I have followed a higher law…I plan to defend myself from the Scriptures."

— A young man known only as Mark B. had presumably accepted his gay Orientation "until he became a Christian" and was made to believe through scripture that he could not be gay and a Christian. Mark committed suicide and left a note addressed to God: "I just don't know how else to fix this."

— 2012 Mollie Olgin and Mary Chapin were shot in a park in Portland Texas. Police believe the shootings might have been gay related. The culprit has not yet been found.

These victims were killed because they were gay. The murderers believed that society wanted the gay men dead because the assailants had been told by certain community members and some ministers that gay men were worthless, lower than scum, and hated by God.

Altogether, there were thirteen gay, hate crimes reported in Texas in 1994. Who knows how many were not reported. In 1997, it was reported that Austin, known to some as a liberal college town, had more hate crimes (52) than any other American city. Dallas had 40 reported cases. Austin had bragged about their reporting of such crimes, which allegedly revealed their interest in tracking and eliminating such happenings in the Bible belt.[23]

The *Austin American-Statesman*, on February 17, 1995, reported that,

[Chisum], leader of an influential caucus of conservative legislators, asserting that some gay men who are victims of violence **bring it upon themselves**[24] through their actions, said Thursday, "he will lead a fight to exclude homosexual victims from the state's hate-crimes law.[25]

---

23   http://www.austinchronicle.com/vol18/issue23/pols.naked.html

24   Author's emphasis

25   http://nl.newsbank.com/nlsearch/we/Archives?p_product=AASB&p_theme=aasb&p_acti

Scan the archives of any major urban center's new papers and you will find reports of numerous hate crimes directed toward the gay and lesbian community. Hate, often promoted by religious communities, can be found everywhere. Rictor Norton has written an interesting essay on the *Historical Roots of Homophobia From Ancient Israel to the End of the Middle Ages.* Norton points out that homophobia is really born of the ancient Hebrews' desire to distance themselves from the Assyrians and their homo-erotic religious practices. He writes,

> What is really interesting in this respect is that the identical male homosexual religious rites were commonly practiced in the Temple of Jerusalem itself, and were an integral part of early Jewish worship (see II Kings 23.7). But, burning with anti-Assyrian nationalistic fervor, the good King Josiah (640-609 BC) zealously burned out the room of the *qadesh i*n the Temple, scattered and reviled them (though again there is no clear evidence of them being killed), and began the campaign against homosexuality that has never ceased since. So militant homophobia began in what was basically the historical accident of a local sectarian feud. Unfortunately this prohibition of a specific religious practice quickly became a prohibition of male homosexuality in general.

> Norton's essay can be found at:
> http://www.infopt.demon.co.uk/homopho1.htm

Some States have passed legislation to protect individuals from discrimination based on sexual preference. Unfortunately, this protection is not yet nationwide. Not uncommonly, God-fearing Christian legislators don't feel such special protection is warranted for what they call *deviates.* Even where legalized job protection exists, many employees are literally afraid to disclose their sexual orientation for fear of losing, or not being nominated for, promotions, choice positions on committees, or other selective work situations. There are a few exceptions to this perception.

The Indianapolis Star reported on March 28, 2007, that the Eli Lilly Company (a major pharmaceutical company) had concerns about proposed Indiana legislation that would ban certain employment benefits for gay couples. Tony Murphy, Lilly's senior vice president for human resources, sent a letter to House Speaker B. Patrick Bauer, D-South Bend, and other legislators saying, "…the amendment could hinder Lilly's ability to attract employees and also paints an image of Indiana as an intolerant state."

The amendment, Senate Joint Resolution 7, read, "…that the constitution or any other Indiana law 'may not be construed to require that marital status or the legal incidents of marriage be conferred upon unmarried couples or groups'…" As a result of this uncertainty over what the amendment's impact might be, Murphy wrote,

…some employees may choose to leave Indiana to work in a state where these benefits are perceived not to be threatened. Given the great lengths Lilly takes to attract and retain top talent from around the world, we oppose any legislation that might impair our ability to offer competitive employee benefits or negatively impact our recruitment and retention…

Spokespersons for Indiana companies Cummins Inc. and WellPoint testified, "…that the amendment could hurt their efforts to recruit employees and could also jeopardize domestic-partner benefits." A third firm, Dow Agro Sciences sent a letter voicing similar concerns.

The U.S. armed services have not been such a concerned employer. In the military, "don't ask, don't tell" reduced the numbers of gay Americans who could have or have served their country. This program was a political coward's way to ignore the inequalities facing the gay person wishing to serve his / her country and fellow Americans. There were numerous reports in many popular media sources detailing how hundreds of gay Americans were being discharged from various branches of the armed services because they are gay. Among those discharged were West Point and Annapolis graduates. Noteworthy was the fact that large subsets of these discharged people had much desired and rare language interpretation skills needed in the defense of our country. It appeared our leaders thought it worth risking the loss of foreign intelligence information that might have been learned by these interpreters than some bizarre risk of maintaining gay men and women in service to the country.

New regulations approved by Congress were implemented in 2011. It allowed members of the gay community to openly work in all branches of the armed services.

The *Globe Gazette* of Des Moines, Iowa, the heart of conservative America, reported (March 23, 2007) on a bill to prohibit discrimination against gays and lesbians in that state. The bill passed 32 to 17 with the majority of dissent coming from conservative Republicans. They argued, "…the bill would lead to a wave of costly lawsuits against employers, small businesses, and schools." Republicans wanted to exempt all schools and the Boy Scouts from the legislation. State Representative Hartsuch said, "…this bill makes radical changes in the fundamental understanding of our society." Civil rights and equality escaped their logic. The expressed fear of lawsuits seemed like a clear indication that there was already overt discrimination against Iowa's gay population. Iowa Republicans, and the religious-right, clearly wanted to keep such discrimination legal. State Representative Hartsuch was correct in stating, "…society will change, but for the better!" Indeed that did happen in 2009 when Iowa's Supreme Court decided that gays had the right to marry.

What did all the earlier noted hypocrites have in common? They had a fear of being known as an openly gay American? Why should they fear being exposed or known as a gay person? In some circles, to be known as a gay American is to be:

- loathed
- disdained

- hated
- feared
- disgusting
- a sinner
- an abomination
- scum of the earth
- a faggot
- fucking faggot
- fag
- a pansy
- a homo
- a fairy
- a gay
- a sissy
- a queer
- a bugger
- queenie
- sick
- unworthy
- a girly man
- a disgrace
- a pervert
- a "prervert"
- nellie
- light on the feet………..

This incomplete list of adjectives/synonyms used as abusive insults should provide some insight as to why people, from all walks of life, do not want to be stigmatized with the title of "gay." Most interesting is how these adjectives gained their usage in regard to that five to ten percent of the American population we know as "gay." No doubt, these titles are used as a result of certain cultural factors, ignorance, bigotry, and fear, but they are also derived from those who should be full of love for all people—Christian fundamentalists.

On August 30, 2007, the Iowa District Court issued its opinion in Varnum v Brien. The court held that Iowa law, which prohibits individuals of the same sex from marrying, violates "due process and equal protection rights [because of] the absence of a rational relationship to the achievement of any legitimate governmental interest."[26]

The court had this to say in reaching their decision to allow marriage rights to same sex couples:

---

26   http://lawprofessors.typrpad.com/trusts_estates_prof/2007/08/iowa-court-says.html

Historically, and to the present, lesbian and gay people have been subjected to discrimination, harassment and misunderstanding because they are perceived as departing from the gender roles expected of each sex. Lesbians and gay men (as well as heterosexuals perceived to be gay or as acting or appearing gay) are commonly debased though slurs, jokes and stereotypical references to same-sex attraction, appearance, dress, mannerisms, sexual practices, occupations, and the like. These remarks reflect personal and/or societal animus, and fear or discomfort with gay people's perceived departures from sex role norms; such remarks seek to and do coerce conformity with those norms.

Hypocrisy covers a multitude of sins. It often causes great personal pain and inflicts tremendous hurt on others. It produces fear, doubt, disbelief and sarcasm upon those who hear and suffer from it. It undermines our government, our sense of justice, and our religious institutions. It hides self-interest and soothes self-deception. It often camouflages homosexuality, as in the Hamlet scene about protesting too much.

In some cases, homophobia may be fear about dissatisfaction with one's own sexuality causing such people to lash out at the gay community. In Shakespeare's *Hamlet Act 3*, a question is answered, "The lady doth protest too much, methinks." This quote could be directed toward some people who complain in excess about the actions of the gay community. By deriding gays, the sexually insecure person believes, consciously or unconsciously, they deflect gayness from themselves. Such public protestations may cloak deep-seated sexual fears in protestors.

"We have just enough religion to make us hate but not enough to make us love one another."

LYNN LAVNER, COMEDIAN

In March 2007, *The Minneapolis Star Tribune* printed an article in which one of the leading fundamentalists of a Southern Baptist Seminary, the Reverend Albert Mohler, stated,

…someday, science may prove that gay people may have their inclinations because of genetic abnormalities. Nevertheless, the actions of these gay people are still a sin. [He goes on to say that] certain future hormone injections, given to the mother discovered to be carrying a gay unborn child, would change the person into a heterosexual before birth.

This minister of Christian faith is on record as opposing any attacks (abortion) on unborn children for any reason. However, for unborn gay babies, the reverend makes an exception. On the one hand, he stated that God works in mysterious ways to work his wonders, yet Mohler's biases do not permit him to believe that IF God created a genetically gay person,

God must have had a reason to do so and that such persons are normal. A common fundamentalists' bumper sticker read, "God doesn't make mistakes!"

Who is Reverend Mohler to say that God made a mistake when a child is born gay? The reverend appeared to be a closed minded, biased (perhaps bigoted) Christian who had been brainwashed to believe that *his belief* in Christianity was the only authentic one. He and other fundamentalists refused to see or consider another possible truth!

An article, "Pas de Deux of Sexuality is Written in the Genes," appeared in the *Health Section* of the April 10, 2007, issue of the *New York Times* was written by Nicholas Wade. It shed new light on genetic issue of homosexuality. His article revealed brain changes of gay men that are most probably due to hormonal differences prior to birth. Heterosexual attraction is probably hormonally dictated as well, and hence God given, as is same-sex attraction.

A medieval religious writer, Albertus Magus (1193-1280), wrote the *Evangelium Lucae* 18:29, in which he tried to combine his knowledge of medicine and theology to produce a concept of "sodomitical physiology." He wrote, "…some men are *constructed* so that they can exercise their reproductive power only with other men…" (Jordan, p. 135). Since DNA and genes were unknown at that time, the writer was unknowingly ahead of his time to suggest a biological basis for homosexuality.

The antigay stand of some religious leaders is, fortunately, not true of all ministers. The *New York Times* reported on an Atlanta Baptist Church minister, Reverend Dennis Meredith. When Reverend Meredith began preaching acceptance of gay men and lesbians a few years ago, he attracted some gay people who were on the brink of suicide and some, who despite the fact they had left the Baptist faith of their childhood, wanted badly to return. Simultaneously, his Church lost many of its most loyal, generous parishioners who could not accept a message that contradicted what they believed and had been taught as the Bible's condemnation of same-sex relations. Over a span of three years, the Church's Sunday attendance shrank from 1,100, to 800. This did not deter the pastor from his acceptance of his gay congregants which included his son.

The Church of Jesus Christ of Latter-day Saints (Mormon) is not well understood by many practicing Christians. One of the religion's former members is D. Michael Quinn, who was professor of history at Brigham Young University.

He suggested that the religion's founder, Joseph Smith, was relatively accepting of gay and lesbian relationships. Professor Quinn wrote a book titled: *Same-Sex Dynamics Among Nineteenth-Century Americans—a Mormon Example.* The 1996 book stated that "Evan Stephens, once the director of the Mormon Tabernacle Choir and author of many church hymns, maintained close male relationships." Joseph F. Smith, a church patriarch (1942), was allegedly homosexual and apparently had two long-term male relationships.[27]

---

27   http://connellodovan.com/abom.html November 5, 2008

This tolerance was apparently in place until the mid-1950s. A study on gay life in Utah, *Lesbian and Gay Men in America Between 1916 - 1938*, by Mildred J Berryman, was published, using Mormon Church documents along with information from other sources. The work strongly suggested that Salt Lake City was never as straight as some would have us believe.

Mormons have had moments of enlightenment in regard to polygamy and their anti-African-American attitudes. However, Harold Brown, the Church's spokesperson on homosexuality, said, "…no amount of press coverage or activism is going to influence God to change the rules about homosexuality…" The Mormon Church believes that a gay person chooses their homosexual lifestyle; therefore, willing one's self to go straight is all that is needed to become heterosexual. The Mormon Church probably has the dubious record of causing, directly or indirectly, the suicide deaths of more gay university students than any other educational institution. I invite you to read the Suicide Memorial in the Book of Remembrance on the Mormon Affirmation Webpage.[28]

The Mormon Church has not only caused great suffering within their community, as regards their gay constituency, they have attempted to block anti-gay hate crimes and anti-gay legislation to fight gay marriage rights in several states outside of California in the 1990s. Preceding the 2000 marriage legislation in California, it is rumored that Mormons contributed forty percent of the funds used to support the Proposition 22 vote. Those interested in this can read about the story according to Christopher Calhoun, Public Policy Advocate, LA Gay and Lesbian Center, in his letter to the *Los Angeles Times*, July 24, 1999, B7.

Hypocrisy is the title of this chapter and a subject in religion most often spoken about by older adults. Interest in this subject is, however, not limited to adults. A recent survey published in *USA Today*, revealed that seventy percent of surveyed Protestants stopped attending religious services by age twenty-three. Author, Cathy Lynn Grossman, reported that of those who ceased attending religious services, twenty-six percent did so because of church members' hypocrisy. Another twenty percent felt disconnected from fellow church members, and approximately eighteen percent disagreed with the social/political stance of the church they had attended. These statistics suggested that the modern church was not very successful at establishing relationships with younger, potential church members.

Hypocrisy is seen as the major reason for this loss to the church. No doubt, the political and religious leaders noted at the beginning of this chapter have contributed to this flight from the church.

In the end, hypocrisy hurts everyone—no one more than the perpetrator. When exercised in the name of, or defense of, religion, it devalues one's faith. Its cutting edge has harmed the gay community and in some cases led to death.

Hypocrisy often arises in the context of ignorance about the homosexual as a human being.

The subject of homosexuality will be explored in the next chapter.

---

28   http://www.affirmation.org/suicides/

The fact is that the radical or religious-right breaks the Ninth Commandment (that prohibits false witness) every day, using ignorance and fear of homosexuality and homosexuals to raise millions and millions of dollars. But they are not alone. The whole Church and other religious bodies have given false witness about gays and lesbians for at least a millennium.

REVEREND NANCY WILSON,
OUR TRIBE: QUEER FOLKS, GOD, JESUS AND THE BIBLE

CHAPTER IV

Definitions of Homosexuality

Some say the homosexual lifestyle is unnatural. Homosexuality Is found in over 450 species. Homophobia is found in only one. Which seems unnatural to you?

ANONYMOUS

*I*n the last chapter, we saw how hypocrisy could harm the gay community but protect a denouncing individual from various harms. Ignorance of homosexuality is often at the root of hypocrisy and denied self-exploration.

In this chapter, homosexuality is explored in search of ways to explain its proper place in modern society.

Homosexuality is not an ancient term. The word was unknown to the ancient Hebrews, Egyptians, or Greeks from whose language the component parts are assembled to create the word, *homo-sexual*. The word was first seen in the nineteenth century in an Austrian pamphlet written by Karoly M. Kertbeny. The 1892 edition of the *Oxford English Dictionary* was the first

English Language dictionary to include the word *homosexual*. Present usage of the word "homosexuality" involves several things:

- gender
- gender identity
- sexual orientation, drive, interest
- gender role
- sexual acts

What most people call gender is generally established at birth by the presence of either male or female genitalia, barring the occasional occurrence of ambiguous sex organs due to congenital abnormalities. Studies have shown that boy babies who had lost their penises through various kinds of trauma or intentional surgery and who were subsequently raised as female, being exposed to every possible social inducement to be female, grew up desiring females as partners, not men. As J. Michael Bailey of Northwestern University said, "If you can't make a male attracted to other males by cutting off his penis, how strong could any psychosocial effect be?" (J. Michael Bailey, p. 46)

Gender identity is the way in which a person perceives him or herself in relation to his or her sexual peers, i.e., another man or a woman. Sexual orientation seems to be determined before birth. Doctor Breedlove said,

> …most of the scientists working on these questions are convinced that the antecedents of sexual orientation in males are happening early I life, probably before birth, whereas for females, some are probably born to become gay, but clearly some get there quite late in life.

Canadian researchers, Ray Blanchard and Anthony F. Bogaert, reported that siblings, consisting of older brothers, have a substantially increased chance that a man will be homosexual. He goes on to say that fifteen percent of gay men can attribute their homosexuality to this finding. Based on his assumption, up to four percent of men are gay, and each additional older brother increases his odds of having homosexual orientation by thirty three percent.[29]

Transgender or transsexual persons may have the body of one sex But the mind feels as though the person owning the body is of the opposite sex. Sexual orientation defines a condition in which the person is erotically oriented or attracted to another person. This attraction might be to a person of the opposite sex or of the same sex. If the attraction is to a different sex, the person is a heterosexually oriented, or if the same sex, the person is homosexually oriented.

Sexual orientation is the very essence of a person's being, an innate drive creating one's love of gender and sexual interest. While one's orientation can be repressed, covered up, denied, or allowed to become overt, it is irrefutable.

The gender role is the way in which a person conforms to certain societal "norms" of behavior. Generally, the role and acts are commensurate, however, the acts may be private or public and may change based on circumstances.

Modern, educated Christians would not consider alcoholics or drug addicts to be sinners because of their obsessive use of either alcohol or drugs. Addiction is classified as a medical illness and is treated by using modern medical methods.

Through research, we know that people who are addicted to alcohol and drugs have developed increased numbers of certain receptors in their brains that "attract" these

---

29   http://www.nytimes.com/2007/04/10/health/10gene.html?pagewanted=2&ei=5087& em&en= e4c2df6308d0edcb&ex=1176523200

addictive substances, and when denied, the receptor's hunger for them (addiction) leads to signs and symptoms of withdrawal—a psychological and physically painful process. This pain can be relieved by taking the substance to which the person is addicted.

If we can see and understand that alcoholism and drug addiction behaviors are attributed to certain receptors in the brain, why do conservative

Christians have difficulty understanding that heterosexuality and homosexuality are mind sets constructed within the brain that respond to certain external sexual stimuli and create our sexual orientation?

Well, maybe they have. Boston's Roman Catholic newspaper, the *Pilot*, printed an article in October 2011 entitled "Some Fundamental Questions on Same-sex Attraction." It was written by Daniel Avila, Director for Policy and Research for the U.S. Conference of Catholic Bishops. Avila had this to say:

> ...the scientific evidence of how same-sex attraction most likely may be created provides a credible basis for a spiritual explanation that indicts the devil...disruptive imbalances in nature that thwarts encoded processes [DNA][30] point to supernatural actors [**devil**][31]...who do not have the good of persons at heart...natural causes disturb typical biological development, leading to the personally unchosen beginnings of same sex attraction...imputed to the evil one not God.

The article was withdrawn from the *Pilot* website a few days later, offering an apology from Avila for any hurt and confusion the article caused. He said his article did not represent the Conference of Catholic Bishops' point of view.

Ancient peoples had a strict interpretation of what maleness and femaleness was and what constituted the overtness of the roles demonstrated by each sex. It was the responsibility of the male (as father figure) to give rise to an unborn child in the womb of the mother. According to Aristotle's *Generation of Animals,* it was the mother's menstrual blood which aided in the molding of the unborn child. This blood was considered a kind of female semen utilized by the developing fetus. After all, menstrual flow ceased during pregnancy. However, Aristotle believed that it was the father who provided the essence or forms of the child, not the mother.

Once born, a child was expected to carry out the societal roles identified with its external genitalia. The male was to be the dominant sex and become a leader in his family and society. Little was expected of the female, except to create and care for the children of one father. During ancient times, the woman was considered a second class citizen whose primary role was that of a mother totally subservient to her husband.

Because of the societal aspects of gender and gender roles, the male was never to take a subservient role in anything (except for certain social, religious and political roles) and this included sex. To do otherwise was to lose maleness, shame himself, his family, his society, tribe, people, and country. Eckart Otto, in publishing the *Ancient*

---

30   Author's addition

Assyrian Law, revealed some harsh examples of punishment for men who ignored this prohibition.

The law stated that if it could be proven that a man had had sex with a comrade, he would be gang raped and then castrated. How could heterosexual men get sufficiently sexually aroused to participate in such punishment? Were animate or inanimate objects used?

Ancient laws did, however, provide a death penalty for what we today call adultery. Now, as in Biblical days, adultery was the sexual act that was condemned under certain circumstances but NOT for same-sex desire. The latter is never mentioned or even hinted at in the Bible.

Reverend Mohler and conservatives of major religions (Jewish, Muslim, Christianity, etc.) like to define homosexuality in terms of sexual behavior only. They consider homosexuality or heterosexuality as something that a person ***does*** not ***is***—a homosexual engages in some form of same-sex act; a heterosexual engages in opposite sex acts. People who have sex with males and females are often called homosexuals, while, all too often, ignoring what is commonly known today as bisexuality. Many conservative Christians seem to believe that a person's homosexual orientation can be changed by an act of self-will. However, heterosexuals have little to say about the process through which a person wills themself to be gay or how heterosexuals maintain their heterosexuality.

If a person is sexually attracted to women and men, many religiously conservative persons believe that the bisexual person has chosen to broaden their interests and sexual activities to include both sexes. Many conservatives believe that people who are only attracted to members of the same sex should remain celibate since any sexual activity between same sex couples is an abomination in the eyes of the Lord (love the sinner, hate the sin).

The religious-right considers the gay lifestyle as chose and seriously wrong, immoral, changeable, abnormal, and unnatural. Some believe that it is an addiction that is hated by God and destructive to individuals choosing to follow the so called gay lifestyle.

The Reverend James Dobson, a noted fundamentalist of Virginia holds a Ph.D. degree from the University of Southern California in child development. As such, one would expect him to be a man of science. On the contrary, he insists that homosexuality is a mental disorder as stated in his book, *Bringing up Boys*, p. 115. His protestation is in contrast to the 1973 announcement that the American Psychiatric Association no longer considered homosexuality to be a mental disorder. In 1975, the American Psychological Association took the same stand. The organization went on to say in their Statement on Homosexuality, July, 1994, The research on homosexuality is very clear.

> Homosexuality is neither mental illness nor moral depravity. It is simply the way a minority of our population expresses human love and sexuality. Study after study documents the mental health of gay men and lesbians. Studies of judgment, stability, reliability, and social and

vocational adaptiveness show that gay men and lesbians function every bit as well as heterosexuals.

The same organization went on to state that attitudes such as Dobson's may Create problems rather than curing them. They said,

> As with any societal prejudice, anti-homosexual bias, negatively affects mental health, contributing to an enduring sense of stigma and pervasive self- criticism in people of same-gender sexual orientation through the internalization of such prejudice.[31]

These two organizations, along with the American Counseling Association and the National Association of Social Workers have taken similar stands. These organizations represent 500,000 professional workers in this field. As a group, they stand opposed to Doctor Dobson whose biases tell him that science explains homosexuality as a sickness, yet this man of science will take, as science, a weather forecast which may be fifty percent correct while denying the science and opinions of the majority of professionals in his own field. What Doctor Dobson is doing is protecting his interests in male dominance, as he denigrates the gay community and feminism which he is also opposes. Why should anyone care what sexual orientation another person may have? Author, Mark Jordan, in *The Invention of Sodomy in Christian Theology,* wrote,

> …the worst troubles linked to condemnation of sodomy have to do with misogyny…and misogynistic logic. [It] condemns violently anything feminine, but especially anything that seems to surrender masculine privilege. A man cannot have sex with another man because to do so makes him less, degrades him, subordinates him…implies a disapproving link with the essentialized feminine…They depend on the familiar male horror tales about women…to be a woman is to be something defective, something already half-polluted, something disreputable.

Among the ancient writings of several peoples, male-to-male sex was thought of in terms of domination and subjugation. Not until the *Epic of Gilgames (Gilgamesh),* do we find a loving tenderness portrayed between two men in literature. This 4,000-year-old Sumerian story is about Gilgames' lover, Enkidu, who becomes the archetypical "butch" guy for modern gay men. The story goes in to great length about the love and lamenting centered around this tragic love story. In the story, Gilgames' mother is the one who interprets Gilgames' dream and informs her son of his male lover-to-be. She was probably the first fictionalized person to be so supportive of a gay relationship. This mother, unlike many mothers, did not insist that her son take a wife and have children.

There are hundreds of thousands of gay Americans who were born between 1930 and 1970 and were taught that they must get married and raise a family. Many did.

---

31   http://www.apa.org/pubinfo/homosexuality.htm

However, years later, biology won out. These men and women have confronted their repressed homosexuality and came out of the "closet" to their families and their children. Fortunately, most of these children were born in an era where there is greater understanding and acceptance of homosexuality; many are quite understanding and accepting of their gay parents. The raising of normal children within marriages containing at least one covert gay parent should be convincing evidence that two gay parents, as adoptive parents, can be great role models.

Members of the helping professions such as therapist, psychiatrists, psychologists, religious liberals, gays, lesbians, bisexuals, and human sexuality researchers define sexuality in terms of the total self.

This includes internal feelings and self-identification where sexual acts flow from one's orientation. If a homosexual refrains from homosexual behavior, the person is still a homosexual. If a heterosexual person refrains from sex, they are still heterosexual. Sexual orientation is considered, by people of science, to be fixed for life [by God?] and cannot be changed by therapy or prayer, only subverted or repressed.

There are a number of organizations, usually religiously based, claiming to assist gay persons change their orientation (be cured of their gayness). Few people, outside religion, hold such a belief. The Los Angeles Times Newspaper printed the following article on conversions.

3 Former Leaders of Ex-gay Ministry Apologize[32]
They cite psychological harm they caused gays as the ministry,
Exodus International, meets in Irvine.
By Rebecca Trounson, Times Staff Writer
June 28, 2007

Three former leaders of Exodus International, often described as the nation's largest ex-gay ministry, publicly apologized Wednesday for the harm they said their efforts had caused many gays and lesbians who believed the group's message that sexual orientation could be changed through prayer.

One highly documented book on the failure of conversions is *One Nation Under God* that chronicled forty years of people in search of a cure for being gay. One example is Gary Busse and Michael Cooper, founders of Exodus, a ministry aimed at converting gays into ex-gays. After years of preaching this dubious gospel, via pamphlets titled *Unhappy and gay? Join the Exodus,* they admitted that they had fallen in love, quit the movement and started preaching tolerance and acceptance of the gay lifestyle. They had become ex-ex gays.[33]

One Nation exposed attempts by change-groups to appropriate terminology of other therapies du jour—calling their services a Recovery Movement, while simply peddling

---

32   http://www.latimes.com/news/printedition/california/la-me-exgay28jun28,1,4252152.story?coll=la-headlines-pe-california

33   http://www.beyondexgay.com/article/busseeapology

Victorian values and using fear and intimidation to scare people "straight." This can lead to suicide. Some conversion experts suggested that gay men ought to play football. Lesbians just need a makeover and a good manicure. This approach to change was a joke, false, and destructive to many whose only "sin" was being who God made them. Those that turned to Exodus International or the defunct organization, Quest, were asking for more turmoil and inner-hatred. They found only a life of continued guilt and despair. That was the only thing such groups could offer gays and lesbians struggling to come to terms with their true self in a hostile and rejecting world, including churches that join in condemnation of the gay community based on Biblical mistranslations and their misapplication.

Kent Philpott's book, *The Third Sex*, presents the testimonies of six homosexuals who supposedly converted to being heterosexual. Within a year of publication, all of the book's subjects sent notarized affidavits to the publisher, stating the book was untrue and that they were still homosexuals.

Nevertheless, the book was printed and sold, as originally copyrighted with no repudiated stories, for eight years. Even today, people are praising God for conversions that never took place. The continued publication of the book highlighted the deception fundamentalists were willing to promulgate in order to foster their belief in a goal based on illusion and hope rather than reality. Honesty and truth are expendable items for some fundamentalists.[34]

Straight To Jesus: Sexual and Christian Conversions in the ex-Gay Movement was written by Tanya Erzen. She wrote about her years of interviewing conversion movement devotees and noted that the religious aspects of the movement may be over turned if it is proven that sexuality is truly fixed or not chosen. The religious community prefers to think that homosexuality is chosen and therefore changeable. However, Erzen notes that even if one's orientation is created at birth, the converters believe that through Jesus' mercy, victims can convert to heterosexuality. (P. 15)

Those who claim to be healed or cured of their homosexuality are few in number and have not yet lived their entire life to ascertain whether or not they will ultimately return to their original, God-given orientation. For those who claim to be cured, I have this to say, if you can fool yourself, you can fool anyone.

Jack T. Chick, publisher of a massive number of fundamentalist, Christian religious books and tracts produced a small tract, similar to a modern comic book, for young children. He called the tract *Birds and the Bees*. In the tract, he writes that the events at Sodom and Gomorra were as follows,

> God gave us a true picture of the Gay lifestyle in the Bible. Centuries ago, there were four cities under the control of Satan and his devils. The worst city was Sodom. These Sodomites, who worshipped Satan, were possessed with devils and they hated God. Their stink reached heaven and God was fed up with them. He planned to destroy them to keep their

---

34   <http://www.lionking.org/~kovu/bible/section10.html> November 09, 2008

filthy lifestyle from spreading…As soon as they got Lot and his family out of Sodom, God fire bombed the cities and turned them into ashes. Today, those same kind of people are back, but now they are called Gays!"

Reverends Mohler and Click are only a few of the so called religious-right. The phrase, religious-right, is not only synonymous with Christian fundamentalism but also carries certain political overtones. Just what is this fundamentalism and who practices it? Former President Jimmy Carter said in his book, *Back to Fundamentals*,

> I would describe fundamentalism as, first of all, a movement led almost invariably by authoritarian males who consider themselves to be superior to others and who have an overwhelming commitment to subjugate women and to dominate their fellow believers.

In keeping with Carter's train of thought, it might be useful to examine a part of the "Adorno Study" from *The Authoritarian Personality* published in 1950:

> …belonging to a religious body in America today certainly does not mean that one thereby takes over the traditional Christian values of tolerance, brotherhood and equality. On the contrary, it appears that these values are more firmly held by people who do not affiliate with any religious group…People who reject organized religion are less prejudiced than those who accept it.

Fundamentalists may be relatively uneducated or may hold advanced college degrees. They appear to have great emotional ties to their faith and seem to be attracted to strong male ministers who have great oratory skills and often threatening messages delivered with "fire and brimstone." They often possess great musical and oratory techniques. Some ministers involve religious rock music in order to appeal to the younger members of their faith. All preach about God's hate of certain sins among which are those alleged of the gay community. Their rhetoric often focuses on the fear of the loss of God's love unless the nonbeliever accepts, word-for-word, what the minister says is the word of God. More often than not, what the minister means is acceptance of the word of God as written, word-for-word, in the Bible without even attempting to understand other possible interpretations of the written word. The other unspoken ministerial message is, "My way or the sin way." It has been said that participants of this religious-right movement, such as the Jehovah Witnesses, frown on advanced education because an education may lead members to question their fundamentalist beliefs and thus stray from God.

A large number of the religious-right relies on the *King James' Version of the Bible*, for the final word in religious matters. Some seem to think that this version is God's direct voice, as if dictated by him, word for word, to King James' scholars. They do so without giving any recognition to the Catholic monks who carefully hand copied the early documents–and perhaps any biases of these early translators. Nor do they countenance any of the recent scholarship based on findings of the last hundred years that adds to our understanding of the context in which the scriptures were conceived and written, e.g., Dead Sea Scrolls, Nag Hammadi Library (Gnostic Gospels) and the ancient Ugarit Library of Syria.

It is as though the religious-right did not want to be bothered with facts or to consider alternate ways of reading and interpreting religious documents. This rigid adherence to a fundamentalist reading of the scriptures reveals an emotional attachment, based on biases firmly held within a closed mind that has the ability to hurt those who are in conflict with such fervently held conservative beliefs. While such beliefs can hurt the so called nonbeliever, they also deny the fundamentalist a deeper understanding of the faith they claim as their own.

Many of the rigid religious-right persuasion in the United States seem to claim only the most rigid and severe elements of the Judeo-Christian past. The main body of work framing this religious heritage is the Old and New Testaments. It is this body of religious work that is often quoted as the absolute and God-given "truth" for millions of believers. Many fundamentalists profess to believe every word in the Bible, as written, and that every statement in it is true. They don't seem aware that the Roman Emperor Constantine convened a council of early century Catholic leaders in 325 CE to establish the first uniform Christian doctrine, create the Nicene Creed, and set a precedent for establishing Church law via ecumenical councils of Bishops (Synods) and to create statements of belief and canons of doctrinal orthodoxy. The intent was to define unity of beliefs for the whole of ancient Christendom.

One of the matters to be considered during the first writing of the Creed was to prohibit self-castration. Canon1. (Jackson, p. 141) This action may have, in part, been taken because many early pagan religions practiced self-castration as a sacrifice to pagan gods and more closely simulated men taking on certain female sexual roles in pagan rituals. Not until 367 AD did church father Athanasius suggest the listing of the 66 books of the canon we know as the Bible. Not until 451 did we see the Creed we know today, thanks to the Council of Chalcedon.

When pressed about the contradictions between the Old Testament and the New Testament, we often hear fundamentalists say that the latter is the clarification of the "don't" in the Old Testament, or that the doctrine of the New Testament is the new rule of God through his son Jesus Christ. They say "this new rule is what we need to follow," as they continue to cling to certain select passages from the Old Testament. Other believers don't try to explain the differences. Yet fundamentalists find reasons in both the Old and New Testament for not liking the alleged sin, or the sinner, identified as a gay American. One should note, where the fundamentalist doesn't, that where ever the conditions of salvation are outlined in the Bible, sexuality or orientation is *never* mentioned. (Acts 4:12, Acts 16:30-31, Romans 10:9, Ephesians 2:8-9, John 3:16-17). Surely there was a reason for this exclusion.

Too frequently, the natural law is used to exclude gay persons from various modern sacred and secular privileges. This so called law is interpreted to mean that it is not the nature (unnatural or not occurring in nature) of humankind to love and lust for one of the same sex. Apparently, St. Thomas Aquinas, the principle author of the concept of natural law later adopted by the Catholic Church, did not know or suspect that same sex attractions are rampant in nature, i.e., natural. The author, Bruce Bagemihl, Ph.D., in his book *Biological Exuberance—Animal Homosexuality and Natural Diversity* has shown that homosexual attraction is very common (natural) among many animals, birds, and marine mammals. Some creatures form life long bonds. His scholarly work should put the myth of natural law and homosexuality to rest in terms of discounting human homosexuality as being against nature (not natural). Homosexual attraction does occur, and is common, in the animal world. This includes homosapiens as well.

The natural law argument has led to hate and persecution of members of the gay community for hundreds of years.

> These persecutions range from the torture and execution of Sodomites during the Middle Ages and the early modern period to the imprisonment of thousands of homosexuals on charges of crimes against nature in the nineteenth and twentieth centuries to say nothing of the guilt, alienation, and despair (sometimes leading to suicide) that millions of members [of the broader gay community] have felt as the result of the Church's pronouncements.[35]

The argument of natural law basically states that if God had wanted same sex attractions to be acceptable, He would have made it known, in nature, and if he had, sex between same sexed things would be ok that it was okay to be gay, but He hadn't. On the contrary, God has made it known to all willing to examine nature that homosexuality is okay because it is manifested in his animal world (nature), as well as in human beings, as a non-learned (natural) behavior. Homosexuality is as natural for the person as heterosexuality if for the straight person. To argue religion as the basis to dispute this is fallacious and based on no more information than a misunderstanding of the Bible gay and ignoring homosexuality in the animal kingdom of which mankind is a part.

That thing most valued by the fundamentalists' community is what we often hear referred to as "manhood" or "maleness." The essence of *straight* maleness is implied and this usually means the maximum amount of testosterone and all its manifestations. After all, man is to be the role model in the fundamentalist's Christian model of family. A closer look at family, however, reveals that somewhere between ten and forty percent of children grow up in a family without a father figure. In cases where there is a father, but divorced, about half of the fathers lose contact with their children in about three years. After ten years, the father is missing totally in about fifty percent of their children's lives. According to a study by the Children's Defense Fund, men are more

---

35   http://www.glbtq.com/social-sciences/roman_catholicism.html

likely, forty-nine percent, to defect on child support payments than their used car payment, where the default rate is only three percent.

Katherine Wynne Edwards, a Canadian biologist, and psychologist, Anne Storey, have reported on certain male hormone levels and noted some interesting results. Fathers who spend time bonding with their children, comforting their children or holding a child's recently worn clothing will have a drop in their blood levels of testosterone and a rise in estrogen and prolactin levels. In other words, the *good* father becomes hormonally less manly and hormonally more like a woman or mother as the man cares for his children. Hormones win out against the fundamentalists' ideal of a masculine male.[36]

Reverend Erwin W. Lutzer, in *The Truth About Same-Sex Marriage*, is a very outspoken opponent of the gay community and its quest for marital rights, but he does admit,

> …our sexual desires are rooted in creation, proof that sex was created by God as an expression of unity and love…Yes, the pursuit of a sexual partner is, for the homosexual or heterosexual, at root a search for God…but sex, separated from God's holy intention [represents] the presence of an alien, impure spirit…homosexual[s] seldom have an abiding commitment to alien bonds. And because they have experienced intimacy outside the proper boundaries, they will have a tendency to forgo any process of courtship and almost immediately seek genital intimacy.

I know nothing of the reverend's personal experience with homosexuals, but I have seen the activity he describes above as common in male heterosexuals. Just visit any club or bar on Saturday night and observe. I also know of hundreds of gay, committed couples who have lived together as a family for decades. One such family has been together for fifty one years. It is these members of the gay community that seek what the reverend wants to deny them, the legal right of marriage.

Homosexuality has been with us forever. Whether hidden, denied, forbidden, thwarted, misunderstood, overlooked, or suppressed, it has never ceased to be, nor will it ever. Evolving, modern scientific research has added greatly to the understanding of sexuality's circumstances and what it means to be gay. A modern reading of the Bible has shed light on its prohibitions and will be explored in the following chapter.

---

36   http://www.mayoclinicproceedings.com/inside.asp?AID=1207&UID=

CHAPTER V

Overview of Leviticus 18:22

a previous review of homosexuality produced information about the biological facts of homosexuality. In this chapter, we will evaluate Biblical references often used to condemn the gay community. It should become obvious that its alleged prohibitions are not as "Biblical" as some have thought and taught.

The Living Bible (a scripture of modern interpretation) greatly broadens the spectrum of the original Hebrew text to include any and all homosexual acts by men or women. This conservative view is confounded by not distinguishing between homosexual orientation and / or homosexual behavior.

A passage in Hebrew, "*Ve'et zachar lo tishkav mishkevei eshah to'evah hi.*" is taken from the Mosaic Code and often used to condemn homosexual *behavior*. The beginning of this verse is literally translated as, "And with a male you shall not lay lyings of a woman." Let's explore the possible meanings of this verse.

The first part of this verse is often interpreted as "homosexuality is absolutely forbidden." Yet many highly qualified religious scholars believe the beginning of this verse referred only to homosexual activities among men participating in ancient pagan temple rituals known to the Israelites at the time of the writing of the verse. If the verses were to be liberally translated, the Bible might read, "Ritual anal sex between two men in a pagan temple is forbidden." Most theologians and Biblical commentators agree that the verse is directed toward men who engage in some form of male-to-male sex. However, there is not full agreement about the spectrum of the so called forbidden act(s). This leaves room for more scholarship and biases.

The Living Bible greatly expands the scope of the original Hebrew to include **all** homosexual acts by men or women. The religious pundits who created this translation caused further confusion in the matter by not differentiating between homosexual orientation / drive and homosexual behavior. It should be remembered that one can have a homosexual orientation and never act on the inclinations associated with it. As far as pundits are concerned, "homosexuality in any form is absolutely forbidden." This is not, however, how the original scripture reads. Indeed, the Bible never mentions homosexuality. It couldn't. Homosexuality, as we know it, was an unknown concept to the ancients. The word did not exist in their time. Not until 1958 did a Biblical translator add to the Bible the word *homosexual* despite the fact that there is no such word in Greek, Aramaic or Hebrew.

The second part of the above Hebraic verse categorizes the type of sin to which this particular transgression is assigned. In the Mosaic Code there are two types of sin:

1. Moral Sin

This is brought about by rebelling against God. Most of The Biblical translations imply this when they translate the Hebrew Word "*to'evah*" into modern English as *abomination, enormous sin*, or *detestable.*" This could mean to give false testimony, to kill, to steal, etc.

2. Ceremonial Uncleanliness

This is caused by contacting a forbidden artifact or engaging in a behavior which might be quite acceptable to non-Jews, but which is, or was, forbidden to the Israelites. Eating birds of prey, eating shellfish, cross breeding livestock, gathering stones or sticks on Saturday, planting mixed seeds in a field (growing two different crops in a single field), and wearing clothing made of a blend of two textiles are examples of acts of ritual impurity which made an Israelite unclean.

Some of these offenses were not considered minor. A few transgressions called for the death penalty (stoning). It is, however, unclear how many, if any, people were actually stoned to death for these offenses.

In *"Ve'et zachar lo tishkav mishkevei eshah to'evah hi,"* the verse appears to be fragmentary and incomplete. The precise meaning of "and with a male you shall not lay lyings of a woman" is unclear. The interpretation of the words "lay lying" is far from being precise and has no absolute clear interpretation. There have been attempts to make more sense of the original Hebrew by editing the phrase and injecting a short phrase into the original verse in several modern Bibles as seen below.

First, table your religious biases.

Consider:

1. In the *Net Bible* translation, two words are inserted into this famous verse to yield,

    And with a male you shall not lay [as the] lyings of a woman.

    The intent of many conservative interpreters is to have this verse read,

    A man shall not have sex with another man as he might have sex with a woman.

Some say this means anal intercourse between two men is not permitted. From this proposed literal word-for-word translation, a smoother English translation might read,

    You must not have sexual intercourse with a male as one has sexual intercourse with a woman.

First, I would contend that two men cannot have sex "as with a woman." While sex between two men might include anal intercourse, one would presume that the phrase "sex as with a woman" is a male having vaginal intercourse. Therefore, men cannot have sex with a man as with a woman because men don't have vaginas. This is not to say that a woman cannot be anally penetrated by a male. However, Jewish men allegedly did not have anal sex with their wives. That would have been considered unnatural, unclean, and non-reproductive. This misunderstood verse cannot be used as a prohibition against a male-to-male sexual encounter in today's parlance. However, the ancients may have had sex, man-to-man, where one male symbolically fulfilled the role of a female (with or without having been castrated) in certain pagan sex rituals.

Secondly, male-to-male sex need not be limited to anal sex; therefore, other forms of male-to-male sex are ignored by this narrow interpretation. People like to argue that same-sex partners have parts that don't fit, therefore these people should not engage in same-sex activities. Those promoting this complimentary parts argument overlook the fact that the parts do fit, in many ways. If they didn't fit in some meaningful way, people would have given up same-sex activities centuries ago.

2. An alternative translation to this famous verse might be to insert different words to yield,

    And with a male you shall not lay **[in the]** lyings of a woman.

This could be interpreted to mean that two men must not have sex on a woman's bed. Presumably, they could go somewhere else to have sex without offending anyone, including God.

The ancient Hebrews believed the bed of a wife should be considered sacred and to be used only for sleeping and heterosexual sex. In this case, the "lyings" is interpreted as the bed of a woman (wife).

There is another Hebrew verse that *may* have some association with the intent of this discussion.

> [a man who touches anything] she slept on shall wash his garments
> and bathe in water and is impure until the evening (a ritual impurity).

We know that some ancient Arabs, also a nomadic people, had a special way of housing a person who was sick or menstruating. This p r o c e s s may have held for the ancient Israelites as well. The ill or menstruating were separated from the remainder of the family and the tribe. This may have been accomplished by using a separate tent, or in some cases, they erected a section of tenting in such a way to create a wall within the tent and thus created a separate room for the *unclean* person.

We know the ancient Israelites considered menstruating women as unclean, or untouchable, and w e r e separated from her community during the period she was considered unclean. We also know that nomadic desert people did not always have sufficient water for bathing or to wash clothing. Limited water supplies were collected and stored in animal skins, and were probably used only for drinking between stops at springs or oases. Soap was not to be invented for thousands of years in the future, and personal hygiene was far from what modern man would consider acceptable.

Two to three thousand years ago, clothing was probably not washed but worn until it fell apart. For the ancients, everything had to be reused and this included bedding. For the Israelites, bedding used or touched by a menstruating woman was unclean but not forever. Since the Israelites were to be fruitful and multiply, Hebrew families were probably large and probably included several females menstruating at the same time. Bedding was not believed to be plentiful for these nomads. Given such a situation, the bedding or *lyings* of these women may have been unclean for weeks under Jewish law. Consider a menstruating daughter serially using the bedding of her m e n s t r u a t i n g mother, grandmother or sister(s)

If we were to presume that a male Israelite was having male-to-male sex, he might have been a married man because of cultural pressures. If he wasn't, then where did he live and sleep? Where was his bed? Since family and family structure was so important to the ancient Hebrews, an unmarried son was not likely to leave his father's home and live independently. Such a man probably lived with his father, mother, and probably some brothers and sisters. Where then might a single or a married man have sex with another man and avoid being seen or discovered by members of the tribe? There were few if any trees in the area where the nomads pitched their tents, so there was no forest to hide in. Sometimes there were rocks that might provide a place for a secret rendezvous. Or—a place where men would not be suspected to go? I suggest that they might have gone to the area of the unclean women. The male lovers may have used the bed (lyings) of another person, perhaps the menstrual bed of his mother's / sisters' bed or that of his male friend's mother / sister. Could this use of an area and unclean bedding (lyings) be the abomination mentioned in the scriptures and not sex itself? The men would have been committing a ritual sin for use of the lyings (bedding) of a woman.

What is considered to be the correct translation of Leviticus?

It is imperative for a student of the Bible to determine, as accurately as possible, what behavior is forbidden before pontificating on the subject. Is it:

- Any or all homosexual inclinations, thoughts or acts between either two males or two females?
- Sexual orientation, thoughts, or behavior of any kind between two men?
- Only anal sex between two males?
- Anal sex, only, between two males in a pagan temple ritual
- Male homosexual acts committed in a woman's bed?

Such things as oral sex, mutual masturbation, consensual touching and faux copulation with the penis between a partner's thighs are not hinted at in these prohibitions of the verse mentioned above. Are they, therefore, permitted behaviors? There is no consensus on the possible interpretations of this controversial verse.

Many people prefer to select the interpretation that most closely mirrors their personal beliefs, biases and prejudices about Biblical homosexual behavior. Conservatives have their biases, and the gay community has theirs.

Some English translations of Levitical verses

English translations of the above, and other parts of the Bible, are in general, along traditional biases. Book publishers, including publishers of Bibles, are under tremendous economic pressures to make their endeavors profitable. If a new translation of Leviticus 18:22 did not include the general condemnation of male homosexual behavior, sales and profits would drop. Bible publishers are not likely to stray from predetermined, conservative, or traditionally accepted interpretations of the Bible, unless they want to sell a translation specifically printed for non-fundamentalist Christian and Jewish liberals. This approach harkens back to an old adage of sales and marketing. "Give the public what it wants." Never mind what the truth might be.

This concept might be paraphrased to mean, "don't bother me with facts, my mind is made up."

Translations of the Hebrew verse "*Ve'et zachar lo tishkav mishkevei eshah to'evah hi*" are handled in differing ways. Below are examples of some of the different Biblical translations:

> **English Standard Version** (ESV): *"You shall not lie with a man as with a woman; it is abomination."*

> **King James Version** (KJV): "Thou shalt not lie with mankind as with womankind: it is abomination."

> **Living Bible** (LBV): "Homosexuality is absolutely forbidden, for it is an enormous sin."

> **Net Bible** (NB): "You must not have sexual intercourse with a male as one has sexual intercourse with a woman; it is a detestable act."

> **New International Version** (NIV): "Do not lie with a man as one lies with a woman; that is detestable."

> **New Living Translation** (NLT): "Do not practice homosexuality; it is a detestable sin."

> **Revised Standard Version** (RSV): "You shall not lie with a male as with a woman; it is an abomination."

The LBV and NLT translations use the term homosexuality, which was coined in the nineteenth century. It can be confusing and deceptive for the following reasons. The ancient Hebraic verses refer only to *some* sexual acts between two men. Selected use of the English word homosexuality in some of these passages is obviously intended to condemn lesbian activity as well. Lesbian sexual behavior is definitely not mentioned in the original text in question. In fact, lesbian sexual behavior, per se, is never addressed anywhere in the Hebrew Scriptures. One might argue that females, in general, were too inferior to socially matter, or two women would never bear children to confuse heritage and inheritance issues. Most importantly in regard to the Old Testament, God did not care! He ignored the subject.

The word *homosexuality* has two very explicit meanings in modern English. Occasionally, it refers to certain sexual acts that people prefer and in which they participate. At other times, it might refer to one's sexual orientation, preferences, or basic concept of self without acting on those preferences. One could conclude from an English translation of the Hebrew Bible that homosexual orientation alone is frowned upon; others might conclude that only homosexual behavior is forbidden. Context will later be shown to be of paramount importance in determining which assumption is correct. However, let me state here that the ancient Hebrews were people who considered actions or behavior more than thoughts.

The word *homosexual* is from our Victorian past. There is no Hebrew word meaning homosexual. Wherever the word is found in English translations of the Bible, you should be aware that someone (or some group) might, consciously or unconsciously, be imposing their prejudices upon the sacred text. No matter which person or group of people creates which translation, the translators want their belief to be the reader's belief above all other Biblical considerations, including sexual matters. If they hadn't believed that their translation was correct, they would not have released it. The gay community is often demeaned by Biblical language constructed out of conscious or unconscious personal prejudices proffered as absolute truth.

As part of my interpreting the Bible, I like to take the approach of looking inside the lives of the ancient Jews and their scriptures to discern for myself what the writers were trying to convey to their ancient peers. The God of the ancient Jews was in fact God only to the tribe of Israelites. God spoke only to the Israelites of the Old Testament (or Torah). Prior to this covenant, the Israelites had worshiped a number of pagan gods. Even while Moses was receiving the Ten Commandments, some of the Israelites reverted to idol worship.

The Israelites and God had bargained as to what they would give unto God and what God would give them. Jews, and they alone, had a covenant with God. They and they alone were *his* chosen people! The Torah, or Old Testament, was the written word of God to his single, chosen tribe! We don't know if God tried to covenant with other peoples, or if so, did they refuse him. We only know that God chose the Tribe of Israel with whom to covenant.

One has to remember that there were several life situations that threatened the existence and longevity of the ancient Jewish people. Among them were wars and the hardships of every-day life, including high infant mortality. Because of these losses, the Israelites needed to continually repopulate the Tribe of Israel. It is believed that the average life span of an ancient Jew was about thirty five to forty years. Girls were married by the age of fourteen and were expected to be "fruitful and multiply," often by the age of fifteen, in order to provide:

- a legitimate heir to family wealth,
- workers for the fields, herders, etc., and
- an increase to the numbers of the Tribe of Israel and
- to produce future Israelite warriors.

Sex for the purpose of sexual enjoyment might have been considered a waste of potential seed, or life, by the ancient Hebrews. Hence, the ancient Israelites were encouraged to have sex that produced children and downplay sex that did not produce new Israelites. To do otherwise, even by heterosexuals, could have been seen as going against nature and God's will.

Homosexual acts produced no children and were probably equated, in the minds of the ancient Hebrews, to certain religious rituals performed for a pagan god who sometimes received child sacrifices, semen, genitals, and ritual sexual acts. Several writers described the Canaanite sacrifices as occurring while chanting and drums drowned out the screams of the child being burned alive, held in the arms of the bronze god, Mo' lech.

II Kings 23: 10,

> And he defiled the *Tophet*, which is in the valley of Ben-hinnom, that no man might make his son or his daughter pass through the fire Mo' lech.

Jeremiah 32: 35,

> And they built the high places of the Ba'al, which are in the valley of Ben-hinnom, to cause their sons and their daughters to pass through the fire Mo' lech; which I did not command them, nor did it come into my mind that they should do this abomination, to cause Judah to sin.

The ancient scriptures frequently make mention of man's seed. It would appear that the ancient Jews thought of a man's ejaculate as containing an entire life form that needed only an appropriate place to grow (much like a seed planted in the ground) and to produce another person. As such, man's seed should not be wasted or allowed to fall in such a place as to deny it a chance to grow and mature into a human being. In particular, it should become a Jewish male.

Accompanying this concept was the apparent belief that a woman's womb could somehow deny the seed a chance to become a male. Instead, a less preferred female would be born or *given* to a husband. Given this concept of *seed*, one can understand why the Jews were so upset about the pagans offering their ejaculate to pagan gods or that Onan did not ejaculate into his sister-in-law as Jewish law prescribed. He spilled his seed on a place where it could not grow into a person thus ignoring the Jewish law which offended God and God's law.

This law was for the protection of a woman whose husband had died without leaving a son to inherit the father's goods or to care for the widow in her old age. Without such a caregiver, the woman would become a burden to the tribe.

The ancient Israelites were originally a nomadic people but later became city dwellers as camping sites and small villages slowly grew larger. Jerusalem grew quite large, becoming the center of Jewish religious life. It was the only place where blood sacrifices could be made to the Jewish God who was believed to inhabit only the "holy of holies" of the Temple in Jerusalem.

Ancient Israel had indistinct borders and was surrounded by peoples of various religious faiths who intermingled with the Israelites for political, social, and financial reasons. A common religion in and around ancient Israel was what we would today call a mother-earth religion. The mother goddess was Astaroth (known by many other names, depending on the culture or nation in which she was revered). Astaroth or Astarot is derived from Ashtoreth as in 1 Kings 11:5, "the goddess of the Sidonians." She was worshiped as the goddess who was responsible for all life. Cosmic sex between her and a male god, Mo'lech, was believed to promote the creation and growth of plants, animals, and people. Ritual sex, sometimes male-to-castrated-male sex, was a regular part of Astaroth's religious celebrations. Such acts were to symbolically join the earthly and theologically conceived planes of religious beliefs in these ancient religions. Even King Solomon built a temple to the god Mo' lech where small children were burnt as sacrifice to this pagan god depicted as a male image with a head like a bull. This Solomon-built temple was not a place for Solomon to worship but the people of this pagan faith who lived in his Israel.

In charge of the celebrations and daily care of Astaroth were priests, some of whom were castrated, perhaps self-castrated (Dods, p. 754). At designated times of the year these men, and perhaps very young boys, would dress in women's clothing and present themselves as "female" disciples of the goddess. In this role, the boys and castrated men would have sex with (presumably heterosexual) community men who came to the temple for certain religious activities. Celebrants would lie with the temple boys and castrated priests as though these members of the temple staff were women. One can only guess as to what, if any, type of sexual penetration may have occurred. However, one would assume that some of the community men did engage in female anal intercourse if the priestess wanted to avoid pregnancy, but there is no known evidence to decide this question. As a general rule, it is believed that most men of that time preferred vaginal copulation. Otherwise, one might assume that there were enough prohibitions against anything out of the heterosexual norm to impede such acts except religion.

It appears that a primary concern of the Hebrews was the waste of one's seed in pagan worship. This was probably at the heart of the matter regarding the Hebrew's and God's stated abominations. The ancient Jews were surrounded by Canaanites. The pagan religion of these people involved orgies (Falk p 129, Gordon p 88-94, 160-163, Seiglie p 29). Male and female prostitutes were sacred to the followers of these religions. Money (offerings) derived from the prostitute's religious activities went toward the support of temples devoted to the pagan gods. It was this ritual sexual activity, known to the Jews, which was prohibited by ancient Hebraic law. Prohibition was a way to set themselves apart from the pagans and to protect the integrity of their ancient Jewish culture, society, and religion.

These pagan forms of worship were referenced in ancient tablets found in Ras Shamra (Ugarit) n o w known as northern Lebanon. Worship involved the use of a lcohol and sexual promiscuity resulting in a drunken orgy…they saw semen and rain as symbolic equals in their fertility rites."[37]

Rick Brentlinger (p. 296) believed that St. Paul referenced these practices.

Romans 1: 26, (*King James Bible, Cambridge Ed.*)

> For this cause God gave them up unto vile affections: for even their women did change the natural use into that which is against nature:

Paul did not believe this verse represented lesbianism as known today. This pagan form of sex may have been chosen for its avoidance of unwanted pregnancies within the temple and an act performed as part of worshiping a pagan god. Therefore, I question whether or not these celebrants (presumably heterosexual) had anal intercourse for sexual pleasure alone, since prostitutes were known to be available to heterosexual men in the ancient world.[38] However, I know of no one who can say with 100 percent certainty that ancient Jewish men never had anal sex with their wives or prostitutes.

It appears that the primary concern of the Jews was that someone might engage in idol worship instead of worshiping the true God. This is seen in the two verses below.

Leviticus 18: 21,

> And you shall not let any of your seed pass through Mo'lech, neither shall you profane the name of your God: I am the Lord.

Leviticus 20: 2-5,

> Again, you shall say to the Sons of Israel: Whoever he be of the Sons of Israel or of the strangers that sojourn in Israel, that gives any of his seed Mo' lech; he shall surely be put to death: the people of the land shall stone him with stones. And I will set my face against that man and will cut him off from among his people; because he has given of his seed Mo' lech, to defile my sanctuary, and to profane my holy name. And if the people of the land do at all hide their eyes from that man, when he gives of his seed Mo 'lech, and do not kill him, then I will set my face against that man, and against his family, and will cut him off, and all that go astray after him, whoring after Mo' lech from among the people.

---

37   http://www.theology.edu/ugarbib.htm

38   http://www.theology.edu/ugarbib.htm

The ancient writers of the Old Testament no doubt presumed heterosexual intercourse was performed in the "missionary position." If true, this may explain the phrase "…man lying with man as with a woman." Why then would a man approach a castrated male for a woman-like sexual experience, if a female could be engaged for sex? One might argue that the pagan male celebrant approached the castrate as though the castrate was the true mother-earth-goddess and to enter him (the symbolic goddess), in any way, would be considered as having "normal" sex with the goddess and therefore a religious experience. I believe it was this connotation of temple sex and the phrase "lying with men" about which the ancient Israelites wrote their prohibitions. This type of sexual union was considered to be an abomination (disgusting), if it was performed by an Israelite, since it was duplicating a religious act reserved for a pagan god. Such worship placed that god above or equal to the God of the Israelites.

I doubt this ancient prohibition against male-male sex had anything to do with homosexual love and / or homosexual sex as known today, yet male-male sexual acts are considered by today's religious-right to be an admonition even in the absence of a pagan god. This present day mistaken belief is based on the *presumed* face value (and biases) of the written word presented as law and command to the ancient Jews alone.

The Laws of the Old Testament were given by God to His people, the Israelites. The laws concerned *only* the Jews and while in *their* land, wherever they ruled.

Deuteronomy 4: 5,

> Behold, I have taught you statutes and judgments even as the Lord my God commanded me, that ye should do so *in the land* whiter ye go to possess it.

Deuteronomy 4: 14,

> And the Lord commanded me at that time to teach you statutes and judgments, that ye might do them *in the land* whither ye go over to possess it.

Deuteronomy 5: 31,

> I will speak unto thee all the commandments, and the statutes and the judgments, which thou shalt teach them, that they may do them *in the land* which I give them to possess it.

Deuteronomy 6: 1,

> Now these are the commandments the statutes, and the judgments, which the Lord your God commanded to teach you that ye might do them *in the land* whiter ye go to possess it.

Jacob Milgrom (p. 1569, 1750 1790) seems to hold the same thoughts as those expressed above. Only Jewish males and residents from other lands, living on Israeli land, were prohibited to have male / male sex. There was no generalization of the law to others.

To ignore the cultural and non-Jewish religious connotations of the ancient peoples and lands where the Israelites lived has helped to create biased beliefs regarding today's gay community and the earlier list of negative adjectives foisted upon America's gay men and women. This brief look at the Biblical source, which is so often used to condemn the gay community, should help remove some biases against homosexuals and provide insight into how the community might argue for change in the misguided religious condemnations against it.

Homosexual cult prostitution was the primary form in which homosexual intercourse was practiced in Israel.

ROBERT GAGNON,
THE BIBLE AND HOMOSEXUAL PRACTICE

CHAPTER VI

What's in a word?

It is difficult to get a man [minister] to understand something when his salary depends on him not understanding it.

UPTON SINCLAIR

*I*n the last chapter, we briefly explored portions of the book of Leviticus. Leviticus is often used as a source of the words frequently used to denounce homosexuality. Words have the ability to heal and they can hurt, when used to intentionally or unintentionally inflict harm. In this chapter, we will examine certain Hebrew Biblical words and how they have been misused to hurt or damage the gay community.

English translations of 1Kings 14.24, 15.12, 22.46, along with Deuteronomy 24: 17, 21, Kings 23: 7, Job 36: 14, and some fundamentalist Christians have used the Hebrew word *qadesh* to mean homosexuals. Current scholarship suggests that this word should be translated as "male temple prostitute" (*Theological Word Dictionary of the Old Testament*). It may also simply mean "unclean." Qadesh comes from the Hebrew word *qadash* which means sanctified, clean or holy. The suffix change (-ash to -esh) causes the opposite meaning of the root word. The Hebrew word *qadeshah* refers to a female sexual priestess. It is also linked with *zanah,* meaning whore or prostitute, as in Genesis 38:21-24 and Hosea 4:14.

In **Hosea 4: 14**, God associates prostitutes (*zanah*) and cult prostitutes (*qedeshah*).

I will not punish your daughters when they commit whoredom, (zanah, prostitution), nor your brides, daughters in law when they commit adultery, naaph idolatrous worship: for themselves are separated with whores, (zanah, female prostitutes) and they sacrifice with harlots, (qedeshah), female temple prostitutes.

Leviticus 18: 22 and 20: 13 is linked with I Kings 14: 23,

And there were also sodomites (qadesh) male temple prostitutes in the land : and they did according to all the abominations (towebah).

Similar sentiments are expressed in other chapters of Kings.

I Kings 15: 12,

And he took away the sodomites (qadesh, male temple prostitutes) out of the land.

I Kings 22: 46,

And the remnant of the sodomites (qadesh) male temple prostitutes.

II Kings 23: 7,

And he brake down the houses of the sodomites (qadesh, male temple prostitutes), that were by the house of the Lord where the women wove hangings for the grove (asherah) sacred poles set up to worship the goddess.

Doctors Gagnon (p. 48-49) and Greenberg (p. 94) write that male cultic prostitutes were common in the Mediterranean and Mesopotamian areas. They acted as the submissive partner in male / male sex during certain pagan rites dedicated to fertility idols, especially those of the Canaanites. However, there is no indication anywhere in the Bible that the word *qadesh* should ever be used to refer to *all* homosexual practices, *if* it refers to any sexual activity at all.

Genesis 18-19 and Jude 7 are two of the passages classically used by the religious-right to condemn homosexuality. However, neither of the two sexual words *Ekporneuo* and "going after strange" (or different flesh) *sarkos heteros* used in Jude 7 have anything to do with homosexuality. The literally meaning of the latter phrase "different flesh" is the one that has caused the disastrously erroneous connection with homosexuality.

If homosexuality was to be inferred, the prefix *homo* could have been substituted for *hetero* (prefixes of Greek, the language of the early Bible).

It has been implied that in the Sodom story, the male mob at Lot's door wanted to *know* (have sex with or rape?) the angels (who were actually non- human). The human men allegedly wanted interspecies sex with those inside Lot's house. Some have interpreted the phrase "going after different flesh" to mean wanting to have homosexual sex (with the angels who were not men but may have appeared as men or possibly women). However, I find this interpretation to be problematic. First, the mob at Lot's door was exactly that—a mob of men (maybe boys as well). They might have wanted to gang rape the angels which *appeared* to be ordinary people (men).

The concept of angels appearing as normal people needs some clarification. First, I believe that there is consensus that defines angels as nonhuman. Angels might have appeared in human form in order to carry out their function as messengers of God, but such images are illusionary as well as illustrative.

It seems most people think of angels as being male. The ancient Hebrews gave Hebraic male names to only three angels:

1. Gabriel: meaning my God's strength will save me
2. Michael: meaning no one can rival my God
3. Raphael: found only in the Apocrypha

There is, however, no evidence that they were in fact male or had any real human gender qualities at all. The Hebraic names were, no doubt, a reflection of male dominance among the ancient peoples. In fact, there are stories of (male) angels having sex with human females and producing interspecies children, the Nephilim.

Genesis 6: 1 - 2,

> Now it came about, when men began to multiply on the face of the land, and daughters were born to them, that the sons of God saw that the daughters of men were beautiful; and they took wives for themselves, whomever they chose.

The wickedness of these creatures caused God to bring about a flood to destroy these undesirable offspring. Other similar stories were excluded from the Bible, perhaps because they made God appear to be too cruel or possibly the story was not believable in the first place.

The doubt about the gender of the angels raises a question. Can a group of men have male homosexual sex with a non-male, non-human thing that only looks like a man? The mob could not have committed *sodomy* (as we know the word today), if there was no *person* to *sodomize*. The question alone should be enough to call into question whether the Genesis passage is relevant to contemporary, committed, gay relationships based on mutual love and respect.

Modern archeologists, Doctor W. Nash of Valparaiso University in Indiana and Doctor Thomas Schaub, Co-director, Dead Sea Plains Expedition, Jordan, worked in the south eastern plain area around the Dead Sea and unearthed a burial site and ruined city, now known as Bab edh–Dhra.[39] While exploration of this site has not revealed any evidence of mass destruction by fire, some evidence of fire has been found leading many to believe this ancient city might have been Sodom.

The Hebrew name Sodom is said to mean "burned city." A nearby sister city of Sodom is Numeira (Hebrew—meaning buried city) which is believed by some archeologists to be Gomorrah. Numeira was discovered to have massive evidence of destruction by fire whose source could not be easily identified.

These ancient cities were thought to be Canaanite, a people known to the Hebrews as a culture of abominations. Besides Genesis' mention of fire and brimstone falling on the plain cities it also mentions *overthrowing* of the cities.

Isaiah 13: 19 also mentions the cities being overthrown. This could mean destruction by earthquake as thought by some archeologists and suggested by the Hebrew name, *Numeira*, meaning buried. For those who demand to see evidence of massive fire-destruction of Sodom in order for such a city to be accepted as the Sodom of Genesis, perhaps they could accept what is now called Numeira as the real Sodom, since there is massive evidence of fire in this ruined city, and what is now suspected as Sodom could be Numeira since it was buried as might occur along with the destruction of an earthquake.

These ancient cities of Sodom and Gomorrah were thought by many to have been only fabled cities of the Old Testament. However, in 1979, an ancient library (17,000 clay tablets) was unearthed in Northern Syria. These were the Ebla Tablets and date to around 2,300 BCE. In the collection are references to Sodom and Gomorrah and the other plains cities mentioned in Genesis.

If these ancient cities are the fabled twin cities of the Bible, there is enough science available to account for a natural disaster causing the cities' destruction. Archeologists found *Numeira* to be surrounded by a deep layer of ash, implying widespread destruction of the ancient city by fire. The exact cause of such a calamity cannot be known from the archeological evidence, but geologists believed that an earthquake caused the City to collapse.[40] Experts believe the collapse was accompanied with the release of a large quantity of underground gas at the time of Sodom's destruction. This explosion and related fires caused large quantities of burning sulfur (still found in the area) to be thrown into the air and then fall back onto Sodom as fire and brimstone (burning sulfur).

Tar is another commonly found substance in the area of the Dead Sea. From time to time, large chunks of tar can be seen floating on the Sea's surface after being released from underwater tar pits. This too could have added to the intensity of the fire which

---

39   http://www.nd.edu/~edsp/index.html

40   http://www.accuracyingenesis.com/sodom.html

destroyed Sodom. Sulfur and tar balls are still used as fuel by modern Bedouin tribes, who continue to live and tend flocks in this sparsely inhabited area. The author, Rami G. Khouri, has written extensively about this subject.

Earthquakes are quite common in the area of what is thought to have been the destroyed twin Biblical cities. There have been seventeen recorded earthquakes in the past 100 years in and around this area, giving credence to the argument that the cities were destroyed by earthquakes and associated phenomena.

Authors Astronomer Mark Hempsell[41] and engineer Alan Bond[41] have another theory for the incineration of the plain cities of Sodom, Gomorrah, Admah, and Zeboim. The clue came from an archeological artifact from ancient southern Iraq. The so called Planodisc had been stored in the collection of the British Museum for decades. The disc was made of clay and engraved by a very skilled ancient Sumerian astronomer, but there was no clear understanding of how the disc might have been used or what one of its strange engravings meant. After much study, Hempsell and Bond concluded that the disc contained a very accurate depiction of the ancient Iraqi (Sumerian) night sky. They also deduced that a long misunderstood line on the disc represented a point which started in the constellation of Pisces and represented the path of an ancient asteroid across the Sumerian sky. Using modern NASA-like software and that of other institutions, the men were able to extrapolate the line out across the universe. One end extended into the Aten asteroid belt (belt of near-earth asteroids). The other end of the line extended into the Alps of Austria.

We know that if a large asteroid strikes the earth, we expect to see its after effects, i.e., a crater like Meteor Crater in Arizona. But there is no crater in Austria. Hopsell believes the ancient Sumerian asteroid, depicted as a line on the disc, exploded in the Austrian atmosphere much like the asteroid that created the destruction over the Tunguska region, which occurred near the Podkamennaya Tunguska River in what is now Krasnoyarsk Krai, Russia on June 30, 1908.

Astronomer Hopsell goes on to write that when the asteroid exploded, it released 100 times the energy of the world's largest bomb—10,000 megaton blast. The blast raised billions of tons of debris into the atmosphere that spread over much of the world. This caused several major earth changes. One was sudden climate change. It is believed the effects of the debris caused the once verdant Sarah and Middle East to become desert. Second, snow covered mountainous areas became flash frozen glaciers.

The University of Ohio has studied glaciers for years by drilling ice core samples in the earth's major glaciers. One such Peruvian sample contained flash frozen plants whose carbon dating is equal to that of the supposed date the Sumerian Asteroid was first seen.

The Sumerian asteroid debris fell heavily over the Dead Sea area as burning debris that had temperatures of 500° F. Such temperatures would have caused instant incineration of all flammable substances in the area of the cities of the plains.

---

41   Authors: *A Sumerian Observation of the Köfels' Impact Event*

With the aid of the computer and its graphic ability to "turn back the heavens" to the time of the asteroid event, Hopsell and Bond have pin pointed the date of the Sumerian event, June 29, 3123 BCE. This is a Bronze Age date and coincides with the general time period of the destruction of the ancient plain cities and the findings of earth climatic changes in all the glacier samples in the collection of Ohio University.

The ancient ruined city, thought to be Sodom, is believed to have housed about 1,000 people. One would presume that fifty percent of the inhabitants were women and about fifty percent were men. This in turn would suggest that a high percentage of the male inhabitants were heterosexual males. Some might have been bisexual and some may have been totally homosexual. Surely, all the approximately 500 males living in the city were not interested only in homosexual sex as the religious-right would lead us to believe. Likewise, I cannot believe that all the women living in Sodom were lesbian. San Francisco, known as a "gay" city, has a large gay community that is made up of approximately fifteen to twenty percent of the city's gay men and women. Most gay people find it hard to conceive of a city constituted of 100% gay inhabitants.

The Arabs living in the area of the Dead Sea have for centuries referred to this body of water as the Sea of Lot or Lot's Sea. As early as the sixth century, early Christians had made their mark on this piece of geography. Just south of Amman, Jordan, is a city known as Madaba. Here one finds the remains of Saint George Church, an ancient fifth century Greek Christian church. It is near the ancient city known as *Zoar* that is mentioned in the Sodom story. While the church was being renovated, an ancient mosaic map was found covered in part of its younger church floor. This early map of the region clearly identifies Jerusalem, *Zoar,* and other ancient cities of the area.

Identified on the map is a church that is thought to be the church dedicated to Saint Lot of the Sodom Story. In the rear of an actual nearby church site (thought to be Lot's Church) is a cave in which early bronze age artifacts have been found. It is believed that these items coincide with the time period of the Sodom destruction story. One will never know for sure if this is the cave in which Lot and his daughters hid, but early Christians must have thought so for them to have devoted so much effort in building a large church there so long ago. These findings add some credence to the general story of Sodom's destruction.

It could be argued that the *reporting* of the Sodom story was a publicity stunt. A *natural* "fire and brimstone" disaster may have occurred in both these ancient cities but was claimed, by the ancient Hebrews. They may have bragged that their God was responsible for the destruction and gave him credit as a way of magnifying his might. Canaanites were known to live in this region and were known for their pagan gods. The Hebrews could have claim that God was angry at the Canaanites for their pagan religion, involving homosexual religious acts, and that God destroyed the cities because of their citizen's wicked ways.

Aside from the archeology, scriptural context, and history of the Dead Sea area, another way of looking at the phrase "different flesh" might be to see the phrase as describing a *promiscuous* sexual relationship of any kind, but not a contemporary loving and committed homosexual relationship. None of the wording in the passages has any implication of homosexuality as known today.

It is possible that the words could be seen as being counter to the passages (Genesis 2:24, Mark 10:8, I Corinthians 6:16, Ephesians 5:31) where two flesh become one. Conservative traditionalists' reading of this Biblical passage assumes the natural law argument in which creation requires that sex should be limited to male and female relationships with the intent of producing children.

Jude 1: 7,

> Even as Sodom and Gomorrah, and the cities about them in like manner,
> giving themselves over to fornication, and going after strange flesh, are
> set forth for an example, suffering the vengeance of eternal fire.

Some Christians believe that "going after strange flesh" is a desire for homosexual sex or any sex that is contrary to the natural law and not performed in the "missionary position." By natural law, I mean the mistaken derivation from St. Paul's "nature theology" as found in First Romans, i.e., acts that are only found in nature and performed for procreative purposes.

While the concept of natural law can be quite broad, the strange flesh phrase may refer to women who engaged in anal sex in service of pagan gods—a practice known to Paul in Corinth. Those proposing the "natural law" argument often say that gay men use their genitalia for acts they were not designed to perform, therefore these men sin. Look around. How many people do you see wearing glasses? We constantly use parts of our body (the nose) for functions they weren't designed to fulfill (noses support reading glasses). Did nature give us ears so we could wear earrings?

Leviticus tells us that we should not eat shellfish. Why then do many Christian fundamentalists enjoy shrimp, oysters, clams, or mussels? Why are members of the religious-right not clamoring to close down seafood restaurants?

Leviticus informs its readers that they are:

1. to be circumcised
2. not to shave your beard
3. to observe Jewish Law
4. not to eat pork
5. to follow Moses—perhaps an indirect command
6. to follow the ten commandments
7. to make sacrifices
8. to observe the Sabbath
9. not to eat shellfish
10. not to engage in pagan ritual homosexual acts
11. not to use cloth woven of different elements, e.g. wool and flax

The Bible is filled with a plethora of things that a God-fearing person should not do. We should not speak against our parents, women should not wear red, and women should be quiet in church, avoid work on the Sabbath, etc. Nevertheless, modern American Christians have *chosen* to ignore these prohibitions, primarily because they do not conform to people's interpretation of the Bible and modern lifestyles. Ignoring these directives is a *conscious* choice.

We may *choose* not to obey these directives of scripture. If we choose to ignore them and feel comfortable with that choice, why then do fundamentalists choose not to re-evaluate their (mistaken) choice to single out the gay lifestyle as the supposed main Biblical admonition to observe? It is because people derive some measure of self-approval from such denouncements? All too often, this chosen belief provides a bully pulpit for conservative religious leaders to rally their sexually insecure audiences, and a way to create a cause around which votes and money can be garnered. In a sense, the choice is a political tool. For some fundamentalists, it is a power source.

From the perspective that Jude 7 is counter to the above referenced marriage texts, the point concerns someone having sex with a person that is *not* bone of your bone, and *not* flesh of your flesh, i.e., *different* flesh. A reading of Jude 7 does not negate the support of a relationship based on a loving commitment and faithfulness. A valid interpretation of this condemnation in Jude concerns having sex with whomever or whenever one wants. The "going after different flesh" may simply imply having sex differently (non-missionary position) and nothing to do with homosexuality. It may also mean that Jews should not have sex with non-Jews or pagans. Such a possible reading of the text appears to be more faithful to the original Genesis 19 passage where the focus is not on *any* possible homosexual aspect of the story but on promiscuity and aggression. The mob was bent on *raping* the angels. The men in the Sodom story were not looking for consensual sex!

An enlightened reading of the Jude passage reveals that the sin of Sodom (and perhaps Gomorrah) was something other than homosexuality that caused God to destroy the cities. Ezekiel clearly identifies the sin in question.

Ezek 16: 49,

> Behold, this was the iniquity of thy sister Sodom, pride, fullness of bread, and abundance of idleness was in her and in her daughters [*not sons*] neither did she strengthen the hand of the poor and needy.

I have wondered why the author used the word *daughter* if the *men* were wicked. As a literary convention, it would not be unusual to combine *daughter* with *her* but the fundamentalists would not do so if they ignored context or took the Bible to be inerrant. We find in,

Ezek 16: 50,

...they were haughty, and committed abomination before me; therefore I took them away as I saw good.

Flavius Josephus, an ancient Jewish historian, wrote in *Jewish Antiquities* 1: 194 –195:

Now, about this time the Sodomites, over weeningly proud of their numbers and the extent of their wealth, showed themselves insolent to men and impious to the Divinity, insomuch that they no more remembered the benefits that they had received from Him, hated foreigners and avoided any contact with others. Indignant at this conduct, God accordingly resolved to chastise them for their arrogance, and not only to uproot their city, but to blast their land so completely that it should yield neither plant nor fruit whatsoever from that time forward.

Homosexuality is not identified as the sin which led to the two cities being destroyed. As we know, the Bible is filled with abominations, however, homosexuality, per se, is never defined as an abomination. It appears that the inhabitants of Sodom (and perhaps Gomorrah) were accustomed to engaging in city wide pagan orgies (possibly homosexual / heterosexual) and gang-rape at any time, any place, whenever and wherever they wanted. They were, to say the least, a pack of drunken sociopaths preying on the weak or defenseless with no thought of the kinds of relationships God desired for humans beings, namely, an intimacy with God and each other. God, in his discussions with Abraham about the city of Sodom, decided that the city would be spared if ten righteous men could be found in the city. I have often wondered what might have happened within the city, if those ten righteous men had been found. God said that he would spare the city, but would God have permitted its inhabitants to continue their wicked lives? Would he have permitted the alleged homosexual acts to continue? Does God's agreement to spare the city mean the physical city but not the inhabitants? The larger question: was God "toying" with Abraham since God should have known ten righteous men of Sodom did not exist?

Genesis 19: 4 - 5,

But before they lay down, the men of the city, even the men of Sodom, compassed the house round, both old and young, **all the people from every quarter**:[42] And they called unto Lot, and said unto him, where are the men which came in to thee this night? Bring them out unto us, that we may *know* them.

---

42   Author's emphasis

The above verse may present a hurdle for some conservative Christians who prefer to read the Bible literally. Many such Christians prefer to construe this Genesis story as referring to men bent on engaging in a specific homosexual act. Note, however, that Genesis states "...*all* the *people* from every quarter" came to Lot's door. Surely some women lived in Sodom. If they did, why would they join the mob? Were the women interested in heterosexual sex (interspecies sex) or did they simply want to watch homosexual rape being committed by the men against the angels (inter-species sex)? I repeat an earlier question, can a man have homosexual sex with an angel who only appears to be a man or is this all just a question of Greek versus Semitic language skills?

As in the text above, the two key passages, Leviticus 18.19-22, and 20.13-18, concern some people when they try to painlessly mesh homosexuality with Christianity. Some people have thought the word *tow'ebah*, often translated as a ritual uncleanness, refers only to temple prostitutes and homosexual acts, such as anal sex (however this could involve men with women). These same people often see *tow'ebah* as meaning homosexuality in general. Others disagree with this interpretation. The antigay author, Robert Gagnon, has written, "Homosexual cult prostitution was the primary form in which homosexual intercourse was practiced in Israel." Current social, sexual and religious biases certainly play a role in our interpretation of scripture where fact cannot be clearly delineated. It should always be remembered that we never choose an interpretation that negates our belief. We must first negate a belief if interpretations are to be changed.

Leviticus 18 and 20 present reasons for readers to believe certain sexual activities rendered one ritually unclean, but not civilly or morally liable. Leviticus prohibits a man from having sex with a menstruating woman. Such sex rendered both unclean. In Leviticus 15: 2-5, there are codes or laws relating to restricted sexual relations with post–partum women (sixty six days after having a girl and seven days if a son was delivered). It should be clear that the Hebrew word t*ow'ebah* in Leviticus 18: 22 and 20: 13 was intended to indicate *ritual* uncleanness.

In the footnotes of the Boswell book, referenced below, note that Eusebius of Caesarea, and the *Apostolic Constitutions* state that the uncleanness that was derived from this behavior is ritual, not moral (not sinful?).

John Boswell writes in his book, *Christianity, Social Tolerance and Homosexuality,* 1980, the University of Chicago Press, p. 102 - 103,

> ...early Christians were exempt from Jewish Law as decreed by the Council of Jerusalem (ca, A.D. 49) except for: idol worship, from contact with blood, from eating things strangled.

Homosexuality could have been specified by the council, but was **not**. If the ancient Jewish Christians were apparently willing to permit homosexuality among Christians, or did not see this abomination as very important or not worth mentioning, why not modern society, which often chooses to quote only those passages of scripture that meets some need to denigrate the ten percent of the modern-day population known as the gay community.

There are only two passages in the New Testament that associate sexual sins with Sodom. We read in,

Second Peter 1: 10,

> Above all [God] will punish those who walk according to the flesh in the desire of uncleanness (*immunditia*) and who condemn authority.

> The desire of uncleanness might be thought of as same-sex desire except we read later in **Second Peter, 2: 14,**

> They have eyes full of **adultery** and [are] unceasingly sinful.

Let's remember that adultery is not homosexuality.

Jude 7- 8,

> Just as Sodom and Gomorrah and the nearby cities, fornicating and going after other flesh in the same way[as the aforementioned angels] were made an example, suffering the punishment of eternal fire, so too it will be with those who stain the flesh and spurn authority and blaspheme against majesties.

The aforementioned angels are the bad angels who exist in hell; not the good angels who came to help Lot. The writer of Jude understands the sin to be sexual, analogous to fornication and "going after other flesh." This last phrase may be an analogy to Genesis 6:1 and the sons of God copulating with the "daughters of men." There is NO clear indication the sin had anything to do with homosexuality unless one *chooses* to think so (each to their own bias). The distinction is between a *conscious* desire to read homosexuality into the verse but with no clearly defined scriptural reason to read it as such.

Church Father, Jerome, acknowledges that Sodom had taken on several spiritual and allegorical meanings. In one of his letters he responds to a question,

> Can a woman whose husband is an adulterer and a "Sodomite" count her marriage to him as dissolved?

Jerome responds with an emphatic NO.

...So long as a husband lives, be he adulterer, be he sodomite, be he addicted to every kind of vice, if she left him on account of his crimes, he is her husband still and she may not take another.

Letters 55: 3 [A.D. 396]

Jerome makes clear that to be an adulterer is different from being a Sodomite. However, he does not define what a Sodomite is.[43] Another church father, Ambrose, morally centers Sodom within a narrow meaning of sexual or bodily sin. He recognized the threats aimed at the angels with Lot to be a violation of hospitality.[44] In his treatise, *On Abraham*, he equates Sodom with fleshly indulgence, lasciviousness and disordered desire (*libido*).[45]

A Latin doctor of the church, Gregory the Great, prefers to think of stressed in his *Moral Readings of Job*.[46] His work would come to greatly influence medieval moral theology.

At one point, Gregory writes the words "the crime of the Sodomite." In two, tenth century handwritten copies of the text, there is an obvious bias of the scribe who transcribed "the crime of the Sodomite" as "of Sodomy."[47] Some reference books list Gregory's letter as the location of the first appearance of the term Sodomy. It is not! The term appears *after* Gregory.

For ten centuries, there was *no* abstract term to refer to the sin(s) of Sodom. If the early Christians wanted to focus on sex, as the "sin" of Sodom, why had they not chosen a word to describe that sin?

These aforementioned Levitical verses reference male-to-male sexual relations. Only one passage in the Scriptures *possibly* deals with lesbianism. Romans I was written with knowledge of ancient Rome's pagan religions and their rituals. St. Paul had, no doubt, passed many such temples as he traveled about Greece. As an apostle, he deplored these religions and wrote and spoke of his disdain for them. One must read carefully, not only his words, but his intention when reading Romans I.

Romans 1: 26 - 27,

For this cause **[idolatry**[48]**]** God gave them up unto vile affections: for even their women did change the natural use into that which is against nature **[priestess engages in anal sex for religious purposes**[48]**]**: And likewise also the men, leaving the natural use of the woman, burned in

---

43   Jerome Epistulae 55.4(3) (Hilberg 492-493)

44   Ambrose of Milan Hexaemeron 5,16.54 (Schenkl 32/1:181.10)

45   Ambrose of Milan DeAbraham 2.8.45 (Schenkl 32/1:599.9)

46   Gregory the Great Moralia in Job 14.19.23 (Adriaen 143A:711.8)

47   e1 (Milan, bibl. Ambrosiana MS C238 inferior, tent or eleventh century from Bobbio) e2(Paris, Bibl. Nationale MS Nouvelles acquis. lat.1452, tenth or eleventh century from Cluny), Norberg 140A:827-9

48   Author's addition and emphasis

their lust one toward another **[anal sex in service to pagan gods**[48]**]**; men with men working that which is un- seemly, and receiving in themselves that recompense of their error which was meet.

I believe the additions make reading and understanding Paul's work easier and clearer. The first addition helps to establish a context for explaining the activities of the women—idol worship. The women assumed the role of temple prostitute. The same is true for men who acted as temple prostitutes. Paul had no obvious reason to conceal his intent regarding homosexuality, unless he feared homosexuality within his own being. He wrote and spoke Greek fluently and could have declared that ALL forms of same-sex activity was wrong if he so intended, but he did NOT. Why not? Is it possible that this worldly man never thought that homosexuality could or would be practiced outside a pagan religion? I doubt such an assumption because "man-boy love" was still practiced in his day. His words have to be read in context, and I believe that they exclude homosexual acts outside of pagan / idol worship.

If one chooses to believe that lesbianism is sinful, then use the Roman passage alone, for Leviticus does not apply to lesbians. There is no single Hebrew word for any sexual act between two men or two women. In using the phrase "a man lies with a man," one **cannot** interpret this to mean a woman lies with a woman. This passage clearly refers only to men. To condemn male homosexuality and not female homosexuality is absurd if, indeed, homosexuality is wrong or forbidden because it is unnatural. Female homosexuality may have been ignored since it concerned females (who were of low social or monetary value). Sex between two women would not cause the birth of males who might challenge someone's inheritance, or were possibly ignored because women were considered only as incubators for a man's "seed."

Rick Brentlinger (p. 77) believes lesbianism is excluded from scripture because women do not penetrate each other. They can't transfer semen; therefore, lesbians presented no threat to established avenues of inheritances. Their form of same-sex acts produced no children and was relatively unknown to the Jews and hence no reason to legislate against it. There was no manly honor at stake. Lesbianism posed no threat to male dominance. Women were second class citizens and of little importance to ancient writers except possibly as a priestess.

- In the book of Jewish prayers. Jewish men are taught to say, "Blessed be the God who has not created me a heathen, a slave or a woman."
- A Buddhist prayer states, "I pray that I may be reborn as a male in a future existence."
- In Plato's *Republic,* we read, "Do you know anything at all practiced among mankind in which the male sex is not far better than the female?"
- Xenophon said, "The ideal woman should see as little as possible, hear as little as possible and ask as little as possible."

- The Koran teaches us that a woman is regarded "half a man" and that… "forgetfulness overcomes the woman. They are inherently weaker in rational judgment."

As a group, it appears that some Christian evangelicals struggle to retain the integrity of the Old and New Testament from a literal standpoint. Without this integrity, they could pick and choose scriptures that they like and throw out those they don't like (and some cases they do). Such an act would be unsound and theologically unwise. The religious-right has often created blinders that prevent them and others from seeing outside their biases. Homosexuality is one of those biases. The religious-right hopes to prove their biased point of view by quoting select passages from the Old Testament that are used out of context. They also selectively take passages from the New Testament they believe supports their viewpoint. In doing so, they become hypocrites because in devoting so much time to hating homosexuals and homosexuality, they are failing to fulfill the laws of love.

Examine Leviticus and you will find a list of crimes for which the punishment is death. These death penalty crimes are repeated again in Deuteronomy. However, homosexuality is **not** once mentioned, even though every one of the other death penalty crimes is listed. Do you think God forgot to inform the writers of these passages about what some call one of the greatest abominations of all times? Deuteronomy, however, mentions male sacred prostitution. It was called *to'evah*—an abomination. It may also mean something religiously unclean and / or associated with idols. This likely involved cross-dressing, mask-wearing, male prostitution rituals that were part of the Canaanite religion. In Leviticus 18:2-5 you find these acts referred to as the "doings of…Canaan."

The Septuagint (pre-Christian Greek translation of the Old Testament) translated *to'evah* in Leviticus 18:22/ 20:13 as *bdelygma* suggesting religious dirtiness and idolatry. The end of chapter 20 says all things declared *bdelygma* were *bdelygma* because they were the idolatrous practices of the Canaanites' involving cross-dressing, male prostitutes. The previously mentioned goddess Astaroth, and the god Mo' lech, are called the to'evah or *bdelygma* (2 Kings 23:13). Some of these prostitutes were boys, which explains why Leviticus 18:21 prohibits Jews from dedicating their offspring to serve Mo'lech as religious prostitutes.

The Jewish philosopher Philo (of Alexander), who died about seven years after Christ's crucifixion, had this to say about priests in pagan rituals.

> They [pagan priests] would apply themselves to deep drinking of strong liquor and dainty foods and forbidden forms of intercourse. Not only in their mad lust for women [? bisexual men] did they violate the marriages of their neighbors but also these men mounted males…then little by little they accustomed those who were by nature men to submit to play the part of women…

Philo, *On Abraham*, Chpt. 26, p. 134 - 136

Deuteronomy's passage on male temple prostitutes echoes Leviticus 20 instead of First Kings. Most telling is the instance in,

I Kings 14: 23 & 24,

> For they also built them high places, and images **[idols]**[49], and groves **[pagan sites]**[49], on every high hill, and under every green tree **[pagan fertility symbols]**[49]. And there were also sodomites **[pagan priests-castrates]**[49] in the land: [and] they did according to all the abominations **[pagan cultic sex and idol worship]**[49] of the nations which the LORD cast out before the children of Israel.

I Kings 15: 11, 12, 13,

> and Asa did [that which was] right in the eyes of the LORD, as [did] David his father. And he took away the sodomites **[cultic homosexual priests]**[49] out of the land, and removed all the idols that his fathers had made. And also Maachah his mother, even her he removed from [being] queen, because she had made an idol in a grove; and Asa destroyed her idol, and burnt [it] by the brook Kidron.

Traditionalists believe Leviticus prohibits homosexuality in general, but only in Deuteronomy is male temple prostitution directly addressed. One would therefore expect the writer of Kings to echo the themes of Deuteronomy where the subject of male prostitution is mentioned.

Deuteronomy 23: 17 & 18,

> There shall be no whore of the daughters of Israel, nor a sodomite **[pagan castrated priest]**[50] of the sons of Israel. Thou shalt not bring the hire **[fees]**[50] of a whore, or the price of a dog **[male pagan temple prostitute]**[50], into the house of the LORD thy God for any vow: for even both these [are] abomination unto the LORD thy God.

There is a parallel here with female prostitutes and the concern over bringing their pay into the temple. However, all the echoes of male homosexuality aren't repeated. What kind of oversight can that be? Instead, I Kings echoes several of the specific themes of Leviticus 18: 27-28, calling the practices *to'evah* (echoing the phrase "…

49   Author's emphasis

50   Author's emphasis

did all of the abominations"). These acts are characterized as practices of the former inhabitants of the land Canaan stating that those inhabitants were driven out of the land because of their religious practices. That the writer did not allude to the supposedly more specific passage in Deuteronomy is a bit odd—unless the writer regarded the Leviticus passage as similarly specific to the practice of cult prostitution."[51] According to Elmer A. Martens (p. 113), the Canaanites' religious rites included:

1. incense burning
2. sacrificial offerings
3. eating of sacrifices
4. idol worship
5. sacrificing children
6. prostitution (male and female)

What is there about male-to-male sex that got the ancient Israelites so uptight about this kind of sexual relationship? I like the explanation given by Ronald Long in his book, *Men, Homosexuality and the Gods.* The ancient Israelites lived at a time of hand-to-hand combat. The sword was a commonly used weapon whose purpose was to penetrate (kill) the enemy. They would be physically and symbolically wounded, bleed, and therein dominated and subjugated. The enemy could then be enslaved or killed. If enslaved, the enemy may also have been raped as well. To have been so mistreated was the ultimate defeat—the loss of manhood. Long (p. 76) has this to say,

> …raping the enemies themselves is a way of showing they lack the power to defend even their own persons, whether that assault is with the spear or arrow or…the erect phallus of the victor. Homosexual intercourse in this case is not an act of love but a demonstration of complete power over and humiliation of another. Indeed, the rape of the unwilling male may so impress itself on the mind that it overshadows knowledge of homosexuality among one's own people and eclipses the sense that homosexual intercourse might be an act of love.

Orthodox Rabbi Steven Greenberg notes that in the ancient near east, people were either penetrators or penetratees. To be a free male and to be penetrated was to be demeaned. Women, boys and slaves could be penetrated as part of their lot or society's expectation. However, penetration was done **to** a man not **with** a man. For an ancient Israelite (and some modern peoples) to be willingly penetrated by a male of equal or unequal status was to be womanized, reduced in social standing, humiliated, and demeaned. Rabbi Greenberg suggests Levitical prohibitions on same-sex acts pertain to (Author's paraphrased listing):

---

51   Royce Buehler <http://www.religioustolerance.org>

1. degradation of the penetrated person as the primary motive for sex,
2. motives as the primary focus, not the anatomy,
3. avoidance of idol cultic sexual practices and worship.

According to Rabbi Steven Greenberg, in *Wrestling with God and Men: Homosexuality in the Jewish Tradition,*[52] homosexual acts outside these parameters are permitted (not prohibited). Rabbi Greenberg readily admits that many rabbis will not agree with him.

The Greek term for male genitals, *medea,* was a straightforward anatomical term. The Hebrew term, *erva,* means "hideous flesh." Perhaps this is why Hebrew ritual, ceremonial circumcision is symbolic castration or ridding oneself of "hideous flesh" and perhaps uncleanliness. Circumcision is not necessary for hygiene and is currently in decline in The United States.

In Leviticus 15: 16 - 18 even semen is declared unclean, and men are admonished to bathe after they emit it. Any garment, or the *skin,* of another person upon which semen has fallen is similarly considered to be unclean. This prohibition is presumed to exclude intra-vaginal depositions.

Ancient Jewish attitudes towards sex, the male genitals, semen, and nudity seem extreme to modern peoples, but they may have grown out of an attempt to politically and religiously separate the ancient Jewish people from the advocates of pagan religions that surrounded them. In the various rites of the non-Hebrews or pagans, nakedness, masturbation, and the spread of semen on idols was a symbolic way of fertilizing a god. This form of worship was thought to be common with Baal in his idol form. During the time the Jews were captive in Egypt, they surely knew of the ritual in which Pharaohs spread their semen (seed) on agricultural fields and into the holy waters of the Nile. This ritual was part of the worship of Min, the god of fertility.

The condemnation of semen being used in idol worship is different from the sin of Onan, an ancient Hebrew, who refused to ejaculate into his widowed sister-in-law. Her husband had died without leaving a male heir. The Hebrew Law required Onan to marry and have sex with his sister-in-law—so much for the sacredness of marriage. However, Onan feared his newly acquired wife might give birth to a son (the law's intent) that would not be seen as Onan's son but that of his dead brother. To avoid this, Onan spilled his *seed* upon the ground (coitus interruptus).

Prohibitions regarding male genitals and nudity were directly linked to Hebrew laws specifically imposed against homosexual acts in the ancient world. In my opinion, these acts were pagan ritual acts **only**. Those prohibited acts were included in the religions of the Assyrians, Canaanites, and others in contact with the ancient Hebrews. The Hebrews felt obligated to renounce and refrain from anything even resembling these pagan religions and their rites.

Assyrian priests engaged in homosexual acts, often donning women's clothing to ritually acquire the magical powers of the Mother Goddess Ishtar. Some priests would

---

52   http://www.globalgayz.com/jewishgay.html

castrate themselves in religious imitation of the god Attis. According to one legend, three days after dying, Attis was resurrected as a female goddess. The lower acolytes in the religion (called *qadesh*, meaning holy ones) were those blessed or consecrated for divine pagan service. They would ritually prostitute themselves to all men who came to the temple as a symbolic way to collect fertilizing semen for the deity. These prostitute priests collected a fee from the community males who engaged these servants of the pagan god for ritual sexual activity. The funds were used for maintaining the pagan temple.

The same word *Qadesh,* meaning holy ones, was used by the Hebrews as an equivalent for sodomite. *Qedheshah,* was used for a priestess prostitute and as an equivalent for whore (see **I Kings** 14: 22-24, 15: 12, 22: 46; **Deuteronomy** 23: 17-18; **Leviticus** 18: 3, 24-30, 20: 23) all of which relate specifically to ancient Egyptian and Canaanite religious sex and homosexuality.

Most interesting in respect to these ancient pagan services is that the identical male homosexual religious rites were once commonly practiced in the ancient Temple area of Jerusalem. These activities were apparently an integral part of very early Jewish worship.

II Kings 23: 7 & 8,

> And he brake down the houses of the sodomites **[cultic pagan priests]**[53], that [were] by the house of the LORD, where the women wove hangings for the grove **[pagan holy place]**.[53] And he brought all the **[pagan]**[53] priests out of the cities of Judah, and defiled the high places where the priests had burned incense, from Geba to Beersheba, and brake down the high places of **[beside the]**[53] the gates that [were] in the entering in of the gate of Joshua the governor of the city, which [were] on a man's left hand at the gate of the city.

Here is mentioned the removal of the grove from the Temple. This may refer to a small place of vegetation where the mother earth goddess was worshiped. We are told religious items used in the ritual worship of other gods were also removed. King Josiah (640-609 BC) zealously burned out the room of the *qadesh* which was by (or in) the Temple. This room was used by weavers of tapestries (or hangings) for the grove. The King scattered and reviled the *qadesh*, but there is no clear evidence of them being killed. At this early date, the story of Sodom and Gomorrah had not yet acquired a homosexual interpretation. That developed much later. On May 14, 390 an imperial decree was posted at the Roman hall of Minerva, a gathering place for actors, writers and artists. The decree criminalized, for the first time, the sexual practice of those whom we call "homosexual" men. (Rev. M. Hyamson, p. 82 & 83)

---

53 Author's emphasis

Modern militant homophobia began in what was basically the historical accident of a local sectarian feud i.e., Hebrews vs. pagan neighbors. Unfortunately, the prohibition of a specific pagan religious practice quickly became a prohibition of male homosexuality, carte blanche. From this doctrine, we are left with Josiah's alleged anti-gay pronouncements, "Thou shalt not lie with mankind, as with womankind." It is an abomination, "If a man lie with mankind, as with womankind, both of them have committed abomination; they shall surely be put to death; their blood shall be upon them." (**Leviticus** 18: 22, 20: 13).

These passages (laws) occur in what is known as the "Holiness Code," which according to Rick Brentlinger (p. 109, 357) should have lost its sway over mankind when Christ died and was resurrected. Presumably, Brentlinger applies this reversal of rules to Jews as well, since many Christians believe Christ was the Jewish Messiah and the New Testament supplants old religious law.[54]

When Jesus was asked by the rich young ruler, "Which of the commandments do I follow to inherit eternal life," Jesus mentioned only six commandments—all relate to behavior:

Matthew 19: 18 - 19,

1. You shall not murder;
2. You shall not commit adultery;
3. You shall not steal;
4. You shall not bear false witness.
5. Honor your father and mother
6. Love your neighbor as yourself.

In these verses, Jesus edited the Ten Commandments and listed only those that were universal rather than particular (Hebrew) religious principles. These six commandments of Jesus could hang in any government building without violating the separation of church and state rule. They were, and are, part of the religious teachings of all the world's religions and many cultures' moral life. They are concerned with how one treats the other (don't engage in murder, adultery, thievery, lying, etc.). The omitted commandments have to do with how one honors a particular religious tradition. By the time the Gospel of John was written, this list of commandments was reduced to one (and the most important commandment).

John 13: 34,

I give you a new commandment, that you love one another.

---

54 <http://www.religioustolerance.org > December 30, 2006

If the religious-right is going to intentionally select one Biblical verse on which to mount a campaign regarding the gay community, why isn't it Jesus' new commandment to love and not the Old Testament verse, contrived by the fundamentalists, to impugn gays and generate hate toward the gay community?

In this chapter are examples of words that can be misinterpreted in ways to do harm to gay people and the gay community. The next chapter will further examine the ancient word *abomination* and how it too has been used stigmatize modern men and women.

CHAPTER VII

Exploring the meaning
of *To'ebhah*

(Often translated abomination)

Jerry Falwell:
[homosexuals are] brute beasts…part of a vile and satanic system
[that] will be utterly annihilated, and there will be a celebration in
heaven.

CHEADLE, RAND, HILL, JIM,
"THE BIBLE TELLS ME SO," ANCHOR BOOKS (1996), P. 69-70:

The previous chapter concerned itself with one word and how it could cause harm if inappropriately used. In this chapter, we will focus on other words often meaning abomination, and examine whether or not they should be applied to the gay community.

To'ebhah, which the ancient Hebrews understood to mean unholy, is currently used by Jews and many non-Jews to mean abomination, and a denigration of a sacred pagan practices or non-Hebrew religions. *To'ebhah* occurs many times in the Old Testament in the context of idolatry. At times, it is a sexual metaphor for "lusting after strange gods." In general, the word means something that is offensive to someone. "Joseph's brothers should not eat with strangers for to do so is an abomination." Its application to things not having to do with cults is unusual. Another Hebrew word, *sheqets*, is also translated as *abomination* or an *idolatrous object* (Strong's Hebrew Dictionary) and is applicable to unclean foods not to be eaten by the Israelites. The Bible uses the word abomination to condemn:

1. Canaanite idols and
2. the metals from which they are cast,
3. casting spells,
4. practicing magic, and
5. idol worship etc.

The Hebrew word *to'ebhah* (or a form of the word) appears over 100 times in the Hebrew Scriptures (Old Testament). This is where they can be found:

In the Torah 26 times:

- in Genesis 2 times,
- in Exodus 1 time,
- in Leviticus 6 times,
- in Deuteronomy 17 times.

In the Major Prophets 58 times:

- in 1 & 2 Kings 5 times,
- in Isaiah 3 times,
- in Jeremiah 8 times,
- in Malachi 1 time,
- in Ezekiel 41 times.

In the Writing of:

- Psalms 1 time,
- Proverbs 25 times.
- It is also scattered throughout Ezra and II Chronicles.

It is **not** used by the Minor Twelve Prophets, or in Numbers.

To'ebah is often translated as *abomination* or *detestable* in English. It can refer to the breaking of either a moral or ritual law. Examples of ritual codes involving *to'ebhah* in the *New King James' Bible* translation (a common source for fundamentalists) are:

- **Genesis 43:32**, ...because the Egyptians could not eat food with the Hebrews, for that is an abomination to the Egyptians.

The President of Egypt meeting the Prime Minister of Israel and sitting down to a meal together would be committing an abomination, IF this law held in modern times.

-   **Leviticus 11:10**, But all in the seas or in the rivers that do not have fins and scales, all that move in the water or any living thing which is in the water, they are an abomination to you.

    Eating a lobster, shrimp or shellfish is an abomination to the Hebrews and should be to the fundamentalists if they hold to their often touted belief in every word of the Bible as written.

-   **Leviticus 11:41**, And every creeping thing that creeps on the earth shall be an abomination. It shall not be eaten.

    We have been told that rattlesnake and alligator tastes just like chicken. However, it is not to be eaten by Hebrews or fundamentalists who believe in every word of the Bible as written.

-   **Deuteronomy 17:1**, You shall not sacrifice to the LORD your God a bull or sheep which has any blemish or defect, for that is an abomination to the LORD your God.

    When engaging in ritual animal sacrifice, it is an abomination if the animal is not perfect.

-   **Deuteronomy 22:5,** A woman shall not wear anything that pertains to a man, nor shall a man put on a woman's garment, for all who do so are an abomination to the LORD your God.

    Presumably this would include a woman wearing jeans or slacks and would include Scots wearing kilts and some professional clowns' costumes. Fundamentalists should refrain from these ward- robes if they believe in the Bible as written.

-   **Deuteronomy 24:4**, then her former husband who divorced her must not take her back to be his wife after she has been defiled (married a second man); for that is an abomination before the LORD.

    This relates to a woman who has been divorced by two husbands. If she decides to be loyal once more to her first husband, then she commits an abomination. The passage suggests that the husband may also be committing an abomination.

When *to'ebah* refers to the breaking of a Jewish ritual law, it might be better translated as ritually improper or unclean or involves foreign religious cult practices. Some of the *to'ebah* passages are considered to be without significance to Christians. Many activities which were *to'ebah* (transgressions to the ancient Israelites) are not held so by modern cultures. Nevertheless, it is interesting how some fundamentalists pick and choose religious laws (their biases) they say pertain to our twenty-first century religious lives. Rabbi Gershon Caudill wrote,

> Jews do not obligate any other religion to the observance of the Torah laws, which were given specifically to the Jewish people and their descendants including converts. This is with the possible exception of the seven Noahian Laws, and there is dispute among the halakhic authorities as to which seven laws non-Jews need observe IF they are indeed required to observe any Torah laws at all.[55]

Of interest is the fact that this rabbi (and others) question whether or not any non-Jew need obey or religiously recognize any Jewish laws, yet many fundamentalists would have all Christians obey at least one, the one that they believe has to do with modern homosexuality.

In the ancient language of I Corinthians 6: 9-10 and I Timothy 1: 9-10, we find *malakoi*, a term most often incorrectly applied to **all** men who take the receptive or passive role during sex. The word *malaka* is found three times in the New Testament and is translated as *soft* (Matthew 4: 23, 9: 35, 10: 1) or effeminate. It would be incorrect to interpret the word to mean homosexual as the word is used in the twenty-first century. In fact, there are multiple ways in which the word can be interpreted other than "gay" by several authorities:

- Dale Martin: broadly means effeminate for members of either sex or orientation.[56]

- Doctor Robert Gagnon (p. 306): effeminate men in the sexual roles of Females

- Reverend Alan Readpath, Moody Memorial Church, Chicago, self-centered, undisciplined Christians of weak religious values.

- Dr. Greenberg (p. 213): homosexual cult prostitutes

---

55   http://www.affirmation.org
56   The Corinthian Body, Dale Martin, Westminister, John Knox Press

- Robin Scroggs (p. 34, 35, 42, 44, 108): effeminate male prostitute

- Josephus, *Antiquities of the Jews, Book I, 11.3,* "…they resolved themselves to enjoy these beautiful boys by force [rape] and violence." [57]

- Dr. Boswell (p. 341): moral weakness

- Dionysius of Halicarnassus, Roman Antiquities, Book 7.2.4: "…the tyrant of Cumae…was called by the citizens *malacus* or effeminate… when a boy was effeminate and allowed himself to be treated as a woman…he was of a mild nature and slow to anger…"

- Dionysius' words suggest that the meaning of *malakoi* was not a definitive term even for the ancient Greeks, and it clearly is not an inclusive term for all forms of homosexuality.'

- Philo, a peer of St. Paul (according to Scroggs p. 88, 89): linked *malakoi* to pederasty, a common bonding of older men and younger men for education and sometimes sex. Such relationships were quite acceptable to the ancient Greeks and Romans.

- I Corinthians 6:9, according to Boswell, *malakoi* refers to male prostitutes who serviced men and women. Others say the verse refers to passive males serving other males and yet others believe the verse refers to sexual oppression and rape but not modern homosexuality. Another interpretation is softness, effeminacy and general moral weakness. In the New American Bible a foot- note suggest the word means young men kept for prostitution.

As the author, Rick Brentlinger (p 355), stated so often in his book, "Scripture cannot mean now what it did not mean then [the time of Christ]." It was not until 1958 that the word *malakoi,* in the *Amplified Bible,* took on the meaning of homosexual as we know the word today. This shift in semantics, driven by cultural and personal biases, causes all forms of homosexuality to be condemned, contrary to intellectually honest interpretations of scripture. Writers living in the first century, around the time of Christ and the apostles, used *malakoi* to mean soft and effeminate as well as things being soft to the touch, not a modern, mutual, respecting same-sex relationship. Here is what other ancient writers have to say:

- Dio Chrystom, 49:25, (40-120 CE): "to be made soft through too much education"

---

57   http://www.ccel.org/j/josephus/works/ant-1.htm

- Josephus, (37 - 100 CE), *War of the Jews*, 7.388; *Antiquities of the Jews*, 5.246; 10.194, "…warriors without courage and hence soft or weak, men who sought too much luxury."

- Epictetus, (55 - 135 CE), (noted by Boswell, p. 106): "people unable to absorb philosophy due to soft brains or soft headedness"

In this same time period, other authors had different interpretations of *malakoi*:

- Plutarch's, *Erotikos*, (46 -127 CE), *malthakos* (similar to malakoi) "refers to passive sexual roles by heterosexual men."

- Caelius Aurelianus noted in Boswell's, *Christianity*, p. 107, footnote 52, "malthakos as in heterosexual men in passive roles."

Malakos is found four times in the Greek New Testament and is used in reference to physically soft and luxurious things. In Luke 7:25 and Matthew 11:8, the word *malakos* is used by Jesus in referring to showy clothing—not homosexuality. Second Kings 9:30, Jeremiah 4:30, and Ezekiel 23: 37-43 find softness referenced as: crimson clothing, makeup on men, men wearing jewelry, etc.—not homosexuality per se. *Malakos* is translated as disease in the *King James Bible* (choice Bible of many fundamentalists) and as sickness in the *NAS Bible*. These are malicious references based on antigay biases.

Among those males who might have worn bright colored clothing, long hair, makeup, eyeliner, etc., included *androgynoi* (castrated men called Galli) who were priests in service to a fertility goddess such as Ceres or Demeter. These priests dressed as women and engaged in passive, pagan sexual rituals involving male-to-male sex, as a religious experience. The active partner was most likely a heterosexual male, acting out of religious fervor or seeking religious favor of his goddess.

Paul's use of the word malakoi must be read and interpreted in the context of his day and its generally agreed upon usage (Connoley, John, p. 1; Brawley, RL, p. 117-126):

1. dressing as a harlot
2. moral weakness
3. adultery in all its forms
4. love of the soft life i.e., luxury
5. moral weakness
6. excessive heterosexual intercourse
7. wearing jewelry and fine clothing

Paul used the word *pornoi,* in I Corinthians 6, to mean male prostitute, so there is no reason to believe he meant to encompass modern homosexuality through the word *malakoi.* To suggest such usage is to seek to do harm to the gay community (a choice of biases).

Doctor Gordon Fee, a noted New Testament textural critic, equates m*alakoi* to a pederastic relationship but only as a "best guess" (p. 244). He states "...*malakos* is seldom, if ever used to describe a passive male partner in a homosexual act." A*rsenokoitai* is the word often used for the active role in male-male sex. It is not correctly or generally translated as "...abusers of themselves with men."

The word *Arseno* (or arsenokoitai) may come from:

-    the Ionic word *arsen,* meaning: "man, to be made wet with semen" or
-    the Doric word *orson,* meaning "arse, buttocks."

Koitai means

-    to lie with or
-    to have sex with.

However, these two roots (*Arseno* + *Koitai*) do not equal the sum of the meaning of the two words.

Rick Brentlinger (p. 343) argues that the word *arsenokoites* was never used by ancient peoples, or St. Paul, to refer to males of equal status in a homosexual relationship and should not be so used today. More likely than not, the word was not so defined by those who used it in their ancient writings. Ancient writers suggest that they and their contemporary readers knew its meaning from the context in which it was used, i.e., not general homosexuality between consenting males of equal status. Slaves and poor men (not boy prostitutes) were most often thought of as un-equals compared to those who paid for male sex. Another case of inequality was that of pederasty (sex between a man and a boy).

The *Thesaurus Linguae Graecae* lists *arsenokoit* 73 times with some attempts at defining the word. [58]

Romans 1:27 condemns men who "leave the natural use of the woman, and burn in their lust one toward another." This may be a reference to gay sex or more likely it may relate to heterosexual men who engaged in homo sexual acts in a deliberate rebellious attempt to be perverse and lecherous as in pagan rituals or possibly among male prisoners.

Romans 1:26 has been used to condemn "women who change the natural use of their body into that which is against nature." This phrase is extremely vague and may refer to nonconventional sexual practices that were non-procreative. Clement of

---

58   http://www.jeramyt.org

Alexandria was one leader who may not have thought this verse referred to lesbian acts. In "Discussions of Procreation" (*Paedagogus 10*) Clement explains that sexual lust in the hare (rabbit) results in it growing a new rectum every year due to heavy sexual use. He goes on to say that both sexes of hyenas grow non-vaginal and non-anal passages structured for penetration. Clement uses this belief to explain why pregnancies do not occur, because sperm is diverted to channels which do not permit conception.

This he calls παρὰ φύσιν "contrary to nature" (86.1) Clement then goes on to tie this idea back to St. Paul by quoting Romans 1: 27 - 27 (86.3). He concludes (87.3) we should refute man-to-man sex, copulating with the infertile, anal sex with females, and sex with androgynous persons (castrated and effeminate male priests, the galli). He seems to think we should observe nature's prohibition against improper use of our genitals. Men should discharge, not receive semen.

On the other hand παρὰ φὰσιν (contrary to nature) is a direct reference to men wasting sperm and not sex between women. The original reader of Paul's word would have known he was referring to pagan practices directed to goddess cults. These religions dominated Paul's world.

Augustine seems to believe Romans is actually referring to non-procreative, hetero-genital intercourse.[59] Paul may have referred to certain sexual positions, perhaps anal intercourse in pagan rituals, or any activity not producing children. These acts were in general condemned for several reasons. Clement expressed concern that sperm was wasted and pagan rites denied the true God his worship. Pagans placed idol worship above the Hebrew (early Christian) God.

All of these unusual activities were usually the result of drunken bacchanals held in celebration of a pagan god and led to conflicts between Christians. The anti-Christian riot at Ephesus (Acts 19) was important enough to be preserved in the Bible. Additional evidence suggests that other conflicts between the goddess cults and early Christian groups occurred.[60]

Rick Brentlinger (p. 334-339) lists 19 possible interpretations of the word *arseno-koites*. In general, the word may refer to male prostitutes (serving males or females), male rape, anal intercourse with one's wife, sexual exploitation, pederastic relation-ships, humans having sex with angels, non-procreative sex, etc. Biblical scholars tend to agree that lesbianism is nowhere mentioned as such in the Bible. Romans 1: 26b is the only verse that hints at homosexuality. However the reference most certainly has to do with sexual affairs involving pagan idol worship in the milieu of a drunken religious party. The concern may also have to do with non-procreative sex wherein no offspring will ensue (wasted sperm). The Talmud (a kind of religious handbook to the Old Testament or Torah) mentions lesbianism but considers it "an obscenity that dis-qualifies a lesbian from later marrying a priest." That's it—nothing more.

The translators of the Twentieth Century *Revised Standard Version of the Bible* chose to use the word homosexual in the passages mentioned above. This is a grossly

---

59   Augustine, Marriage and Desire 20.35 (trans. Roland Teske; ed. John E Rotelle; Answer to the Pelagians, II ; New York: New City Press, 1990), 75-76.

60   Roscoe, "Priests," 205

unjust distortion of the text, because it extends the prohibition to all male and female homosexual practices and *personalities* rather than what was scripturally prohibited: *cultic, ritual* anal intercourse between men as part of pagan ceremonies—nothing more. The choice of the much broader translation may be either a conscious or unconscious biases against modern homosexuals. Such a translation may help improve the sales of the Holy Bible. However, this bias may be personal and incorrect.

All the aforementioned prohibitions were probably more formal theological concepts than practical ones, for there is no recorded evidence that any death penalty was ever inflicted for breaking these laws even though the Mishnah and Talmud prescribed stoning to death for certain acts, as does Leviticus. There have been reports of agreements among rabbis who believed that a thirteen year old sodomite (i.e. minor) could not be guilty of a religious sex crime, because the Biblical phrase "*men* with *man*kind" referred only to adult males. Therefore, one might conclude that a thirteen year old child cannot be a homosexual even if they willingly participated in a homosexual act. In turn, the act would not be a civil or religious crime since those who participated, if underage, cannot be found guilty or stoned by reason of their age.

The Jews were the only ancient peoples to condemn homosexuality. From a small, ancient nomadic tribe, we have inherited a tradition that has shaped the world on an unprecedented scale. The ancient Jewish religious culture created what became an anti-gay and anti-sex tradition that has spread into Eastern, Arabian, and Western cultures. Homophobia was originally a condemnation of ritual male-to-male sex that was a major feature of some mid-eastern ancient pagan religions. As a pagan religious act, it symbolized humility and subservience to pagan gods, but to the Hebrews it was a crime of humiliation and a sacrilege to their God. Law codes in the ancient Near East—including those of Urukagina (2375 B.C.), UrNammu (2100 B.C.), Eshnunna (1750 B.C.), and Hammurabi (1726 B.C.)—virtually ignored homosexual acts. (David Greenberg p. 124) Vern Bullough (52) notes these codes had an influence on later codes and were to deal with specific behaviors (not general moral principles), and were not to be observed in all cases or at all times.

The Hittites, who flourished in eastern Anatolia (Turkey) and Syria ca. 1700-700 B.C., had an interesting law, "If a man violates his son, it is a capital crime" (Pritchard p 196, section 189c). The same judgment held for father-daughter incest and mother-son incest. As Hittitologist Harry Hoffner, Jr., observed, "A man who sodomized his son is guilty of *urkel* [illegal intercourse] because the partner is his son, not because they are of the same sex." Later, Hoffner added, "[I]t would appear that homosexuality was not outlawed among the Hittites." (Naphy, p. 20) More than two millennia would pass before these Hebraic religious "crimes" would be made illegal. King Henry VIII of England and Wales was determined to show the Pope that he was the master of church and land by taking control of, or dissolving institutions, within the Roman Catholic hierarchy.

He had Parliament enact the Statute of 1533—25 Henry 8, Chapter which begins,

> "Forasmuch as there is not yet sufficient and condign punishment appointed and limited by the due course of the Laws of this Realm, for the detestable and abominable Vice of Buggery committed with mankind or beast."

He goes on to define it as a felony punishable by hanging.

The early twentieth century found male-to-male kissing in public to be lewd behavior, which could be prosecuted in the west. At the time of this writing, in the State of Utah, a man may have anal sex with a woman without fear of legal reprises; two men may not. This discrepancy is no doubt due to the fundamentalists' legal sway in that State by the Mormon Church. In some states, it is still illegal for couples to cohabitate without the benefit of marriage.

In considering the subject of homosexuality, we need to look at the Hebrew word, *zachar,* which means male, as does a variant of the word *zekhur.*[61] An understanding of both words affects the true meaning of Leviticus 18:22 and 20:13. In the Kings James translation of the Old Testament, we find *zakhar* and *zekhur* translated as man or mankind (and even birds) 86 times as compared to 160 times for the word *ish* which may also mean man. *Zakhar* and *zekhur* have been used in reference to sacrificed animals and circumcised men as well as Israelite priests. In all cases, the use of the word *zakhar* refers to a male (men and boys) dedicated to the Hebrew God with each having some unique sacred function to perform, e.g., a holy warrior, men returning to Jerusalem to renew worship in the Temple, male newborns, sons dedicated to God, etc. On the other hand, these two words could also be applied to males dedicated to pagan deities.

There are other Hebrew words which need to be considered within the context of these ancient people as well as their pagan peers. The first is *ish,* which means man. The second is *ishshah* which means woman. Both words are commonly used in the Old Testament and may generally translate as father, husband, procreator, wife, or sexual partner. They may also mean concubine or prostitute. In Leviticus 18: 22 and 20: 13, we noted that the Hebrew word *ish*, meaning man, refers to Israelite men; so *zakhar* must be a reference to something other than an Israelite man. Now, combine this information with that of

Deuteronomy 23: 17 - 18,

> None of the sons of Israel shall be a [zakhar] temple prostitute [or bring] the wages of a temple prostitute into the house of the Lord your God.

When understood together, we should see that sacred male, *zakhar*, in Leviticus refers to cultic male prostitutes in Canaan and these temple prostitutes only, not all men, everywhere, for all time.

---

61   http://dictionary.babylon.com/sacr

In this chapter, we have examined several ancient words and their possible meanings. A word frequently used to harm the gay community is the word sodomite. It should be clear that one can interpret these words as a weapon against members of the gay community. Those who choose to do so are gravely mistaken.

In the next chapter we will examine the etymology of sodomite and its usage as a misguided weapon against gay men.

CHAPTER VIII

The Inhospitable Sodomites

*T*he derogatory word *sodomite* was used by the Hebrews to describe sins of an ancient people who lived in the city of Sodom. Today, the word is hurtfully used against gay men without knowing the true meaning of the word or understanding the Biblical verse from which it comes. This chapter should help to discourage the vulgar use of the word sodomite and sodomy.

The Lot account, told in Genesis 19: 4-11 and repeated in Judges 19: 22, can be summarized. Lot decided to settle in Sodom, a city reputed to be as wicked as its neighbor, Gomorrah. In order to determine the truth of this reputation, God sent two angels to investigate. These two foreign travelers (the angels) were met at the city's gate by Lot. They accepted his hospitable invitation to stay at his home. That night, the old and young male residents (perhaps even visiting males as well as females) and **all** peoples from all quarters of Sodom surrounded Lot's house and pounded on his door while demanding: "Bring the visitors out unto us, that we may know them." Lot refused to comply with the demand and instead offered the mob his two daughters.

Lot had lived at Sodom for a while and surely knew something of the sexual interests of the citizens or the reputation of the city. If Lot had considered all the citizens to be homosexuals, he surely would not have offered them his presumably heterosexual daughters to do with as the mob saw fit. If the crowd wanted to have sex with men,

Lot and we would have to presume that the homosexual mob would not have wanted women. Why did Lot offer them?

When the Sodomites would not relent in their demand to have the strangers, the angels caused the mob to become blind.

The next morning, Lot fled the city with the angels and his family, allegedly leaving his future sons-in-law behind. This allegation implies the men who would have married Lot's daughters were at least bisexual or heterosexual, which would negate the argument that all the men in Sodom were homosexuals. As Lot's family fled, God sent a torrent of fire and brimstone to consume the two cities of the plain because of their (Biblically unspecified) wickedness.

The difficulty of accurately interpreting this passage about Lot and his city is that the sins of Sodom and Gomorrah are not specified in Genesis. Christians with little linguistic expertise may assume that *know* means engage in sex. However, the Hebrew term for "know" is *yada,* and it is used in the sexual sense only ten times in the Old Testament. All of these cases are heterosexual in content. *Yada* is used in the Bible to convey a sense of "get acquainted with" 924 times. The odds against *yada* meaning homosexual sex are nearly 1000 to 1. Author Sherman Bailey, in *Homosexuality and the Western Christian Tradition*, argues that sexual intercourse should be expressed with the Hebrew verb *sakab* meaning to lie or to sleep, and that the verb *yada* means to know of or learn about the visitors in Lot's house. Malcom Smith wrote in *Lost Secrets of the New Covenant* a general discussion about the Greek word *ginosko* which translates into Hebrew as *yada* meaning to know, as man can know God—the emotional and spiritual nature of a relationship. Many modern and enlightened Biblical scholars have abandoned the (to know) homosexual sex theory (rape, however, maybe another story), so why haven't the members of the religious-right? I believe the reason is their blind and uninformed adherence to their chosen biases—in a word, prejudice.

The interpretation of the Sodom story, now accepted by many Biblical scholars (excluding most evangelical sects), is as follows. Lot was a *ger*, a sojourner, a resident alien in Sodom. In today's parlance, Lot had a "green card." He had certain civic obligations to the inhabitants of Sodom in return for the protection that the city offered him. There are, however, allegations that Lot was unpopular in the city. Some scholars argue that under Sodom's rules, Lot did not have a right to open his house to foreigners unless they were properly vetted by Sodom's governing body. The citizens (mob) of Sodom were merely demanding to see the credentials of these two foreigners (angels)—that is, to know whence they came and their intentions. Lot had to refuse because he was obliged by his Jewish code of hospitality to provide food, shelter, etc. to his guests.

The sins of Sodom, whatever they might have been, were especially horrific since they offended God's emissaries (angels) and therefore God himself. Lot offered the Sodomites his daughters as the first appeasement that came to his mind, *not* as a heterosexual substitute for homosexual sex but as a political appeasement through, perhaps, sex. Remember that females were second-class citizens and of little value to ancient peoples. The mob was not motivated by lust only, but they wanted to demonstrate their supremacy and power over Lot (the outsider) and his unauthorized guests. These outsiders had to be shown their rightful place, and that was a position of subservience to the men of Sodom.

The Sodom story is similar to the story of the Benjamite city of Gibeah in **Judges 19**. The Gibeahites were notorious for their inhospitality. Yet an old man of the city took a certain Levite and his wife in for the night. Hearing of this, the malcontents of the city began to yell to the owner of the house to send out his male visitor. Trying to honor his duty for hospitality, the old man offered his daughter and then the wife of the guest. When those offers did not satisfy the mob, the old man sent out his wife who was raped multiple times throughout the night and found dead the next morning. The city, unlike Sodom, was not destroyed, but a major war between the Benjamites and other tribes of Israel did occur because of this incident. In this story, the offense was the heterosexual rape of the Levite's wife.

Contrary to the alleged attempted rape in the Sodom story, few fundamentalists condemned the heterosexual activities in Gibeah as they have the alleged homosexual activities in Sodom. Why not? The two stories are similar. In any case, d*omination* is the central theme. First, the visitor was to be dominated, then the daughters of the host, then the wife of the male visitor, then the wife of the host. The rape and death of the host's wife also represented the figurative rape of the host as well. The elderly male host had been dominated in that he could not protect his wife and therefore had failed one of his primary male functions—to protect his property (wife) and provide safe sanctuary for Levite visitors.

The alleged threatened homosexual rape was not the cause of Sodom's downfall. Read earlier in Genesis 18 and you will find that God had already revealed his plan to destroy Sodom because of the *peoples'* (not just men's) wickedness. Literalism for fundamentalists forces them to accept that all persons in Sodom were wicked. More liberal Christians may argue that the word *peoples* refers only to men since women were not worth mentioning by the ancient writers. Nevertheless, God's decision to destroy Sodom is made **before** the alleged threatened homosexual rape. The angels were in Sodom to tell Lot to flee because the city was going to be destroyed.

Genesis 18: 20 - 26,

> And the LORD said, Because the cry of Sodom and Gomorrah is great, and because their sin is very grievous;
>
> I will go down now, and see whether they have done altogether according to the cry of it, which is come unto me; and if not, I will know.
>
> And the men turned their faces from thence, and went toward Sodom: but Abraham stood yet before the LORD.

> And Abraham drew near, and said, Wilt thou also destroy the righteous with the wicked?

> Peradventure there be fifty righteous within the city: wilt thou also destroy and not spare the place for the fifty righteous that [are] therein?

> That be far from thee to do after this manner, to slay the righteous with the wicked: and that the righteous should be as the wicked, that be far from thee: Shall not the Judge of all the earth do right?

> And the LORD said, If I find in Sodom fifty righteous within the city, then I will spare all the place for their sakes.

God's final decision was ninety nine percent in place *prior* to the supposed attempted rape of Lot's guests. Many Biblical scholars have wrestled with the question, didn't God know what was transpiring in Sodom; he should have known without having to send angels to visit the city. At the time of the discussion with Abraham, God knew that fifty *good* men did not live in Sodom, and therefore he knew he was going to destroy the city. It appears the angels were specifically sent to warn Lot of the impending destruction. However, we will never know why God "played the numbers game" with Abraham except to reference literary invention and not history.

The sin in the Sodom story was inhospitality. In the words of the prophet Ezekiel, "They [the people of Sodom] did not help the poor and needy." In fact, neither Ezekiel, Jesus, nor Talmudists ever identify sodomy as the sin of the Sodomites. Only later, around 390 CE, do the church fathers, Augustine and St John Chrysostom, declare sodomy the cause of Sodom's destruction. The basis for their decision is far from clear.

Some Biblical experts say that the two cities of the plains were destroyed because the citizens did not recognize their obligations of hospitality while others say the story is a moral allegory about the dire effects of inhospitality. However, if one insists on believing that the intentions of the crowd were sexual lust, then one should focus on the act that would have been *rape* since consensual sex with non-humans seemed unlikely.

The sins of the Sodomites may have been great and grievous in the eyes of a wrathful God, but the Bible does not cite homosexuality as "the" sin (Genesis 13: 13, 18: 20) in question. Jeremiah 23:14 suggests adultery and lying are the sins of Sodom, and Ezekiel 16:49-50 suggests pride, sloth and idolatry are the sins. Since the word for "idolatry" can be *to'ebhah in Hebrew*, and one form of it *might* have been homosexual temple prostitution, it is remotely possible that homosexuality was included, but it must be emphasized how *remote* this possibility was. If Sodom, or sodomy, was believed to be an example of homosexuality, it is remarkable to the point of being an inconceivable omission that Sodomy was never mentioned in any of the Biblical condemnations discussed earlier. The Apocrypha demonstrates the standard interpretation:

"Whereas the men of Sodom received not the strangers when they came among them. (Wisdom 19.13-14) In Ecclesiasticus (Book of Sirach) 16.8 we find another reason for the destruction of Sodom, "He [God] did not spare the neighbors of Lot, whom he loathed on account of their insolence.""

Jews, over the centuries, developed Midrash stories that filled in the gaps of often enigmatic (and certainly archaic) Old Testament Biblical texts. From the earliest times, there was recognition that certain Biblical word meanings were not clear. A famous 9ᵗʰ century Midrash story about Sodom tells us that the people of Sodom banned feeding the poor and hungry and burned a woman at the stake for doing so. It was her alleged cries that rose to heaven and prompted God's wrath.

"Sodomizing" the Sodomites

Why did the "sins of Sodom" become synonymous with sodomy for the Christian religious-right and perhaps other religious populations? The relationship seemed to result from the nationalistic fervor seen in the ancient history of the Jews. The Jews began reacting against "the ways of the Gentiles" just as they had earlier reacted against "the ways of Canaan" and of Egypt. The Palestinian Jews and Jews of the Dispersion (100 BC to AD 100) were exposed to pagan Hellenistic immorality, which helped to foist a homosexual misinterpretation of the story of Sodom. The inhabitants of Sodom were largely Canaanites who were not highly thought of by the ancient Israelites. One way to belittle the Canaanites was to cast aspersions upon them and their culture as well as their religion, which was pagan and often involved sexual excesses—something seen as unfit for an ancient Jew. These ancient pagan rites may have involved male-to-male sex as well as male-to-female sex perversions. Adherence to ancient Hebrew laws was a way to separate and distinguish the Jews from the outsider Canaanites.

The *Palestinian Pseudepigrapha,*[62] particularly the *Book of Jubilees,* is a product of the most rigid and conservative of Jewish orthodoxy. It considered the sins of Sodom and Gomorrah as uncleanliness and acts "changing the order of nature." The Testaments of the Twelve Patriarchs (109-106 BC), especially the Testament of Naphtali, stated the Sodomites "changed the order of nature." Jude states that they "went after strange flesh." This is still a rather vague religious phrase. However, by 50 BC, the rabbinical interpolators had reached a consensus that the citizens of Sodom were "sodomitic," i.e., committing unnatural sexual acts between men. However, they did not state that these acts were part of pagan worship or committed between heterosexuals.

The Book of the Secrets of Enoch, written in Egypt early in the first century by a Hellenistic Jew, states the Sodomites committed "abominable lecheries, namely one with another" and "the sin against nature, which is child-corruption after the Sodomitical fashion, magic-making, enchantments and devilish witchcraft." This is embellishment when the "…Secrets of Enoch" are compared with the actual Biblical text concerning

---

62   a collection of early Jewish and some Jewish-Christian writings composed between c.200 BC and c.AD 200, not found in the Bible or rabbinic writings

Sodom. The Enoch interpretation is obviously the result of coming into contact with the unseemly side of first century Alexandria where pederasty and homosexual prostitution flourished alongside competing mystical sects, astrology, fortune telling, and cults involving castration and transvestism. Many of these acts were associated with idolatry and cultic homosexual acts.

During this period, Philo presents the story with which we are familiar today:

> Not only in their mad lust for **women** did the Sodomites (heterosexuals) violate the **marriages** of their neighbors, but also men mounted males without respect for the sex nature which the active partner shares with the passive; and so when they tried to beget children they were discovered to be incapable of any but a sterile seed….[these men appear not to be exclusively homosexual and venereal diseases rendered some of them sterile]….little by little they accustomed those who were by nature men to submit to play the part of women.

> De Abrahamo, 26

A similar account of the Sodomites is related by Josephus (who died around AD 96), whose writings emphasize the rape of beautiful boys.

The faith and culture of the ancient Hebrews encompassed the notion of *manhood*. Man-hood was the essence of maleness and made man what he was (and is). Men were to be strong, leaders, dominators, and aggressors. Through these characteristics, men revealed their God given strengths. Men (Adam) had been made directly in the image of God. Eve had been made from Adam; therefore, Eve (woman) was a second order citizen. The female's role became one of passivity, to give birth, to care for offspring, and manage the household in which the husband and the children lived. Women and wives had almost no social or religious role to play in ancient Hebrew culture. When they did, they were separated from men as seen today in Orthodox Jewish temples.

The concept of *manhood* and *maleness* carried over into the religious realm of the Jews where any man, who would permit himself to be sexually violated, was seen as NOT being a man. To the Jews, he had been submissive to another man and therefore a denouncement of what they believed God had created and wanted man to be. The man was no longer a "man." In the eyes of the Jews, this lowered the status of man (manhood) and was an abomination in every sense of the word.

The subject of abomination is explored by Ing Anderson on his website.[63] Anderson states that in modern Christian circles we hear the argument that homosexual behavior is,

(1)   The worst of sins and
(2)   God hates homosexual behavior and homosexuals.

---

63   http://glow.cc/isa/whatisan.htm

He argues that most writers using this interpretation base their opinion on the word abomination. These believers ***assume*** the word abomination indicates that same-gender sex is a sin greater than a heterosexual sex act performed within the same context, e.g., two unmarried people having sex or one married and one unmarried person having sex. The latter case is adultery, which is specifically mentioned in the Ten Commandments as a sin. The Bible makes no direct assertion against homosexual behavior except in cases of pagan worship; however, eating shellfish is an abomination. Had any shrimp lately?

Allegedly all homosexual behavior is an abomination. Are we to believe that one abomination is a greater sin than another abomination? Is this what the Bible says? The answer is No! Why then do fundamentalists still focus on all homosexual behavior? The answer has to be personal biases.

Sexual **sins** of any kind were considered by the ancient Hebrews as abominations to the Lord. See Leviticus 18: 18—30. Pay particular attention to verses 27 - 30, which refer to "**all** these abominations—after various kinds of sexual activities apart from marriage…" A similar list is repeated in Leviticus 20, concluding that God's people [the Jews] ought not to do these things ". . . after the manner of the [ancient] nations which I cast out before you." Allegedly the citizens of Sodom and Gomorrah were not cast out but destroyed. We find that the laws in Leviticus also forbade remarriages of divorced couples, calling such an act an abomination in Deuteronomy 24: 1 - 4. Later, Christ amplified these laws to include the lustful thought.

Dishonest business practices are named as an abomination in Deuteronomy 25: 13 - 16, Proverbs 11: 1 and Proverbs 20: 10. It seems that unscrupulous business practices are forbidden of anyone professing to be of the Lord's people. Oppressive treatment of others and a haughty attitude are considered an abomination in Proverbs 3: 31 - 32, and a "forward [disobedient, turning back] heart" is mentioned in Proverbs 11: 20 as an abomination.

Proverbs 6: 16 - 19 list six abominations. "These six things doth the LORD hate; yea, seven are an abomination unto him (author's listing):

[1]   A proud look,
[2]   a lying tongue
[3]   and hands that shed innocent blood
[4]   an heart that deviseth wicked imaginations,
[5]   feet that be swift in running to mischief
[6]   a false witness that speaketh lies,
[7]   and he that soweth discord among brethren."

Wickedness is equated with abomination in Proverbs 8: 7. "Lying lips" are added to the list in Proverbs 12: 20 and a "proud heart" in Proverbs 16: 15. Some people say that pride and lies to further one's own agenda are every bit as hateful to God as are sexual sins. Others may say that to break one of the Ten Commandments is more sinful than to commit an abomination.

Are all sins of equal value? It is impossible to say for certain? Catholics believe in mortal and venial sins which carry qualitative and quantitative weights. In Proverbs 17: 15 and 24: 9,

"Those that justify the wicked or condemn the just are an abomination as are scorners…" In Proverbs 28: 9, prayer coming from one who turns away from hearing the law is added to the list of abominations. We should remember that one of the laws in the Bible is to love one another as we love ourselves. This includes homosexuals, or should I say this **does not** exclude homosexuals. A much beloved former president, Jimmy Carter, (in *Back to Fundamentals)* promoted love and respect for all mankind and often used this quote. "When an alien lives with you in your land, do not mistreat him." [64] Fundamentalists take note—this includes the gay community!

An abomination refers to something the Lord hates—something totally out of harmony with God's character of purity and love. If we take the Biblical record as a whole, we find that pride and self-sufficiency are mentioned more often than any other qualities as being distasteful to God. Pride feels no need. So much so that even God can do nothing for a self-righteous person. Given the Bible's pronouncement that there is "none righteous," Christ's statement indicates, as clearly as any other, that a self-righteous spirit excludes its owner from the kingdom of heaven. All too frequently, when the religious-right speaks against the gay community and its struggle for equal rights, the tone of the condemnation is that of self-righteousness and pride—a pride that those of the religious-right are not gay. Some such people may actually feel superior because they are not gay and not part of the alleged hated class of deviants.

Bishop Spong, in his book, *Rescuing the Bible from Fundamentalism*, notes that "…Lot protected the messengers by offering to the mob, for their sexual sport, his virgin daughters. You may 'do to them as you please,' Lot asserted." (Genesis 19: 8) The story goes on to say that Lot, despite this violent betrayal of his daughters, was accounted righteous by God.

Can anyone imagine an American father offering his daughters to a mob, as an appeasement to that mob, so some **non-family** member (and **stranger)** would be spared some harm? I dare say, no. If a modern father performed such an act, he would be taken away by the police and sentenced to time in prison for endangering his children. Failing such a legal action today, we would say the legal system was broken or the judge should be removed from the bench. How then can religious conservatives and fundamentalists ignore Lot's actions and God's blessing of the actions while simultaneously clinging to the belief that homosexual activity was the sin of Sodom requiring damnation? The answer is religious bias.

Lot's actions were later complicated by his allowing himself to get drunk on wine and having incestuous relations with his daughters. We know of no chastisement by God for such actions, which today would cry out for justice from our legal system. Bishop Spong has this to say about these overlooked sexual family matters, even though fundamentalists decry the alleged homosexual acts of Sodom.

---

64   Leviticus 19:33

> …the purpose of a claim of Biblical literalism is revealed to be [a truth,] not to call people to the values of justice, but to justify existing prejudice by keeping oneself secure inside a way of life that cannot be challenged by any new insight.
>
> **BISHOP SPONG**

From the fundamentalists' standpoint, we hear not a single questioning word when one reads (and glosses over) such commands from God as what He said to Moses, "…go down into Canaan and kill **all** the Canaanites and take over their land." Moses was a murderer (he planned mass killings at God's command), but no one seems to consider this to be a character flaw.

Adultery and other sinful acts of the ancient Hebrews were said to be evil. Yet no one spoke out about Abraham and Isaac who tried to pass their wives off (lying) as their sisters. In their time, to have lived and had sex with a sister was an abomination to God (Genesis 20 and 26), yet, this was the image certain men were portraying. Tamar, the daughter-in-law of Judah was treated as a prostitute, and later he wanted to have her killed when she became pregnant.

In the desert, some of the Israelites made and worshipped an idol made of gold, while Moses was conversing with God on the mountain. Where do you think desert roamers got precious metals to make an idol? It is possible these captive people had some wealth, but it seems unlikely these alleged Pharonic slaves had significant amounts of gold. These slaves may have borrowed it, or as some scholars suppose, the slaves stole it and other supplies from a small village before leaving Egypt on their way to deliverance (even though Moses had asked to **borrow** the village's possessions, we know nothing of the possessions being returned or being paid for). Some fundamentalists say this action was permissible since the Ten Commandments had not yet been written so there was no religious prohibition against stealing—only civil prohibitions.

The Bible is filled with stories that would make most moral people question such happenings, but, since the Bible is infallible, we assume that even genocide or murder was acceptable if man was commanded to do so by God (this sounds like the modern argument used by Muslim jihadists).

The ancient Hebrews believed, as do many modern fundamentalists, that they are God's

chosen people. Such logic can only lead to the counter equation that all the other people are God's non-chosen people and therefore they are not important but inferior to "true" believers.

In this chapter, the concept of sodomy, as a sexual perversion, leading to God's destruction of the ancient city of Sodom, has been reviewed. A careful reading of Exodus reveals the sodomitic claim about Sodom to be erroneous. The application of the term sodomite to the gay community is itself a sin in that the naming of an act is a conscious effort to denigrate God's children. The choice to so stigmatize gay men (and women) is based on personal biases and ignorance of scripture.

In the next chapter we will explore other words that are often associated with sinful acts in the ancient world and some that are confused with non-sinful acts.

CHAPTER IX

"Sinful" Words

Why do we have to recycle the old conflicts so many times: first we fight about slavery, then segregation, then gender, and now sexual orientation? Why can't people look at the phrase 'liberty and justice for all' and simply accept that '**all**' means '**all**.'

ANONYMOUS

*I*n the last chapter, we saw how the words sodomy and sodomite were examined in light of a careful reading of Exodus and the history of the use of theses "S" words. The words are clearly misapplied to members of the gay community because they denigrate its members. Their use is without any thought as to how the words create harm and prevent objective study of the alleged abomination described by them. There are other ancient words that are similarly misapplied to modern sexuality. In this chapter, we will explore some of the more commonly abused words.

There are two key terms used to refer to sins of a sexual nature in the Christian New Testament. The Greek word *pornea* is often translated to mean fornication. The second Greek word is *akatharsia* which is often translated *uncleanness*" These two words appear numerous times in the Bible. They are often found in the writings of St. Paul in which he overly concerned himself with sexual sins. As is often true with the Bible, not everyone reads the same message of sin in Paul's words.

Pornea

The King James Version of the Bible (often the Bible of choice for fundamentalists) defines *pornea* as fornication. Thirty-two verses in the original Greek versions of the Christian Bible contain this word. Below are a few selected verses containing this translated word. It should be noted that the true translation of *pornea* is hotly debated.

I Corinthians 5: 1, "It is reported commonly that there is <u>fornication</u> among you, and such as is not so much as named among the Gentiles, that one should have his father's wife."

I Corinthians 7: 2, "Nevertheless, to avoid <u>fornication</u>, let every man have his own wife, and let every woman have her own husband."

Matthew 5: 32, "But I say unto you, That whosoever shall put away his wife, saving for the cause of <u>fornication</u>, causeth her to commit adultery…"

Romans1:29-31, "Being filled with all unrighteousness, <u>fornication,</u> wickedness, covetousness, maliciousness; full of envy, murder, debate, deceit, malignity; whisperers, backbiters, haters of God, despiteful, proud, boasters, inventors of evil things, disobedient to parents, without understanding, covenant breakers, without natural affection, implacable, unmerciful:"

Revelation 18: 3, "For all nations have drunk of the wine of the wrath of her , and the kings of the earth have committed <u>fornication</u> with her, and the merchants of the earth are waxed rich through the abundance of her delicacies."

Galatians 5: 19 - 20, "Now the works of the flesh are manifest, which are these; Adultery, <u>fornication</u>, uncleanness, lasciviousness, idolatry, witchcraft, hatred, variance, emulations, wrath, strife, seditions, heresies…"

Jude 1: 7, "Even as Sodom and Gomorrah, and the cities about them in like manner, giving themselves over to <u>fornication,</u> and going after strange flesh, are set forth for an example, suffering the vengeance of eternal fire."

In many dictionaries, Strong's Concordance, and among religious liberals, fornication is defined as sexual intercourse. In *The American Heritage Dictionary of the English Language,* Fourth Edition, defines fornication as,

> Sexual intercourse between partners [heterosexuals[65]] who are not married to each other.

This dictionary discusses the derivation of the word fornication. It is derived from the Latin word fornix. The word means a vault or arch (as in a vaulted cellar or vaulted place) where old world prostitutes took their clients for sex. In modern medical usage, the word *fornix* refers to a part of a woman's vagina near the cervix.

A Dictionary of Modern American Usage, defines fornication as sexual intercourse between:

- two unmarried persons, or by
- one unmarried person with a married person.

Strong's Concordance provides a 19th century Biblical understanding of ancient Greek and Hebrew words. Strong indicates that *pornea*, had a somewhat broader meaning in Biblical times:

> Literally, it includes three types of activity: prostitution, adultery and incest.

Figuratively it means idolatry, or sexual intercourse between unmarried persons.

Many conservative Christian churches have expanded the word fornication to mean many things, perhaps based on their own biases. Writer Chris Freedmen states, that usage of the word now covers:

> premarital sex, orgies, masturbation, oral sex, fetishes, pornography, 'impure' thoughts about the opposite sex, homosexuality, and just about any other sexual sin you could think of.

Freedman also states, "While some of these things are sin…this is a gross misuse of the word [pornea]."[66]

---

65   Author's addition

66   < http://freedom2201.tripod.com> December 21, 2007

Akatharsia and *akathartos* in the New Testament

Akatharsia is a noun. *Akathartos*, is an adjective. They appear in **Romans I**: 24, 2, **Corinthians** 12: 21, and **Galatians** 5: 19 where both words are usually translated as uncleanness. We read in the *King James Version of the Bible*:

> **Romans 1**: **24,** Wherefore God also gave them up to <u>uncleanness</u> through the lusts of their own hearts, to dishonour their own bodies between themselves.

> **Corinthians 12: 21,** And lest, when I come again, my God will humble me among you, and that I shall bewail many which have sinned already, and have not repented of the <u>uncleanness</u> and lasciviousness which they have committed.

> **Galatians 5: 19,** Now the works of the flesh are manifest, which are these; adultery, uncleanness, lasciviousness.

In the Old Testament, there are numerous laws regarding ritual uncleanness. An example could involve a person or a married couple who could become ritually unclean for a prescribed period of time as when:

- a woman is menstruating, or after having given birth. Having a girl baby was more "polluting" than having a boy. A post partum woman remained "unclean" for up to 80 days for delivering a girl and up to 40 days for delivering a boy.
- a man and a woman had sexual intercourse, they were unclean until the evening (of the same day).
- someone touches or is close to a dead body, they are "unclean" for seven days.

Jesus and his disciples intentionally violated Hebrew Scriptures regarding issues of ritual uncleanness. They were setting the stage for transforming the Jewish faith into that of Christianity where rituals were less important. For example, they worked on the Sabbath. In Mark 7: 6 - 23, Jesus makes it known there is no ceremonial uncleanness, only moral and spiritual uncleanness. He repudiated uncleanness by saying a person is "defiled by the things that come out of his heart, evil thoughts, hatred, adultery, murder, etc."

Luke 7: 15,

> There is nothing from without a man, that entering into him can defile
> him: but the things which come out of him, those are they that defile the
> man.

The religious-right seem to believe that ceremonial uncleanness still exists and is applicable only to the gay community and their way of life, e.g., extra-vaginal touching of semen renders one unclean for a period of time.

The gay community is now considered by many Americans to be a (political) minority group. As such, they are often derided without much fear of reprisal from the larger community of heterosexuals, but this is changing. This derision provides a rallying point for hell-fire ministers who gather their flock and praise them for not being like the gays who are allegedly hated by God. This rhetoric confirms the erroneous belief system of the religious-right, promotes church attendance, and financial contributions.

In the 1990s, the Salvation Army used some of their follower's contributions to support antigay political movements in Australia. This organization has long been involved in antigay controversy. [67]

For some churches, hate is good for business. Why isn't some of this hate directed to the "twelve mortal sins" of which gluttony (obesity) is so common in America and prevalent in church congregations? To do so would drive fat members and their contributions away from the church. Perhaps it is because obese people out number gay Americans who would be forced to confront their detractors with fewer numbers of complainers than in the obese population.

Christ clearly taught that a self-righteous spirit is a Teflon-coated defense against God's saving grace. Christ actually used the word *abomination* in describing such a spirit. Luke gives this account,

Luke 16: 15 & 16,

> And the Pharisees also, who were covetous, heard all these things: and
> they derided him. And he said unto them, Ye are they which justify
> yourselves before men; but God knoweth your hearts: for that which is
> highly esteemed among men is abomination in the sight of God.

In the final analysis, *all* our righteousness is an abomination in the sight of God. None can say, "I am better than you." None of us is qualified to "cast the first stone." We are all equally in need of restoration. Let us not focus on heterosexuality or homosexuality as anything before God, but let us focus on Him who is our hope. Let us then embrace each other in love, either gay or straight but together.

---

67   http://www.enotes.com/topic/The_Salvation_Army

In previous chapters, we examined several words often used as weapons against the gay community. Some individuals and religious groups chose to use these words with the intent to do harm. Many chose their language based on personal biases—not an objective reading of scripture.

These hurtful words are often used to underscore how members of the gay community are allegedly threatening the "sanctity of marriage." Rarely is there any discussion as to how homosexuality and the current gay marriage movement will destroy the heterosexual's loosening stranglehold on the institution of civil marriage. What follows is an examination of marriage and how its boundaries could embrace gay marriages as well as "straight" marriages.

Once the idea of maintaining power and influence through male children became established, it became necessary to control female fertility. How could a man be sure that the children borne by his official wife or wives were his own? How could he be sure that it was his eldest son who would inherit his power and status? How could the followers of a powerful chief be sure that it was truly his son who would succeed him as their leader? Unless all this could be guaranteed, the whole patriarchal social system would fall apart.

JULIAN HAFNER, *THE END OF MARRIAGE*

CHAPTER X

The Christian Family and Marriage

…the worst thing that happened to the gay community was the fall of communism…As long as the conservative movement had communism to fight, they could organize and raise their money over that issue. The minute they lost communism, they had to find a new enemy, and that enemy became homosexuality.

STEVE GUNDERSON,
FIRST "OUT" GAY REPUBLICAN CONGRESSMAN

a current topic of discussion in certain media is how the gay marriage movement will destroy the sanctity of marriage. The Bible has often been misquoted in an attempt to bolster this argument by fundamentalists. In this chapter, we will explore the concept of marriage and its place in our modern world.

We will never know when religion and marriage were merged into a single entity or state of being—a special, societally recognized state and religious bonding. No doubt such a union occurred prior to recorded history and was necessitated by two things:

—**First:** society did not want children to be created and raised outside a socially approved system. The institution of marriage would help to insure that children would be cared for by parents and not become a burden to society in general.

—**Second**: some ancient peoples saw the birth of everything as being created by a mother-earth goddess. Through the bearing of children, humans were engaged in a god or goddess like act and therefore the production of children was a religious act.

Children born outside an ancient societally approved family structure led to several problems. Frequently, these children and their mothers were stigmatized. In time, the children would be known as bastards or illegitimate. These titles caused much consternation and embarrassment for the children and involved parent. The children were often outcast from their kin group and denied social and religious, inheritance and political privileges. Their mothers may have been ostracized because they were somehow considered to be damaged goods and not fit for future bonding ceremonies. The non-bonded mother and her child were often a burden for society at large and could become as destitute as what we today call homeless or street people.

Effective birth control was not available to ancient peoples; therefore, intercourse outside socially approved bonding was discouraged because it could produce unwanted offspring. Presumably, families did not want their daughters labeled with some derogatory term associated with being a non-bonded mother. Society's derision of non-bonded mothers was intentional and probably intended to be a deterrent to non-bonded (or extra-bonded) sexual activities. If a daughter bonded and produced children, her family wanted the child and mother to have food and shelter. The societal requirements of a special, social bonding helped to assure virginity, maternal and child welfare and thus removed the burden of communal support while assuring inheritance and other societal rights. In time, this special bonding became known as marriage.

Ancient people wondered about the miracle of birth of animals and rebirth of plants. Even though they did not understand the science of reproduction, they saw it as a function of the earth goddess. This in turn led to religious rites in which fertility figures were paid honor and given ritual gifts. Similarly, a woman's fertility and offspring were seen as gifts of the goddess. It is not difficult to see how marriage and religion, especially the worship of a mother earth goddess, could be merged. Sex and procreation became religious acts and marriage protected the mother goddess' gifts (children). Christians have adopted the thesis of this ancient concept as they regard marriage to be a sacred act (even though it is also a legal institution) wherein children are considered a sacred gift.

Currently, that group of Americans known as the religious-right hold fast to the concept that marriage is:

- holy or sacred
- protects and provides for children
- only for heterosexuals
- should exist only between a man and a woman

Fundamentalists often see marriage as that bonding model promulgated in the 1950s and 1960s where the father worked outside the home, the mother worked in the home (subjecting herself to the control of her husband), and cared for children (on average, 2.3 children in each house- hold). Neither of the parents had been previously married and both (or most) were virgins on the day of their marriage. The woman was subservient to the husband (she said so during the wedding ceremony).

The children were well behaved and mannerly. They were expected to graduate from high school and a few would become professionals. Daughters might become teachers, nurses, or librarians. Sons might become policemen, firemen, doctors, lawyers, or get a labor or industry job with good benefits. Many of these jobs would be life-long with the same employer.

There would be a large family Bible on the coffee table in the living room. The family would attend Church services, and later all would sit down to a large Sunday meal, often with aunts, uncles, and others. Dinner would be cooked by the mother as the father read the Sunday newspaper. When dinner was ready, mother would take off her apron and gather the family around the table for the meal, which would be preceded by a prayer offered by the father, sitting at the head of the table, a la Norman Rockwell.

In that era, no one used curse words around children, and all media was safe for children to watch, hear, or read. The creation story was taught in schools, where each school day started with a public, Christian prayer and the Pledge of Allegiance was recited. Sound familiar? If it does, you are probably horrified by the modifications to this scene reflected in today's vernacular.

This is the family model to which the fundamentalists wish to return, and they will do almost anything to attain their goal. It is backward looking, hoping and almost despairing for the past. The image holds devotees captive to a past that is gone forever. This image includes marriage. Fundamentalists frequently forget (or never knew) that marriage was and is a legal institution originally conceived to protect the rights of inheritance and to provide social, psychological, and economic assets for the protection of dependent children and widows. This was especially true for the ancient Hebrews who lived in a patriarchal society with arranged marriages. How many western brides want to return to that model of marriage?

It would not have been unusual for the ancient Jewish bride to be much younger than her husband, and they may not have known each other prior to their marriage. Romantic love, especially prior to marriage, was of no concern to the ancient Hebrews. Their views about marriage and religion were no doubt affected by their Egyptian and Mesopotamian neighbors, who either predated the ancient Hebrews or were their peers.

David Blankenhorn, in *The Future of Marriage*, has written extensively on what constitutes a marriage. He argues that the Egyptians adopted certain "wisdom writings" of a man known as Ptah-Hotep. He advised Pharaoh Izezi (about 2450 BCE) about family life. Ptah-Hotep tells the son:

> …found thy household and love thy wife at home as is fitting. Fill her belly; clothe her back. Ointment is the prescription for her body. Make her heart glad as long as thou livest…Her eye is her storm wind. Let her heart be soothed through what may accrue to thee; it means keeping her long in thy house….

As for paying attention to other women, Ptah-Hotep warns,

> …beware of approaching the women. It does not go well. …He who has a wandering eye for the women cannot be keen. A thousand men may be distracted from their own advantage. One is made a fool…Do not do it. It really is an abomination—and thou shall be free from sickness of heart every day.

This Egyptian writer had this to say about fathers and how to treat a dutiful son, Ptah-Hotep writes,

> He is thy son, whom thy *ka* [vital force] engendered for thee. Thou shouldst not cut thy heart off from him…If a man converses with his children, then they will speak to their children…

This is a clear affirmation of the importance of fatherhood, but if the son is rebellious or displeases the gods,

> Thou shouldst cast him off: he is not thy son at all. He was not really born to thee.

King Lipit-Ishtar of lower Mesopotamia wrote (around 1900 BCE) some bonding rules concerning marriage that would become the first such legal code. Martha Roth (p. 25) notes that the king wrote,

> With a… [decree], I made the father support his children. I made the child support his father. I made the father stand by his children. I made the child stand by his father.

Blankenhorn (p. 15) argues that, "Childrearing is probably the single most important social need that marriage is designed to meet…"—simply put as "procreation of the species." As part of his argument, he notes the Lipit-Ishtar code as translated in Prichard's, *Ancient Near Eastern Texts*:

> If a man's wife has not borne him children, but a harlot from the public square has borne him children, he shall provide grain, oil, and clothing for that harlot; the children which the harlot has borne him shall be his heirs, and as long as his wife lives the harlot shall not live in the house with his wife.

The recent controversy about marriage rights for gay people should set one wondering about the intent of the words used to define the marriage issue. We often hear that the sanctity of marriage is the foundation of the modern family and society. The rhetoric surrounding American marriage appears to be based on fundamentalists' Judeo-Christian beliefs. Religious and political leaders who oppose equal rights for gay people to marry do so based upon their erroneous selective choice of a favorite religious abomination while choosing to ignore other abominations.

Doctor Laura Schlesinger, a noted columnist and radio personality allegedly received a letter from one of her readers inquiring about Old Testament directives. The writer noted in Leviticus 1: 9 that a bull should be offered on the altar of the temple. It was supposed to create a pleasing odor to God, but the writer's neighbors objected to the smell. The writer wanted to know if they should smite the neighbors. The writer went on to say that in Exodus 35: 2 one should not work on the Sabbath. However, a neighbor insisted on working on that day. The writer wanted to know if the neighbor should be put to death. One might laugh at the humor, but it carries to a logical end the absurdity of the religious-right in selectively insisting on observing some admonitions and ignoring others.

The disdain of homosexuals and same-sex marriage comes from non-Christian ideals such as hate, personal biases, self-righteousness, and hypocrisy. This position in regard to same sex unions has not always been filled with so much ill will. Recent history is filled with positive positions regarding the goals of the gay community. The reader is referred to authorities and such publications as John Boswell's fine book, *Christianity, Social Tolerance, and Homosexuality* (University of Chicago Press, 1980) and his *Same-Sex Unions in Pre-modern Europe* (Villard Books, 1994), *Male Colors: The Construction of Homosexuality in Tokugawa Japan* (University of California Press, 1995), Marjorie Topley's *Study of Lesbian Marriages in Guangdong, China*, William Eskridge's *The Case for Same-Sex Marriage* (1996).

Older references to what we would call a gay lifestyle can be found in the once oral and now written history of the Azande tribe of the southern Sudan. For centuries, Azande warriors bonded, in all legitimacy, with boy-wives, something only now being approached in western civilization through gay marriage and civil unions. The Sacred Band of Thebes (4th century, BCE) is another public example of acceptable gay unions. The warrior group was composed only of male couples. Their culture's rationale was that lovers would fight more fiercely and cohesively than strangers with no strong emotional or sexual bonds. Two hundred fifty-four of them died in battle and are buried in Thebes. A 20th century restored monument stands at their burial site.[68]

Modern marriage is not a cookie cutter image of ancient Jews' culture. The ancient Israelites were nomadic people whose primary financial assets were flock animals and tents. Sons and daughters were also assets. They could be workers, laborers, shepherds, and in the case of females, offered (sold) into an arranged marriage. Jewish children (ours included) and other assets could be significantly affected by what we today call marriage. The ancient Hebrew daughter given (sold) into marriage served as a kind of glue joining two families for economic, ethnic, political, and breeding purposes. Martin Stol (p. 489) has stated the two families often exchanged gifts of equal

---

68   http://en.wikipedia.org/wiki/Sacred_Band_of_Thebes

value as a way of binding the two families. Love or romantic entanglements between the bride and groom rarely, if ever, occurred, for many couples never saw or knew of the other prior to the wedding. Wedding celebrations for the ancient Jews was not a celebration of romantic love between the new couple, but for the hope of children, and various social and economic benefits that would accrue to the bride's and groom's families.

Some people say that only couples in a heterosexual marriage can properly raise children and protect society's family values. To believe otherwise allegedly undermines society and the heterosexual family. This argument is most often offered without evidence for such claims. Those who believe in this demise often fail to note that gay people are the children of heterosexuals who were married and constituted the so-called nuclear family. Some fundamentalists have stated that such families have failed God in that they somehow failed to properly raise non-gay children.

....

> I believe that others have the right to live as they choose, free from discrimination. But I don't believe that this acceptance, that this tolerance should lead to a radical redefinition of marriage.
>
> **SENATOR BILL FRIST** *(R-TN AND FORMER SENATE MAJORITY LEADER),*
> *RELIGION & ETHICS NEWSWEEKLY*

....

Recent census figures reveal that less than fifty percent of America's population, eligible for marriage, is married. Those who choose marriage often cite children as being important to the happiness and success of their marriage. The Catholic Church, through the Code of Canon Law, has stated that the siring of children is a responsibility of married Catholics. The Church has a well thought out set of rules for approving marriage. First of all, the couples should be baptized Catholic. Their marriage is considered consummated (*ratum et consummatum*),

> …if the couple has performed between themselves in a human fashion
> a conjugal act which is suitable in itself for the procreation of offspring,
> to which marriage is ordered by its nature…

Can. 1061§ 1

This means the use of artificial birth control, such as pills and condoms, is not permitted. This carefully worded section of the Canon means that ejaculation must occur as well. The Catholic Church also expects all the couple's sexual parts to function normally.

…Antecedent and perpetual impotence to have intercourse, whether on the part of the man or the woman, whether absolute or relative, nullifies marriage by its very nature…Sterility neither prohibits nor nullifies marriage, without prejudice to the prescript of Can. 1098. [see below]

Chpt. 3, Can. 1084 § 3

A person contracts invalidly who enters marriage inveigled [cajoled, lured] by deceit, perpetrated in order to secure consent, concerning some quality of the other party, which of its very nature can seriously disrupt the partnership of conjugal life.

Can. 1098

In November 2003, the US bishops approved a restatement of long held Catholic beliefs about marriage. Bishop Kevin J. Boland, head of the bishop's Committee of Marriage had the following to say about the document.

- Marriage is a lifelong union of a man and a woman joined by love for life. They commit themselves to each other and to the responsibility of bringing children into the world. Even though equal, men and women are sexually different from each other but made for each other in a complementary way that draws them together in such a way that is open to procreation. This is the argument that the "parts" (penis and vagina) fit together and since men have no vagina their parts do not "fit."

- Marriage comes from God who made men and women in the divine image. He goes on to quote Genesis 1: 27 discussing men clinging to a wife and becoming one body. The man sees the woman as bone of bone and flesh of flesh (Genesis 2: 23). God Commands the man and the woman to be fertile and multiply (Genesis 1: 28).

- The bishops go on to say that a same—sex union contradicts the nature of marriage. Unions are not based on having complementary parts as are marriages. Partners in civil unions (and marriages) cannot cooperate with God to create new life nor or unite in a way to meet the natural purpose of sexual union or create a true conjugal union.

The argument presented in the bishop's document is, first of all, a religious statement of faith. The bishops' and other fundamentalists' faith is just that—faith. Why should they feel that their faith should be forced on Americans who do not believe as they do. The complementary parts argument fails to realize that the parts between men do fit or the members of the gay community would have given up on this means of expressing love centuries ago.

It appears to me that the statement of their faith is still based on ancient biological knowledge. Men or women in civil unions or marriages can cooperate with God to create Children via several paths, but the Church does not approve of these differing coming together of parts.

Given the fact that the seven billionth birth occurred November 1, 2011, perhaps the Committee of Bishops should read the works of the third century Cyprian, Bishop of Carthage,

> …the first commandment given to men was to increase and multiply, but now that the earth was full there was no need to continue this process of multiplication.[69]

Despite all the arguments made for marriage, the Catholic Church did not officiate at weddings until the ninth century.[70] Matrimony, for most of Church history, was a sacrament celebrated (as in the Judaic tradition) without clergy and was done according to local customs.

Recent research by the Pew Research Center has shown that the rearing of children is having less impact on creating a good marriage in America than in the past. Their research has shown that shared housekeeping (62 percent), good housing (51 percent), adequate income (53 percent), happy sexual relationship (70 percent) and faithfulness (93 percent) were more important to a good marriage than children (41 percent). Sixty-five percent of married couples said children were important in a 1990 World Values Survey, but only forty-one percent of couples cited children as being important in 2007—a drop of twenty-one percent. The survey also found:

> …by a margin of 3 to 1, Americans say the main purpose of marriage is the "mutual happiness and fulfillment" of adults rather than the "bearing and raising of children.[71]

Of heterosexual couples who marry, fifty percent of the marriages will end in divorce. Some of those divorced will remain single parents. Yet, many of these heterosexual, single parent families (as well as homosexual families) are shown to be equal to paired heterosexuals in raising happy and psychologically normal children. (*PEDIATRICS* Vol. 109 No. 2 February 2002, p. 341 - 344) Research on gay families, reported by the University of California (UC) at Davis, was used in a New Jersey Supreme Court ruling (October 25, 2006). In her opinion, New Jersey Chief Justice Deborah Poritz referenced an article by UC Davis psychology professor Gregory Herek. That article's scientific evidence aided Justice Poritz in reaching her opinion that same-sex families

---

69   <http://en.wikipedia.org/wiki/Christian_views on_marriage > Nov. 1, 2011

70   Karen Armstrong, *The Gospel According to Women*, London, 1986

71   http://pewresearch.org/pubs/526/marriage-parenthood

provide as stable a setting for childrearing as that of a heterosexual couple. Professor Herek reported that regardless of whether children are raised in heterosexual or homosexual households, researchers have not found significant differences in mental health or social adjustment of the children.

Many married people choose, or choose not, to have children. Should couples electing not to have children be considered a non-contributor to society or do they even constitute a family? Certain segments of society continue to ignore the fact that homosexuals have formed family units equal in most ways to that of heterosexuals? The Christian right persists in praising heterosexual family values but refuse to overtly acknowledge the fact that heterosexual families produce gay offspring (with God's help). To do so would be an acknowledgement that the "gay lifestyle" is not chosen but God given and one not to be persecuted by the religious-right.

A Christian marriage could be viewed as a risky religious and economic arrangement. The Barna Research Group has reported that conservative, born-again Christians are more likely to divorce than couples from other faith groups. Their research found the Christian divorce rate to be even higher than that of atheists or agnostics. The founder of the group, George Barna, said,

> While it may be alarming to discover that born-again Christians are more likely than others to experience a divorce, that pattern has been in place for quite some time. Even more disturbing, perhaps, is that when those individuals experience a divorce many of them feel their community of faith provides rejection rather than support and healing.[72]

Professor Brad Wilcox, a Christian sociologist specializing in family matters, notes,Compared with the rest of the population, conservative Protestants are more likely to divorce.

He also notes, in Ronald J. Sider's 2005 work, *Books & Culture*, p. 9 & 39, divorce rates are higher in the southern United States, where conservative Protestants constitute a high percentage of the population. Kentucky, Mississippi, and Arkansas voted overwhelmingly in 2004 for a constitutional amendment to ban same-sex marriage. At the time, these three states had the highest divorce rates in the United States. The state with the lowest divorce rate was Massachusetts, where the Supreme Court ruled in favor of gay marriage. There is clearly a self-selected disconnect between the problems confronting heterosexual marriage and the conservatives' proposed solution to divorce by banning same-sex marriage in America. Some fundamentalists believe that marriage is sacred for two reasons:

- God made woman from Adam's rib and therefore she was Adam's "wife". They were "married by god" and were husband and wife.

---

72   <http://www.barna.org/FlexPage.aspx?Page=BarnaUpdate&BarnaUpdateID=170>December 28, 2008

- Christ attended a wedding feast where he performed his first miracle of converting water into wine. He, therefore, believed in the sanctity of marriage since he attended and provided a miracle for the bride, groom, and parents of the couple.

A careful reading of the scripture regarding this miracle reveals nothing to indicate that Christ attended what the fundamentalists would call the "sacred" part of the marriage ceremony but only the party. The feast occurred **after** the marriage contract was signed. From the way the verse is written, we can deduce from Christ's actions that:

1. He liked parties;
2. He enjoyed wine;
3. He wanted to please his mother who requested more wine;
4. He saved the hosts some embarrassment at having run out of wine too early in the wedding celebration.

Adam and Eve are often referred to as the first "married" couple. However, in Genesis, there is the suggestion that there may have been a woman prior to Eve. Some scholars believe there is a twice telling of the story about man and woman's creation. Nevertheless, in,

Genesis 1: 27,

> So God created man in his own image, in the image of God created he him; male and female created he them.

As written, this occurrence predates the act of God making man from the dust of the earth. Some religious persons (mostly Orthodox Jews) argue that the man and woman in Genesis 1: 27 were the first male and female on earth. A few believe that a careful reading of the above verse indicates that the male and female may have been hermaphrodites, i.e., "male and female created he them." A subsequent verse has God making "another" man and woman called Adam and Eve.

Some orthodox Jews call the alleged "first" woman Lilith. Some believe she was an equal to the male but was ambitious and separated herself from him (the first divorce?) because she would not place herself under Adam's dominion.

The 13th Century writings of Rabbi Isaac ben Jacob ha-Cohen, tell us that Lilith left Adam after she refused to become subservient to him and would not return to the Garden of Eden after she mated with Archangel Samael.[73] Later, in Chapter 2, verse 7, God creates (another ?) man from the dust of the earth:

---

73 *Eve and Adam: Jewish, Christian, and Muslim readings on Genesis and gender*, Kristen E. Kvam, Linda S., Schearing, Valarie H. Ziegler, p 220-221, Indiana University Press, 1999

Genesis 2: 18,

> …It is not good that the man should be alone; I will make him an help
> **meet** for him.

God (the Bible) makes no mention of a "wife" or a "marriage," only a helper. Some scholars say that this helper was the second female on earth. In verse 22 of Genesis we read, "…made he a woman and brought her unto the man." She was to be called woman because the word meant that she was "taken out of man." The presenting of the helper to Adam has been construed by a few to constitute "holy matrimony" and the establishment of the first family.

Genesis 2: 24,

> Therefore shall a man leave his father and his mother; and shall cleave
> unto his wife and they shall be one flesh.

Note that it is the man who may leave his mother and father—not a woman. **IF** family-leaving constitutes part of marriage, fundamentalists should note that leaving one's family was not applicable to Adam because he had no mother or father to leave. However, one needs to remember that Genesis was written many years after the creation story of Adam and Eve, so the story may be incomplete.

If they were a true couple, it would be interesting to know if they were created speaking the world's first language. Many scholars believe the Genesis story was maintained in oral form for tens of hundreds of years before it was written more than 3,000 years ago. As with all rumors, who knows what aberrations may have crept into the language and story about the first humans later described in the Old Testament.

There is no doubt that the modern word *wife* is one that is associated with a woman who joins with a man to become his life partner. However, wife was a word created by man to describe the earliest Biblical relationship many years after Eve's existence. Eve was first referred to as a helper, **not** a wife. The word wife occurs after Eve's sin (eating the forbidden fruit) in the Garden of Eden. Prior to that event, she was "woman."

Wife is a word that was first associated with a woman who was part of a **sinful** couple. Their relationship is described as one in which they *cleave*. This word may not only mean married or marriage, but may mean *to cling*. The word may also mean *to split*. The interpretation meaning *cling* may have been used to refer to the relationship of a weak woman (Eve) to a weak man (Adam). Their weakness was exposed when neither could resist the Devil's temptation. Today, there are couples who live as *one flesh* (as did Adam and Eve), or as one cleaving unit, without being legally married or having "benefit of clergy." Too much importance has been given to Genesis and its use in fostering the religious biases of the religious-right. The use of Genesis is an improper support for the current legal view of heterosexual marriage or to deny homosexual marriage.

The religious-right and fundamentalists often refer to the "sacred institution" of marriage. An institution is an established relationship, organization, practice standard, corporation, etc. We are all familiar with institutions: churches, banks, The Red Cross, schools, Boy Scouts, Department of Defense, the Presidency, and similar groups of associated people. Membership in these institutions may require time and money along with social and psychological support. In return, the institution grants certain benefits for the exchange of various assets required of members to be associated with the institution. Marriage can be such an institution.

Promoting hatred and bigotry in the name of God is what destroys society, not the marriage of two loving people of the same gender.

RAYMOND MILLER, *TORONTO STAR*

Marriage has members, legal support, societal support, and possibly religious support. Even non-religious marriages have many of the above supports. In exchange for attaining the legal status of being married, our national, state, and many local governments extend certain financial and legal rights to males and females united in such pacts. Leaders of the gay marriage movement have pointed out that married couples have 1138 Federal Government benefits that are not available to un-married gay couples or single people.[74]

The recent law making homosexual Civil Unions legal in New Jersey has helped to reduce the benefits disparity for gay couples. However, many New Jersey residents joined by a civil union are facing discrimination because they are not "married." There were, as of 2010, many attempts to legally change civil unions into marriages but these efforts failed.

The Federal Government continues to discriminate against gay couples by denying them Federal recognition or accepting a state's granting them a legal marriage or a legal civil union bonding. In 2009, a few Federal government agencies extended some partner benefits to its gay employees, but so far, this action has been limited. The religious-right joined this discrimination for various reasons. One being the protection of the legal and financial rights they have. Some of the religious-right believes their rights might be diminished if equal rights were extended to the gay community. The role of the haves versus the "have nots" is to maintain their central belief that Christian conservatives are **better** than or **superior** to members of the gay community. Some Fundamentalists believe that gay people are not loved by God and cannot become

---

74   <http://www.dosomething.org> December 28, 2008

Christians unless homosexuals become heterosexuals—then they would be permitted to marry.

After God created the world, its contents, and man, he declared all was good—except with Adam. God saw Adam as being lonely, so Eve was created to be Adam's helpmate. Even though this couple later produced children, there is no mention of a marriage wherein Eve could or could not agree to any kind of marriage arrangement. No bridal dowry was paid. No wedding feast was held. No contract was signed. There was no "marriage."

Marriage is a legal state of being. Adam had no legal system to call on for a marriage certificate that would permit him to be legally married.

Eve was made from Adam's rib (or side), which was taken via a God-induced-sleep. This anesthetic-sleep can be seen as necessary for two reasons: God wanted to spare Adam the pain of "surgery" or Adam might not be willing to give up a rib. God could have made Eve from the dust of the earth as was Adam but, perhaps, the writers of Genesis wanted to portray Eve as being of lesser status than man or somehow beholding to Adam. We have no way of knowing if Adam knew Eve was made of his rib or if Eve knew of her origins. All we know is that Eve was presented to Adam as a "help meet."

Some Christians still believe that a female is to be subservient to her husband and include such language in their marriage ceremony. No wonder some Christian and non-Christian men want to protect "traditional" heterosexual marriage. For such couples, marriage provides a legal arrangement that is male-centered and one where the female is disadvantaged. History reveals that marriage among ancient, and some modern, societies was one of mutual family arrangement. What was sacred about that? I cannot believe that these brides or grooms were happy or even pleased to be married to a person chosen for by their family. Some of these marriages were conducted under the umbrella of religion, but others were for cultural, financial, or social reasons.

> Gay people deserve the same right to marry that everybody else does. And God cares about our relationships the same way God cares about heterosexual relationships. We're making the same commitments to each other. We have the same responsibilities to each other, and we deserve the same rights and responsibilities under the law that everyone else has.
>
> **HARRY KNOX** *OF THE HUMAN RIGHTS CAMPAIGN*

Many ancient weddings took on religious overtones, because the religion in question was based upon a mother-earth theology in which a proliferative mother-nature goddess was prominent in the religion. A married couple was expected to mimic mother-earth and produce offspring. Continuing the species was only one reason for having children. In some cases, if the couple produced no children (sterility) or failed to consummate the marriage, the couple could divorce. This rule persists in modern Roman Catholic Canon Law. Even today, certain religions still expect couples to "be fruitful and multiply."

The same expectation can be met inside the marriages of gay persons, with the assistance of a female acting as a surrogate or biological mother for gay male couples, or a male can be a sperm donor for gay female couples. However, conception under such circumstances is, for the religious-right, one step forward but two steps backwards.

One important aspect, if not the primary purpose, of arranged marriages was the protection of wealth along a given line of male inheritance. A bride was considered the property of her father and family and as such could be "given" or betrothed to a father-selected bridegroom. Even in some modern marriage ceremonies, the person officiating at the ceremony will ask. "…who *gives* this woman in matrimony?" Many Christian brides are still treated as *property* to be publically given away in a church ceremony.

Ancient Hebrew women were denied certain types of property rights, but their husbands and sons could lay claim to property ownership. Brides were associated with a dowry and in a sense, she was a purchased item. If women of history were fortunate enough to own land, the ownership of that land could become that of a new husband. For this reason, second sons who had no land to inherit often sought to marry women or widows who owned property. Would the religious-right consider these marriages sacred if the true intent was property rights and not "love" as we have come to know it?

Put another way, is love a valid reason for marriage, either civil or religious?

Marriage contracts of the Middle Ages came to be as a way of delineating certain financial and economic parameters between the partners. The modern prenuptial contract also delineates rights and responsibilities of the bride and groom if the marriage is dissolved.

Romantic love was not required for marriage in the Renaissance nor is it always present in a contemporary marriage, i.e., a marriage of convenience, for business, immigration, arranged marriages by some Hindus and Moslems, etc. Heads of different geopolitical powers might intermarry to bond two political entities. Even today, some marriages between members of different royal families seem more to protect the status quo of royal blood lines than for religious reasons. If a royal person cannot find another royal person to marry then a prince, princess, king, or queen may marry a commoner and making him or her a royal person by decree. Hence, the couple becomes royal and their children will be royal.

In the mid-15th century, there was a powerful Italian family known as the Borgias. Alexander, an assumed name after being made Pope, Borgia bought for himself a position as Cardinal in the Roman Catholic Church. After assuming the position of Cardinal, he had several children with a mistress. Later, Alexander became Pope Alexander II (1492 - 1503). His daughter, Lucretia, was betrothed at the age of 13 through an arrangement made by her father. On the wedding night, the pope (her father) accompanied the bride and groom into the bed chamber. While not directly watching the couple have intercourse, the Pope did see the marriage being consummated as the couple copulated under a sheet. Today, this act would seem most unusual. However, in the era of arranged marriages, the issue of marriage as a contract was very important. Many people of that era believed that if the marriage was not consummated, or if children were not produced, the contract could or should be annulled. The most frequent reason for asking for an annulment was impotence, real or not. So it was with Pope Alexander's son-in-law. He made such a claim, out of fear, to save his fiefdom from being confiscated by his father-in-law, Pope Alexander.

European serfs of the middle ages were not permitted to marry because they owned no property and nothing to be inherited. In fact, serfs were considered the property of the owner of the land on which the serf worked. Self-proclaimed marriages among serfs did occur but were without any legal protection or recognition by the state. Until the 12th century, European Catholic priests infrequently oversaw marriage ceremonies.

The Catholic Church's Fourth Lateran Council (1251 CE) ordered prenuptial banns (public announcements) for upcoming weddings, required the weddings be held in public, but did not require ecclesiastical blessings of the wedding. Matters of matrimony were eventually officially resolved in the Roman Catholic Church at the Council of Trent (1545 CE) when it was decided that marriage must take place in a public Christian ceremony where marriage came to be regarded as a sacrament. Thereafter, a public Christian ceremony, combined with consent and consummation, became the basis for a valid marriage. What Catholics know today as a wedding mass grew out of 16th Century church law.

To be married for emotional reasons was once considered to be immoral (lustful). Martin Luther saw marriage as a civil matter from which the church should refrain. Not until 1563 CE did the Catholic Church **require** the participation of a priest in a marriage ceremony for the ceremony to be valid. Some say this was a consolidation of church power over the secular world.

The Bible's ancient peoples knew almost nothing of the concept of today's ideal of monogamous, lifetime, romantic, heterosexual marriage because the Bible portrays marriage in terms of property and business transactions, polygamy, extended family, tribal groupings, Levirate marriage and other lifestyles. However, the anti-marriage bias in some parts of the New Testament and sex-negative emphasis of early Catholic theologians is well known by historians and students of human sexuality.

Do America's religious pundits claim all religious marriages are sacred or only Christian marriage? While one may argue that marriage is a sacred institution, today a marriage cannot exist without the explicit approval of the state. While it is true that many marriage ceremonies are conducted by a member of a religious group, the person conducting the marriage ceremony must be licensed by the state to perform such ceremonies if the marriage is to be legally valid. However, in the eyes of the law, the ceremony performed by a justice of the peace is as legally binding as that of a licensed, religious leader. Are these civil marriages sacred? If so, what makes them sacred? The religious-right would frown on a couple living together without the "blessings" of the state (and in some cases clergy). A simple statement by a couple saying "We are married by God," would not go over very well within the fundamentalists' community. Adrian Thatcher (p. 16) has noted,

> The theology of marriage is…integrated into the institutions of slavery
> and the hierarchical order of social relations which slavery serves.

For this reason alone, many women and feminists abhor marriage ceremonies. Many prefer to "live in sin."

A New Jersey heterosexual or homosexual couple may apply for certain legal protections and rights in a Domestic Partnership, if they are over 62 years of age. These persons may or may not be in romantic love but, for various reasons or limitations of the State, are not married. Gay New Jersey couples may apply for a Civil Union, which carries all the rights and privileges of a heterosexual marriage—except for the title of marriage. The rights so granted are not always easy to access because of the absence of the title "marriage" defining their status.

It is well known that the religious-right has actively worked to deny gay couples National recognition of marriage rights. This denial of equal legal rights to the gay community has centered on a Congressional bill commonly known as the *Defense of Marriage Act*. This bill was authored and promoted by Rep. Bob Barr of Georgia. Representative Barr (approximately 50 years old) had been married three times. When the Defense of Marriage Bill was being discussed, rumors floated around Capitol Hill that asked,

> "Bob Barr…WHICH marriage are you defending?"

New York state not only allows gay marriage, but a New York court announced that legally married gay couples, from states that permitted gay marriage, would be recognized as married in New York despite the desire of the religious-right to maintain the rights of marriage only for heterosexual unions—so much for equal rights in New Jersey where the legislature permitted civil unions but not gay marriage. On the other hand, Massachusetts granted the right of marriage to homosexuals without significant objections of then Governor Romney who, as a presidential candidate, later recanted his support of the gay community and gay marriage. The fact that homosexual marriages do exist in the United States refutes the claim that a marriage is only between a man and a woman and clearly demonstrates that other types of family structure exists.

Many religious persons judge homosexuals to be unworthy of marriage. This reveals moral weakness and a sub-rosa, self-righteous pride often based in religious hypocrisy. In the Christian religion, we are instructed to "judge not lest we be judged." It seems egotistical and illogical for anyone to believe that their personal religious beliefs are perfect and applicable to all mankind. Such beliefs have caused too much hatred and bloodshed over the history of mankind.

In March 2007, General Peter Pace, the then Chairman of the Joint Chiefs of Staff, exposed his personal biases against having gay people serve in the armed services. In regard to a question before the press, the general responded to a question about the "don't ask, don't tell" policy for gay service personnel. The general said,

> I believe homosexual acts between two [same-sex] individuals are immoral, and that we should not condone immoral acts. I do not believe that the United States is well served by a policy that says it's okay to be immoral in any way…and it's against what I have been taught.

One should note that the General was discussing behavior. He apparently knows nothing about orientation or that two men can love one another as he supposedly loves his heterosexual wife. Some heterosexuals seem to believe that love, as they know it, cannot be shared by two members of the same sex.

The general failed to realize that his above statement was not the only time he physically and overtly bragged about his privileged social status. He publicly and openly broadcasted ***his*** sexual orientation (heterosexuality) every time he referred to his status as being married, having a wife, showed his wedding band, etc. Yet, the General wanted gay service personnel to ***lie*** about their sexual orientation by denying it to everyone, even the America these gay service people served. This forced cover up was in itself a lie and therefore immoral. Yet, this type of immorality was actually blessed by this servant of (some of) the American people. The American Family Association of Tupelo, Mississippi and the religious-right supported his announcement.

The gay community questioned whether or not any one person's personal or religious belief system should determine the nation's policy of denying equal rights to gay Americans, including those who chose to serve their fellow Americans and, on occasion, offered their lives in such service. "Don't ask, don't tell" programs are as immoral as the general and fundamentalists' support of the lie.

Doubters, such as General Pace, focus on so called unnatural sex acts among homosexuals. Yet, many heterosexuals perform the same acts. In Utah, heterosexuals can do so without fear of legal repercussions. As an American, this writer asks that the religious-right keep their sacred beliefs, regarding marriage and sexuality, to themselves and their congregations. They should "…Render unto God what is God's and unto Caesar what is Caesar's…" and that includes equal marriage rights for the gay community.

> [t]he military is nominally intended to *defend* what the country is, but as its racial and gender histories show, it is the chief institution by which the nation *defines* what the country is and what is to count as full personhood and full citizenship.
>
> **RICHARD D. MOHR,** *GAY JOURNALISTS*

The religious-right often discusses marriage without defining what marriage *is*. I would like to answer that question within our modern American context. Marriage is:

1. A mutual consenting to be married (legally contracted) with each party fully understanding the rights (freedom) and obligations provided by this institution.

    As previously noted, there are approximately 1138 Federal legal rights provided by marriage. Some are major rights and some are minor. Best known for receiving the Nobel Prize for Economics in 1993, Douglas C. North (360-61) had this to say about marriage,

    …the humanly devised constraints that structure human interaction… are made up of formal constraints (e.g., rules, laws, constitutions), informal constraints (e.g., norms of behavior, conventions, self-imposed codes of conduct), and their enforcement characteristics.

North is most concerned about what the social institution of marriage forbids. Another scholar, A. R. Radcliffe-Brown (P. 10-11), reminds us that marriage is not,

    …a haphazard conjunction of individuals…but one where…the conduct of persons in their interactions with others is controlled by norms, rules, or patterns…and…in marriage a person knows that he is expected to behave according to these norms and that other persons should do the same.

2. Socially approved sexual relations.

    Anthropologist Robin Fox (p. 27) writes: "Copulation produces the relation between the mates which is the foundation of marriage and parenthood." An exception is the case of Mary, the mother of Jesus, and Joseph where it is believed by some Christians that Mary remained a virgin until her death.

    Pierre L. van den Berghe (P.45-47) has this to say about marital sex,

    All known human societies recognize the existence of the sexual pair-bond and give it formal sanction in the form of marriage. With only a handful of exceptions presently to be examined, married pairs are expected not only to copulate with each other, but to cooperate in the raising of offspring and to extend each other material help.

The Archbishop of Hincmar of Reims wrote in 860 CE,

> A true coupling in legitimate marriage between free persons of equal
> status occurs when a free woman, properly dowered, is joined to a free
> man with paternal consent in a public wedding followed by sexual
> intercourse.

3. Social, economic, psychological, etc., support for children (natural or adopted).

4. A new family structure created through self-selected kinship.

5. A "bundle of rights" as described by E. R. Leach (105-113) in 1955. Among
    these rights are:

    > ...sexual rights, the rights of legal maternity and paternity, the right to
    > receive domestic labor from a spouse, the right to a spouse's property,
    > the right of the couple to pass on property to their children, and other
    > family rights...

6. A very special interpersonal relationship of intimacy where people [partners]
    are the most important part of the union.

7. Legally sanctioned interpersonal fidelity between the married couple. A sexual
    breach of this understanding can lead to divorce with significant effects on the
    offenders' financial status.

8. A wealth generating and asset building institution. Author Blankenhorn (p. 102)
    points out that married couples statistically earn more money and accumulate
    more wealth than unmarried people.

9. The sharing of a common life and lifestyle.

10. An institution in which love is shared.

Developmentally, man was biologically driven by lust to mate and then seek another
available female. He is disposed to spread his seed and progeny as far and wide as possible. It has been argued that fatherhood persuaded man to stay with his family. With the
exception of human beings, primates do not provide food for their weaned offspring.
Human fatherhood promoted infant care and later human cultural evolution would see
legal marriage adding weight to the obligations and privileges of fatherhood, family
and to society in general. This is all fair and good if you are heterosexual, but there are

millions of men and women who are not so ordained. Many fundamentalists argue that marriage is (and always has been) between a man and a woman. Author Evan Wolfsan (p. 589) argues marriage is "socially constructed and thus transformable." He goes on to say (p.599-80), that gay marriage is a social issue in the United States which is,

> ...both conservative and transformative, easily understood in basic human terms of equality and respect, and liberating in its individual and social potential.

In the Republican Party Primaries of 2012, many of the candidates went on record opposing gay marriages. These opponents often repeated a phrase so often used by religious leaders to battle proponents of gay marriage—"Marriage is between one man and one woman." This argument is a relatively modern invention by Christian Americans. However, many Islamist countries still permit multiple wives as do some African countries. On the other hand, polygamy is of growing interest as seen in recent TV programing.

The Old Testament is filled with references to God-loving men who had thousands of royal wives and hundreds of concubines. Unfortunately, there is no undisputable reference in the New Testament prohibiting polygamy. In Matthew 25:1-13, Jesus presented the Parable of the Ten Virgins. It deals with a bridegroom and ten virgins. Some believe this to be a positive statement about polygamy. In First Corinthians 5:1, there is mention of a New Testament situation that might have been polygamist. In the story, a son had fornicated with his father's wife. There was however, **no** reference to the man's mother. Leviticus 18:8 refers to a father's wife as specifically separate from our concept of mother. Many experts believe this reference should be applied to the Corinthian passage meaning polygamy did exist in early Christianity.

Earlier in our history, many Christian Americans had more than one wife. In fact it was not until 1862 that America had laws that prohibited a man from having more than one wife (Morrill Anti-Bigamy Act, 1862). This prohibition was strengthened in 1882 when another bill against bigamy became law (Edmunds Anti-Polygamy Act, 1882).

For the gay community, marriage is whatever society decides it to be. Just because society has, in the recent past, formulated the word marriage to convey the idea of a legal union of one man and one woman does not mean that that same society could not hence forward use the word marriage to define the legal union of two people of the same sex. While marriage is a legal right granted by society to heterosexuals, it is also a right **due** the gay community as one of the equal rights expressed in our constitution. The religious-right should be permitted to claim, inside their church, that marriage is a sacred institution as long as they acknowledge that marriage is also a legal convention with civil rights that should be extended to homosexuals.

In order to better understand social-sexual discrimination, I have often wondered how the religious-right would react if they were told that they could only marry people of a faith different from their own, i.e., a Christian could only marry a Jew, Muslim, or Hindu—not another Christian.

If this concept was seriously considered by members of the religious-right, they might grasp the sense of hurt and equal rights denial suffered by the gay community in being denied the right to marry whomever they choose. No human being should be told which other human being they can or cannot marry. Such mandates are unjust and a denial of equal rights under the law. Insisting that men marry only women is one of the most intrusive laws ever foisted upon humankind. Nothing is more damaging to the human spirit of a gay person than the denial of formal societal recognition of the love and special relationship between two same sex people that is supported by all the rights and privileges so associated in a marriage.

In this chapter, marriage has been discussed from a Christian and legal (civil rights) point of view. Should marriage be held hostage to the fundamentalists' point of view? Absolutely not. Marriage is a civil right applicable to all people despite their orientation.

In the next chapter, we will examine family structure and the alleged threats argued against the concept of gay marriage. They will be examined and debunked.

CHAPTER XI

Does Homosexuality Threaten Marriage and the Nuclear Family?

This sort of marriage [interracial] is not in the best interest of children. God has a plan for marriage and this isn't it. Allowing this kind of marriage will pave the way for all sorts of moral depravity.

MILDRED JETER AND RICHARD LOVING
COMMENTS FROM THE 1960S ON THE INTERRACIAL MARRIAGE OF ONE MAN AND ONE WOMAN.

*P*reviously, the concept of marriage was examined and found not to be a socially exclusive structure reserved only for heterosexuals. Worldwide, marriage is being legalized for more and more members of the gay community. However, further legalization is being hampered by fundamentalists who allege that gay marriage will ruin heterosexual family life. This chapter will attempt to disprove that allegation.

For thousands of years, non-Christian families have come together to create a special relationship and raise children. Some of these children were wanted and others were not. The ancient Greeks placed unwanted or deformed infants at some isolated roadside place and then walked away. These children were expected to die of starvation, thirst, heat, cold, or to be devoured by wild animals. Some of these abandoned children might have been rescued and raised to become sex slaves. The society in which these ancient people lived condoned such activities. It is said the Chinese abandoned unwanted female infants well into the 20th century.

Later these female infants were turned over to orphanages. These acts were an acceptable part of the family values for these cultures.

Some acts, unacceptable to modern American sensibilities and our family values, thrived well into the 21st century. The American Inuit (Eskimos) left aged members of the tribe in isolated places where the person was expected to die and / or be eaten by bears. Some aged, infirm people might take such a trek on their own so as not to be a burden to their family or tribe. Despite what we would call loathsome acts, these peoples acted within the framework of their family values and their cultures have survived.

Religious conservatives, the Catholic Church included, have said that man should not become involved in such things as artificial insemination, Petri dish (in vitro) fertilizations or intra-egg injections of sperm, because in doing so, man is playing God. As of 2013, thousands of children have been born thanks to these new technologies. Despite the Church's admonitions, the world has not come to an end, family structure has not crumbled, and many families now have children that they would not otherwise have had. Children born of these modern technologies are as deeply loved as a child born of natural conception. Technology-assisted parents call these children a gift of God and have not caused society to crumble.

Even though liberal and conservative Christians may not condone abortions, the procedure occurs hundreds of times each week. Sometimes they occur within a marriage where the couple is deeply connected to each other through love. For various reasons, they simply do not want to have another child, yet society has not crumbled.

Given these activities so disdained by Christian conservative, neither the family, nor our society, has disintegrated. Given all these cultural and science-based occurrences, how can the religious-right believe that a gay (married) couple living within the same city, or on the same city block of such believers, threatens (Christian) marriage? I have yet to hear a single bit of information that would support the argument that heterosexual marriage will disappear from the face of the earth if gays are given their civil rights and permitted to marry. The anti-gay marriage argument suggests the modern, nuclear, heterosexual family is so weak that it cannot survive in the presence of an alternative life style (gay marriages). I do not believe any of these arguments are valid.

Often, conservative Christians refer to God's definition of marriage as sacred. However, Paul, in I Corinthians 7, has this to say about marriage,

> Now concerning the things whereof ye wrote unto me: It is good for a man not to touch a woman. Nevertheless, to avoid fornication [sin], Let every man have his own wife, and let every woman have her own husband.

Paul apparently doesn't care much for women. He says it is best if a man does not even touch a woman, but if the man cannot control his lust he should get married. Paul says nothing about marriage being sacred. He suggests marriage be used by those who lust to avoid giving into the sin of fornication.

Paul goes on to say,

…for I would that all men were even as I myself.

He means chaste [no sex] and unmarried. Later, Paul goes on to say,

> …I say therefore to the unmarried and widows, it is good for them if they Abide even as I [chase and unmarried].[75] But if they cannot contain, [lust or have sinful sex][75] let them marry: for it is better to marry than to burn [lust or sin by having sex].[75]

How can one find anything sacred about marriage if it is used to avoid the sin of fornication?

I recently received an email concerning the destruction of the institution of hetero-sexual marriage. The email involved the following conservative, religious members of government:

Ronald Reagan—divorced the mother of his two children to marry Nancy Reagan who bore him a daughter 7 months after their marriage. This suggests he got Nancy pregnant outside of marriage.

Sen. Bob Dole—divorced his child's mother who had nursed the senator through his long recovery from war wounds.

Newt Gingrich—divorced his wife who was dying of cancer. At the time he was promoting the Defense of Marriage legislation, he was secretly dating a woman whom he would marry after divorcing his wife.

Dick Armey—House Majority Leader - divorced

Sen. Phil Gramm of Texas—divorced

Gov. John Engler of Michigan—divorced

Gov. Pete Wilson of California—divorced

George Will—divorced

---

75   Author's addition

Sen. Lauch Faircloth—divorced

Rush Limbaugh—Rush and his current wife Marta have six marriages and four divorces between them.

Rep. Bob Barr of Georgia—married three times

Sen. Alfonse D'Amato of New York—divorced

Sen. John Warner of Virginia—divorced (once married to Liz Taylor)

Gov. George Allen of Virginia—divorced

Henry Kissinger—former secretary of state—divorced

Rep. Helen Chenoweth of Idaho—divorced

Sen. John McCain of Arizona and Republican Candidate for President—divorced. The senator obtained his marriage certificate to marry his second wife while he was still married to his first wife. He married a wealthy, younger woman within a few weeks of his divorce.[76]

Rep. John Kasich of Ohio—divorced

Rep. Susan Molinari of New York and Republican National Convention Keynote Speaker—divorced

Gov. Mark Sandford of South Carolina divorced because of extra-marital affair with an Argentinian woman. He used state funds to pay his airfares to visit her in South America.

Senator John Edwards of North Carolina became the father of an illegitimate child while he was still married to his dying wife.

---

76 <http://articles.latimes.com/2008/jul/11/nation/na-divorce11> 12-28-2008

It is often leaders such as those above that deride the gay community and proclaim that homosexual marriages will ruin the institution of heterosexual marriage. This short list of divorced national leaders suggests that they and other conservatives are doing more than their share of the work needed to destroy heterosexual marriage while many of these leaders promote legislation which would deny marriage rights to the gay community.

Throughout much of recorded history there have been men and women who found members of their own sex to be objects of desire and love. Recent sex research has projected that approximately 5 to 10 percent of the general population is gay. There is nothing to dissuade one from believing that this percentage, of gayness in the population, could be extrapolated into history and past peoples. Homosexuals have always been a part of society, even if they lived a covert existence.

In the past, same-sex desire was not understood by most people and countenanced by even fewer. This was probably due to ignorance. I am sure, however, gay people in the ancient world found each other, loved each other, and had sex. They may have lived with each other under all kinds of circumstances, perhaps as the Biblical centurion and his servant mentioned in the Bible and later in this book. John Boswell's book *Christianity, Social Tolerance, and Homosexuality: Gay People in Western Europe From the Beginning of the Christian Era to the Fourteenth Century* takes note of the many civil and legal unions throughout western history.

History's homosexuals probably lived as many gay Americans now live—in quiet communities, next door to religious friends, building a life together, out of the limelight, while building businesses, earning a living, and aspiring to a better life. For thousands of years, heterosexual marriages and family structures have persisted undamaged beside these unsanctioned gay marriages. Across time, gay people living as couples can be seen as valiant warriors (the Sacred Band of Thebes), musicians (Elton John), politicians (Barney Frank), kings (England's King James I), and TV stars: Ted Allen, Kyan Douglas, Tom Filicia, Carson Kressley and Jai Rodriguez (Queer Eye for the Straight Guy), Sean Hayes (Will and Grace). Many became popular icons in the heterosexual world.

The National Organization for Marriage is a not-for-profit organization run by religious conservatives who are opposed to gay civil unions or marriage. I examined their webpage and a particular section entitled "Threats to Marriage." Much to my surprise, I found no mention of actual threats, only what the group perceived as threats to their objectives.

One of the group's 2009 internal documents was made public on March 26, 2012, by court officials in Maine. It disclosed the organization's attempt to split the Democratic Party's base by pitting African-Americans and Hispanics against gay-rights groups. It suggested "interrupting the process of cultural assimilation for Hispanics in hope of curtailing support for same-sex marriage."[77]

---

77   http://www.nydailynews.com/news/politics/gay-marriage-foes-split-gays-blacks-art

The New York Daily News (June 12, 2011) said, "The National Organization for Marriage is a shadowy group, run by religious fundamentalists, that is bankrolling a pitched crusade against same-sex marriage in New York." The Wall Street Journal (July 26, 2011) contained an article written by conservative columnist, James Taranto. He wrote,

> If the National Organization for Marriage were a commercial enterprise, its 'Let the People Vote' [against gay marriage] campaign would be a case of deceptive advertising.

The organization argues that gay marriage is NOT a civil rights issue. The released documents revealed that they wished to "Find, equip, energize and connect African-American spokespeople for marriage, develop a media campaign around their objections to gay marriage as a civil right, provoke the gay marriage base into responding by denouncing these spokesmen and women as bigots."

On September 8, 2011, Archbishop Charles Chaput celebrated his last mass in Denver, Colorado, before assuming his new post in Philadelphia. He replaced Cardinal Justin Rigali who had for years swept under the rug many of the pedophilia cases in Pennsylvania. Archbishop Chaput is quoted in the Philadelphia Gay News (September 2-8, 2011, p. 10).

> Marriage is a natural relationship between a man and a woman for the sake of children. And so same-sex marriage doesn't make any sense, if you understand that's what marriage is. It's about children. It's not about love, it's not just about sex—though sex is always above love and about children…It's naturally procreative, and so the church is concerned about a stable meaning of marriage. We think it's the bedrock of not only the church but society…It [gay marriage] undermines the meaning of marriage for all of us…That is why the church opposes this…[there is a] need to support marriage as a stable relationship for the sake of children.

My response to Archbishop Chaput's interview is to say that marriage is not natural. It is a manmade legal institution to protect property. Religion simply rides the shirttail of the legal contract of bonding and promising. Same-sex marriage is now legal worldwide so the archbishop's pronouncement is behind the times. If children are at the heart of the issue, why not permit gay families with adopted and "natural" children to get married so they can provide the same stability as found in heterosexual marriages? His pronouncement logically leads one to believe that all non-child bearing marriages (either self-determined or biologically determined) should be canceled. This includes deathbed marriages and second marriages of elderly residents in nursing homes. Only since the middle of the dark ages has marriage been considered the bedrock of society and that was when the Catholic church first mandated marriages, but who is to say gay marriage could not, nor does not, contribute to the good of society in support of that bedrock?

The archbishop goes on to repeat the often heard statement that "gay marriage undermines the meaning of marriage for all of us." He offers no logical reasoning for his slander of gay marriage. He, like many other fundamentalists, fails to define "undermines."

I ask what and where is there a homosexual threat to the institution of heterosexual marriage? The only thing I see is a group of so-called religious individuals who believe that all gay people are sinners and therefore not worthy of anything *sacred* such as marriage. Permitting gay marriage would legally mean that gay people are as "good" or equal to religious heterosexual couples, which in the mind of the religious-right is anathema. Legalizing gay marriage might mean detractors would have less ammunition with which to denounce the gay community as they have in the past.

Conservative religious families might fear:

-   having their children hear of or see happily married gay people, or

-   experience gay marriage occurring between the adult children of some fundamentalist parents (who have also produced gay children) living a sane and civil life.

These kinds of life experiences would be counter to what the religious-right has been teaching its children and proclaiming to the world. They might even be surprised to learn that ministers may have gay children or have a closeted gay spouse.

Gay people and unmarried gay couples have for centuries contributed to the economic, political, social, and cultural life of the community in which they live, albeit some as closeted members of that community. Why would anyone believe that acceptance of gay marriage by the general community would decrease the contributions made by legally united gay couples or negatively impact the contributions of heterosexuals? The one thing the religious-right seems to fears is that they would have to admit they had been promoting a lie and hatred in the name of religion.

David Blankenhorn (p. 143) believes a primary rationale for gay people to seek marriage is to "conferring society's blessing on the fortunate couple." He states, "If I were gay, I might well view the prospect of marriage in exactly these terms."

Reporter Paul Varnell, Chicago's *Windy City Times*, thinks of marriage as a route to social equality.

> I suspect that our new ability to marry, even in just a few states, will inevitably encourage most heterosexual people to take us, our lives, and our partnerships more seriously. If the law stipulates our partnerships are the legal equivalent of theirs then that will be considerable encouragement for them to begin thinking of us and our lives as equal to them and their lives. Far more than non- discrimination laws, that

is pretty much exactly what our long sought goal of social equality consists of.

Mental health therapist, Irene Javors (p. 296, 304) writes,

> I have counseled many people who desperately want marriage because of the social validation it offers for their lives and their relationships.

The quotations of these two authors carries some merit and are no doubt a consideration in the minds of some gay people. Gay marriage may help reduce or eliminate the list of hateful adjectives seen earlier in this book.

There are now numerous married gay people in the United States and several foreign countries. So far, absolutely nothing untoward has happened to any heterosexual family secondary to these gay unions. The religious-right pundits fail to acknowledge the numerous changes in society, education, science, law, travel, money, etc., that affect how we live, where we live and with whom we live. All these things have a bearing on the nuclear family and the question of its continued survival. Most of the changes (perceived as threats) have almost nothing to do with homosexuality. They have more to do with increased freedoms and opportunities for heterosexuals than the gay couple who might live next door. In fact there is an urban myth which says,

> when gay people move in, property values go up, art and cultural happenings increase, food in restaurants improve and women's hairstyles are enhanced.

The religious-right and fundamentalists are so frightened of gay marriage that they and their fundamentalist President, George W. Bush, attempted to create a constitutional amendment banning gay marriage or any recognition of it, in any form and by any state. So far that has not happened, but it is difficult to discern which is worse: co-opting antigay sentiment in the church for political gain or attempting to use the constitution as a tool of discrimination.

Four decades ago, in a memorable sermon about American history, Martin Luther King, Jr., reminded us of the broad promises contained in our country's founding document. King compared what we say we believe and our actions. He challenged us to live up to our "holy" constitution and the words, "We hold these truths to be self-evident, that all men are created equal." He then added, "Yes, black men as well as white men." However, within the span of one generation, an American President attempted to use our Constitution in a restrictive way, enshrining a particular (his) religious belief (and an unstated hatred) into a constitution conceived and created to disentangle church from state. The Constitution was created to shield Americans from unjust internal forces, not as a sword to cut off the gay community from justice and equal rights.

Comparative Relationships

Most Americans have little or no knowledge about the various forms of marriage except for the 21st century, American institution of marriage. Since fundamentalists see marriage as mistakenly arising from the Genesis story and the Garden of Eden, let us quickly review part of that story.

Adam uses the name *Eve* for the first time in Genesis 3:20 after both had eaten of the forbidden tree. Not until Genesis 4:1, is it stated that Adam *knew* Eve. I am commenting upon the order in which the Genesis story is presented, not that the story is necessarily occurring in this order. The "knowing" was reported after they had *sinned* and were driven out of the Garden of Eden. I have heard it argued that this means procreation actually grew out of a sinful relationship. Today, according to the religious-right, sex within a relationship is okay as long as the relationship is one of marriage. In fact, sex and children are expected to result from a marriage relationship where sex is a "sacred" thing. Recall that Adam and Eve were NOT married.

We are told by fundamentalists that Adam and Eve were the first people on the earth. Having sinned, they became aware of sexual differences and after leaving the garden had two sons, Cain and Abel. Later on we are told in,

Genesis 5: 4, (King James Version)

> And the days of Adam after he had begotten Seth were eight hundred
> years: and he begat sons and daughters.

In Genesis, we read that Cain slew Abel and was driven from his home and the place of the Lord. Cain went to a place east of Eden, called Nod (a place of wandering), where he met his future wife (perhaps a sister or cousin). Since the word *wife* is used, one might assume the two had a marriage in contrast to Adam and Eve.

Let's take a look at the average American marriage as compared to the alleged marriage of Adam and Eve:

- The American couple comes together on a voluntary basis backed by certain legal protections provided by government.

- Eve had no input into her alleged marriage to Adam. She gave no consent and had no legal protections because there was no state to legally sanction marriage.

- An American couple may elect to have a civil or religious based marriage ceremony but in both cases they are required by the state to obtain certain permissions (license) in order to be legally married.

- Adam and Eve had no ceremony and gave no mutual permission. Some say that Eve was ordered by God to be married to Adam. We know nothing of Eve's wishes about becoming a wife and we know nothing about Adam's wishes about becoming a husband, if indeed they were husband and wife.

- The American wedding is expected to be followed by sex and children. Premarital sex in not unusual for most brides and grooms according to recent research.

- The first people, Adam and female (unnamed until Genesis 3:20), were apparently naïve about sexual relations (or so we are led to believe) when they were first created. Adam and the female were naked but unashamed.

- There is no mention of Adam and the female having sex or children Until banished from Eden, even though we read in,

Genesis 1: 28,

…And God blessed them, and God said unto them, be fruitful, and multiply, and replenish the earth, and subdue it.

- American couples are expected to willingly meet, date and become acquainted for a period of time before they wed.

- Adam and Eve had no courtship.

- A married American couple may delineate how they will or will not care for each other through prenuptial agreements.

- Adam and Eve had no such opportunity.

- Inside American marriage, mutual nudity is not uncommon and is not considered something unusual, shameful or sinful.

- On the contrary, Adam and Eve (if they were married) were unaware of their nudity until they sinned. Then God (himself??) made for them some clothing out of skins (were these created de novo or did God kill an animal?) to cover their nakedness. No other human existed then so why was there a need for the clothing? Was it God who did not want to see them? Presuming marriage, why should a man and woman be bothered by each other's nakedness? A corollary might be that modern religious married couples should not see each other's nakedness.

- The modern American married couple produces about two children. Adam and Eve did the same but they also created a murderer. Fundamentalist would also have us believe the couple passed onto all of mankind what is now called "original sin." According to the Catholic Church, two people escaped original sin; they were the Virgin Mary, mother of Jesus, and Jesus Christ. Atheists and others have asked, "If God can block the passage of original sin to these two people, why not to all of mankind?"

- Adam's and Eve's sin caused them to lose their original home and plush life as well as cause all their children, grandchildren and all of subsequent humanity to be punished with "original sin." This punishment resulted from eating "fruit" (disobeying God)—not sex. However, sex can be associated with sinful parents—Adam and Eve.

- Modern couples who commit a sin don't usually have the punishment for that sin placed against their children. The sinner appeals to God for forgiveness and God forgives them. The sin doesn't linger forever. Some fundamentalists believe baptism "washes away" original sin. This forgiveness can even be granted by God to a seven day old infant who does not ask for or even know he or she is being forgiven at baptism. God gave Adam and Eve no opportunity to ask for forgiveness for their sin.

- After being expelled from the garden, we are left believing that Adam and Eve lived happily ever after and died of old age as "normal" human beings.

- Marriage in our time can and often does end in divorce. The divorce rate for American marriages is about 50%. Modern couples of young age have even higher divorce rates. If American couples were to marry as young as did people in Jesus' time, the modern divorce rate would be expected to rise to as much as 80%.

- Modern married couples take housing as a given. Many do not get married until they can afford to buy a house.

- Adam and Eve's living arrangement closely parallels what, today, we would call a common law husband-wife team. The qualifications for such a modern designation are:

      A. Physical cohabitation (time period varies by state)
      B. Hold themselves out to the public to be husband and wife
      C. Have mental capacity to make such decisions

    This side-by-side comparison should make it clear that Adam did NOT have a legal wife in the person of Eve. She was nothing more than a help meet (mate) and the unmarried mother of his children. As for the argument of being a common-law wife, that is not possible since there was no legal system at the time of their creation. This couple cannot be and should not be held out as the first married couple upon which God supposedly modeled the modern "sacred" marriage.

    In some states, cohabitation arrangements may lead to a legally binding state of marriage even without a marriage license or marriage ceremony. Currently the states of: Alabama, Colorado, Iowa, Kansas, Montana, Oklahoma, Pennsylvania, Rhode Island, South Carolina, Texas, Utah, and Washington, D.C. allow common-law marriage. Once established, a common law marriage can be terminated only by a legal divorce decree from a court.

    Attorneys suggest that couples intending to live together should draft a "living together" document in which they detail that they intend to live together as two free and independent beings and have no plans to form any kind of marriage bond. I call this a pre-non-nuptial agreement. The presence of children may or may not complicate these arrangements depending on how well the unmarried man and woman relate to each other. However, a non-legal, family-like unit may call itself a family. Would the religious-right call such an arrangement sacred, a marriage, or a family? I doubt it.

    The only type of family structure that allows procreation by the spouses is made up of one or more men and one or more women (monogamy and polygamy). Two women cannot procreate together (if we exclude cloning). Two men cannot have children between themselves. It is alleged that God's intent was for marriage to be limited to opposite sexes. God did not initially create one man and multiple women, or one woman and multiple men, or multiple men and women (are we to cast a blind eye to the harem of the Israelite kings). Some allege God's intent was to have opposite-sex pairs of humans marry and create families consisting of one man (father), one woman (mother) and children. This logic omits the fact that the ancient patriarchs were polygamist.

    The religious-right preaches that there is no room in God's plan for same-sex marriage. Given this claim, fundamentalists argue same-sex marriage should not have been legalized by rogue courts and legislatures as seen in the Netherlands, Belgium, Canada, Spain, and the state of Iowa, Massachusetts (and California in 2008), New York, and Rhode Island. Those who make this argument ignore the basis for these legal decisions which are essentially ones of equal opportunity afforded under the laws of the states and countries involved. Secondly, the affected states or countries are not religious institutions to be ruled by religious biases.

    Sex and marriage, the gold-standard of Christian family relationships, have been reviewed. Marital union is no longer seen as the captive domain of Christian heterosexuals, despite the claim thereto. The Exodus story of Adam and Eve does not constitute a married couple which can be held out by fundamentalists as a model for all marriages, but the Bible has been misused for this purpose. Marriage is a civil right and must not be denied to homosexuals. Their rights are equally to those who are heterosexuals.

In the following chapter, the subject of eunuchs and their Biblical relationships to the hetero / homosexual world and marriage will be investigated.

CHAPTER XII

Eunuchs

One place to begin an exploration of ancient family history is the Biblical concept of immortality. According to Simcha Raphael's, *Jewish Views of the Afterlife*, the ancient Israelites were not very clear or consistent in their concept of life after death. The primary way the ancient ones thought they would achieve immortality was through children as their heirs. The worst fate that could befall someone in the ancient world was to be "cut off" from one's people. This could happen by being exiled for certain crimes, by public execution, or by dying without having any children, especially sons. The acquisition of property and the siring of many children were believed to be dual signs of God's favor (Psalm 127:3-5; 128:3-6). An ancient Israelite would live on through his / her children, hence the importance of offspring. Children were surrogates for immortality.

In this context, female barrenness was considered a curse. A woman's worth was connected to her ability to *give* her husband children, preferably sons. The Bible is replete with stories of desperate women who asked God to "open their wombs" (Psalm 113:9; Genesis 30:1; I Samuel 1:10). Barrenness, or infertility, became a metaphor used by prophets to describe Israel's pitiful condition when abandoned or cursed by God. Isaiah presents a poignant retelling of this metaphor. It mentions the curse of barrenness and Israel as a desolate (barren) woman. In later chapters, Isaiah uses the term "dry tree" (a female image of barrenness) for eunuchs. Isaiah also associated the term *"cut off"* with eunuchs. The term *eunuch* in Isaiah 56 is possibly a generic term used to include men and women who do not, or cannot, have children.

The scriptures fail to reveal anything regarding what we today call infertility. About 40 percent of infertility in modern peoples is due to male issues. However, 100 percent of the burden of providing a child, at the time of the ancient Israelis, was born by women. Not being able to conceive is Biblically addressed several ways.

One Biblical reference is Torah law, Deuteronomy 23:1, which may also be the source of exclusion of eunuchs from the Temple. Leviticus 21:17 declares only those who are "unblemished can present themselves before God…" This passage also excluded *eunuchs* who, in ancient pagan religions, might have been temple priests. It is possible the passage also excluded children born of incestuous unions.

Ultimately Isaiah proclaims an inclusive covenant promising eunuchs and barren women full participation in the blessings of God and a *"name better than sons and daughters…an everlasting name that shall not be cut off."* Immortality would no longer require heirs or be constituted by passing on one's family name. Childless couples and eunuchs, of all kind, had found favor in God's eyes.

Most men would never consider becoming a physical eunuch unless their lives depended upon the procedure. Nevertheless, ancient men may have willingly undergone such surgery for either religious or financial reasons. Occasionally modern men must undergo genital surgery (for cancer, accidental genital trauma, and rarely infection) that may render him not only impotent but also a *eunuch*. Fortunately, we live in a world where modern anesthesia makes surgery more bearable than in the ancient world. One can only imagine the pain and suffering that were associated with the cutting procedures required to create a eunuch in the ancient world.

According to Justinian's *New Constitution* 142,

> The majority of the innocent victims died in the barbaric operation in so
> far as it was intended to exclude every possibility of sexual intercourse.

Today doctors administer the male-hormone testosterone to prevent the physical and endocrine characteristics associated with being a eunuch—feminization. With the aid of these drugs, unlike the ancients, the public may not know that they have passed a eunuch on the street.

The procedure to make one a eunuch was performed in the ancient west from primitive times until it was outlawed in ancient Rome. There a Roman surgeon (according to Juvenal, known as Heliodorus) who made his living from performing such surgery. With his surgical help, a certain number of his patients became desired and valuable slaves. In Juvenal's *Satires* 6.366-378, written in the first century, we find,

> There are women who always delight in the unwarlike and soft kisses of
> eunuchs, and in the lack of a beard, and in the fact that an abortive drug is

not needed. However, that lust is supreme when the young crotches are delivered to the doctor after the development of mature heat and black pubic hair; therefore, Heliodorus snatches the awaited and developed testicles only after they have begun to weigh two pounds—to the detriment of the barber. A true and miserable weakness afflicts the slave dealers' boys, and these boys are ashamed of the bag and chickpea left behind. [Two pounds is far in excess of the weight of a normal testicle which weighs between 10 and 15 grams.]

What constituted being a eunuch and who were the eunuchs of Biblical times? The word, eunuch, seems to refer to males who had been castrated (often to make him sexually safe for the purpose of attending or guarding royal females). These "safe" guards could not sire children who might later overthrow the ruler and help their father become a vying ruler. Becoming a eunuch was one way for a child to maintain his youthful beauty. Emperor Constantine had a young eunuch for a lover, as did Nero. He made his young lover into a eunuch in order to preserve the youth's much desired beauty. Nero then went on to actually marry his eunuch lover.

Nancy Wilson, writing in *Our Tribe*, suggested some post pubescent males became eunuchs to gain employment in royal quarters where the eunuch could use their perceived innate skills of hospitality. Eunuchs served as social planners of the day. These males were voluntarily and un-voluntarily exploited for the social, and occasionally sexual, services they might provide. Wilson also suggested that some obviously gay young men could have been selected to become involuntary eunuchs. It should be noted, however, that voluntary court eunuchs were probably of a different mindset than men who chose to become eunuchs in order to serve their pagan god or goddess through homosexual rites. Social and economic pressures may account for some men electing to become eunuchs, but homosexual religious rites may have provided a safety net for others seeking to cover up their homosexuality outside their pagan religion. The same type of argument has been made against some Christian priests who found a certain safety from being labeled as homosexual because they were not married or interested in marriage. For some men, the Catholic priesthood provided a source of sexual prey as revealed in late twentieth century scandals involving Catholic priests and altar boys.

There are references to eunuchs who served as court officials, but some may not have been physical eunuchs. All the eunuchs referred to in Genesis, Isaiah, Jeremiah, and Daniel, as well as those in the New Testament, may not have been castrated males. Eunuch is a generic word that may well have included barren females, physically intact but sterile males, gay persons, gay foreign court officials, magicians, priests, and "wise men," as well as "straight" castrated males.

In Matthew, we read where Jesus spoke about eunuchs:

Matthew 19: 12,

> For there are eunuchs who have been so by birth, and there are eunuchs
> who have been made eunuchs by others, and there are eunuchs who
> have made themselves eunuchs for the sake of the kingdom of heaven.
> Let anyone accept this who can.

One might assume that eunuchs "made so by others" are those who had been sur-
gically castrated, either voluntarily or involuntarily. Those who "made themselves
eunuchs" are voluntary celibates (apparently, Christ was not speaking about Canaanite
priests who rendered themselves physical eunuchs in order to serve pagan gods and
participate in pagan temple rites). This does not, however, exclude those who for other
reasons may have become eunuchs via self-mutilation.

What of those men who were *born* eunuchs? A person born with ambiguous genitalia has been referred to as a hermaphrodite if there was even a suggestion of both male
and female sex organs. In some cases, one or the other of the sex organs may be present
but not easily identified with the simple observational techniques of the ancients. Even
today, newer diagnostic techniques, or surgery, may be required to make a definitive
identification of one's true gender. However, this condition does not reflect what is
most commonly thought of as being a eunuch. In some cases, a person can be born with
what seems to be testicles but without a penis. Could such a person be referred to as a
eunuch? Perhaps. Individuals have been born with no obvious external sex organs but
may harbor either ovaries or testes inside the body. Would these individuals have been
considered a eunuch by the ancient Hebrews? Perhaps. Given the rarity with which
these types of congenital abnormalities occur in human beings, it is doubtful that the
ancient Hebrews would have known enough about these conditions to have written
about them. What then constituted, for the ancient Hebrews, the condition of being a
eunuch from birth?

Since the New Testament is essentially a Greek document, we need to examine
some etymology concerning the word *eunuch*. Those ancients who could speak Latin
could convey the notion of castration in 20 different ways. The twenty-first edition of
Eberhard Nestle's *Novum Testamentum Graece* designates the Greek word *eunouchos*
as the origin of the word we now know as eunuch. This Greek word is derived from
eune (bed) and *echein* (to hold). It is generally believed that these two words mean
"someone who guards a bed." This is obviously in reference to the use of eunuchs for
guarding harems as in Ester 2:3, 6 and 16. Other Greek words conveying the meaning
of eunuch are:

Spadon: torn or removed
Ektomias: cut off
Tomias: animal gelding
Apokops: cut off
Thibias: pressed

Thaisias: crushed
Ithris: eunuch
Apokopto: to cut off / castrate
Temno: to cut / castrate
Apotemno: to cut off / castrate
Ektemno: to cut out / castrate
Eunouchizo: to castrate, make a eunuch
Apospao: to tear from / castrate
Keiro: to crop, cut off / castrate
Therizo: to mow down, cut off / castrate

The ancient Greeks were not ignorant about eunuchs. What had once been a mid-eastern religion, Cybele became a local Greek religion during the several hundred years before and after the Common Era. In Mary Beard's, *Religions of Rome*, (pp. 96-99, 164-166, 263) we read of a temple to Cybele being built in Rome in 194 BCE by Caesar Augustus. Later, in Rome, the religion became known as Magna Mater. Both titles referred to a mother goddess figure known as the Mother-of-the-Gods. She was known to the Hittites as Kubaba. The religions Cybele, Magna Mater, and Kubaba had many similarities with the religion of Dionysus. This religion and its eunuch pagan rituals were surely known to early Christians including St. Paul. After the pagan religion was driven from Rome, the Christians built the Basilica de Santa Maria Maggiore over the former Magna Mater temple. This fact may have led to the relationship of Mary (mother of Jesus) and the "mother goddess" concept.

Of passing interests is that Cardinal Law of the Boston diocese, where numerous cases of child molestation occurred, was transferred by Pope Paul II to the Basilica di Santa Maria Maggiore. The Cardinal serves as archpriest of the church.

During ancient spring celebrations, devotees of the Cybele religion made a grand exposition of devotion to their deity during which they drank a great deal of wine. There was ecstatic dancing, flute and tambourine playing, and much merry-making. The faithful, who sought a more dedicated form of devotion to the mother-earth-goddess, would use curved knives to castrate themselves. The severed body part(s) were then thrown against residential doors where the women inside were expected to come out and present the newly initiated devotee(s) with items of women's clothing which the castrated men donned. Those men not so inclined to self-castration would offer the testicles of a bull to the goddess instead. The religion and its eunuch rituals were extinct by the end of the 6th century AD.

According to Doctor P.C. Remondino, in his *History of Circumcision*, during the Ottoman Period, there were priests in Egypt's Coptic monasteries who were involved in the marketing of eunuchs. The Coptic priests participated in the creation of eunuchs using young, dark-skinned, African boys who were then sold as slaves to Arabs in several countries. Doctor P.C. Remondino states the area in and around the Sudan provided 3,800 eunuchs annually. This figure excluded the 30 percent mortality rate associated with the primitive surgical procedures involved in the process.

In 1945, former Dutch government minister, Wim Deetman chaired a commission that investigate child abuse inside the Dutch Roman Catholic Church. Besides the 1,800 complaints received by the commission, it was revealed that some church leaders had ordered castration of several young men to treat their homosexuality.[78]

The first Bible was written in Greek and conveyed the Aramaic language of the original apostles and Jesus. If Jesus was being truly quoted in his ancient Aramaic language (see below), we would read the "eunuch" scripture differently.

Matthew 19: 12,

> For there are some eunuchs, which were so born **f**rom [their] mother's womb: and there are some eunuchs, which were made eunuchs of men: and there be eunuchs, which have made themselves eunuchs for the kingdom of heaven's sake. He that is able to receive [it] let him receive [it].

Jesus would have used the Aramaic word *saris* for eunuch which is a word borrowed from the Assyrians. *Saris* was believed to mean "at the head." In the Matthew verse above, each use of the word eunuch is given equal weight, since each word is not otherwise associated with any further description or adjective. The question then arises as to what does the word *eunuch* really mean. Different possibilities include:

- Someone who is incapable of having penetrating vaginal sex because the male has no penis.

- Penetrating vaginal sex was possible but there was no possibility of pregnancy because the male had his testicles removed.

- Vaginal penetration and pregnancy was not possible because the penis and testicles were removed. Eunuchs in this state of being were, however, able to perform oral and manual sexual stimulation of either sex. This fact often made the eunuch desirable by certain women. (Clement of Alexandria, *Paedagogus*, Book 3, Chapter 4). Clement warned Christians about this type of servant overseeing women.

- A person has **elected** not to have sex even though they are physically intact. A Catholic priest is such an example.

- There is yet another possible interpretation of the word eunuch. That is, a person who is physically intact but does not have any **d**esire to have sex. Non-desire could extend to either heterosexual or homosexual sex

78   http://www.guardian.co.uk/world/2011/dec/16/thousands-children-abused-dutch-catholic

acts, but in this context, I will omit only hetero- sexual activity. The result, one might argue, is a modern gay man or woman.

The concept that a eunuch is a person (male) who has no desire to copulate with a female can be seen in one book of the Biblical Apocrypha known as Sirach. Here we can read:

Sirach 20: 4,

As is the lust of an eunuch to deflower a virgin; so is he that executeth judgment with violence.

Sirach 30: 20,

He seeth with his eyes and groaneth, as a eunuch that embraceth a virgin and sigheth.

Some say that these ancient verses indicate naturalness to the eunuch's emotional state of aversion to male-female sexual encounters.
Clement of Alexandria, in *Paedagogus III 4.25* writes,

…Many are eunuchs; and these panders serve without suspicion those that wish to be free to enjoy their pleasures, because of the belief that they are unable to indulge in lust. But a **true** [emphasis mine] eunuch is not one who is unable, but one who is unwilling, to indulge in pleasure…

I am sure he was not interested in knowing if these men could have same-sex-relations. Clement goes on to state the following,

…But for one who is a man to comb himself and shave himself with a razor, for the sake of fine effect, to arrange his hair at the looking-glass, to shave his cheeks, pluck hairs out of them, and smooth them, how womanly! And, in truth, unless you saw them naked, you would suppose them to be women. For although not allowed to wear gold, yet out of effeminate desire they enwreath their latches and fringes with leaves of gold…[79]

The *Stromata* is sometimes referred to as the lost book of Clement of Alexander. In Chapter III section 1 of this text we find,

---

79   <http://www.newadvent.org/fathers/02093.htm> April 30, 2007

The Valentinians, who hold that the union of man and woman is derived from the divine emanation in heaven above, approve of marriage. The followers of Basilides, on the other hand, say that when the apostles asked whether it was not better not to marry, the Lord replied: "Not all can receive this saying; there are some eunuchs who are so from their birth, others are so of necessity." And their explanation of this saying is roughly as follows: Some men, from their birth, have a natural sense of repulsion from a woman; and those who are naturally so constituted do well not to marry. Those who are eunuchs of necessity are those theatrical ascetics who only control themselves because they have a passion for the limelight. [And those who have suffered accidental castration have become eunuchs of necessity.][80]

The Hebrews used the word *sarees* to mean a castrated male, as seen in Hayim Baltsan's book, *Webster's New World Hebrew [English] Dictionary*. The word eunuch is defined as a male deprived of the testes or external genitalia [penis] as in Brand, Draper, and England's (ed.), *Illustrated Bible Dictionary*. This Dictionary goes on to say that the Hebrews also interpreted this word to mean any court official. A very early translation of the Bible by the Syrian Orthodox Greek Church substituted the word *mu'omin* for *eunouchos* and *saris* (An English Annotated version of this Bible will soon be available from the Peshittla Institute in Leiden). "A person of trust or person of faith" is often used as one translation of *mu'omin*.

According to Penzer, in his book, *The Harem*, three varieties of eunuchs were recognized in antiquity:

1. Castrati: clean-cut, both penis and testicles were removed;
2. Spadones: testicles only were removed; and
3. Thlibiae: testicles were bruised and/or crushed.

We can read in,

Deuteronomy 23: 1,

> He that is *wounded* in the stones, or hath his privy member *cut off*, shall not enter into the congregation of the LORD.

Here wounded may mean without, diseased or atrophied testicles, however, I believe it may mean infertility in spite of having otherwise normal appearing testicles. Cut off is probably a reference to having lost the penis. In both cases, one should note that the word eunuch is **not** used in this verse. In many other parts of the Bible, there are references to eunuchs without mentioning the word castrated. The question is whether

---

80   <http://www.earlychristianwritings.com/text/clement-stromata-book3-english.html> April 30, 2007

or not this omission was a coincidence or intentional by the writers of the Bible or those who translated it? The *King James Version of the Bible* translates the word *saris* as eunuch, officer, chamberlain, and as a proper name for a person—the Rabsaris (high or chief eunuch). The Lutheran Bible refers to:

Matthew 19: 12,

> Denn es sind etliche verschnitten, die sind aus Mutterleibe also geboren, und sind etliche verschnitten, die von Menschen verschnitten sind, und sind etliche verschnitten, die sich selbst verschnitten haben um des Himmelreichs willen. Wer es fassen mag, der fasse es...[81]

This German Biblical passage is translated below:

> Since several are cut, they are from mother's body thus born, and several are cut, those by people are cut, and several are cut, to themselves have cut for the kingdom of heaven. Who catch it may, that catches it...[82]

Luther uses the word ***cut*** for eunuch. The Martin Luther translation uses the words chamberlain or high (head) chamberlain over and over until he comes to Matthew, above, and in Isaiah. Perhaps Luther's biases are revealed here. The word *sarisim* is the plural of *saris* and means eunuchs. We read in,

Jeremiah 34: 19,

> The princes of Judah, and the princes of Jerusalem, the **eunuchs** [sarisim], and the **priests**, and all the people of the land, which passed between the parts of the calf...

According to Jewish law, these eunuchs were forbidden to participate in religious rites if the participant was deficient in body parts as is noted in,

Deuteronomy 23: 1,

> He that is wounded in the stones, or hath his privy member cut off, shall not enter into the ***congregation*** of the Lord.

This concept of perfection carried over to those animals which were to be sacrificed. The animal should be without blemish, i.e., perfect.

---

81   <http://www.biblecenter.de/bibel/lu1545/cmatt.htm> April 30, 2007

82   <http://translation2.paralink.com> September 2, 2007

In regulating marriage, Roman law concerned itself with castration as can be seen in this section from the Principals of Roman Law *(Catholica Encyclopedia:* Roman Law):

> Marriage (*nuptiæ* or *connubium*) was the association or community of life between man and woman, for the procreation and rearing of offspring, validly entered into between Roman citizens. It was wont to be preceded by *sponsalia* (betrothal), defined as an agreement of future marriage. *Sponsalia* might be verbally entered into, and required no solemnities. The mutual consent of the spouses was requisite, and the object of marriage was kept in mind so that marriage with an impotent person (*castratus*) was invalid…[83]

Here, we are dealing with Roman citizens. Roman slaves were not so accorded. The Roman jurist Ulpian wrote, during the 3rd Century BCE, the *Roman Digest of Laws* which gave some guidance regarding marriage between a woman and a slave eunuch. He states in,

Digest, Book xxiii 3.39.1,

> If a woman marries a eunuch… [and if he]…has been castrated…there is no dowry; if he has not been castrated, then there can be a marriage and so there is a dowry…

Even the Romans made a distinction between the various ways in which the word *eunuch* could be used. It does not always mean a body part is missing. However, another peer jurist of Ulpian believed that a eunuch, even with a penis, was diseased. The above Roman law could be considered as modern in that it would not exclude gay men, born eunuchs, from entering into a marriage of convenience. The ancient Israelites were a people of instincts and drive. As regards their religious philosophy, they were a people of doing or not doing. They knew nothing of psychology. They were concerned with actions and behavior, not mental attitudes. They knew of and saw homosexuality as a behavior, not an orientation. They saw homosexual acts as constituting a major part of ritual worship in pagan religions that surrounded them in the ancient world.

Some present day orthodox rabbis and Roman Catholic Leaders say that homosexual orientation (or drive) is not a sin but acting on such a drive is forbidden. Some members of the religious-right, with deeply conservative religious beliefs, have adopted this concept, however, many have not. If one looks logically at this claim, the argument fails. As human beings, we have many different biologically driven actions. When we feel hunger, we eat. When we feel sleepy, we sleep. When we feel we need to defecate, we do so. Even in sexual abstinence, males have nocturnal emissions. Our endocrine system automatically produces various chemicals when our body deems them necessary.

---

83   <http://www.newadvent.org/cathen/0907a.htm> April 30, 2007

The church allows heterosexuals the right to exercise their biological sexual interest, so how can we favor these various internally driven urges and deny the homosexual outlets that are normal for them? We do so based on our biases.

Too many religious conservatives believe that being gay is a consciously selected lifestyle and is sinful at its core. One might argue that the ancient Hebrew people helped frame modern homosexuality as a sin simply because of their socio-religious belief system of their primitive times.

The Talmud contains some thoughts of the first-century AD scholar, Rabbi Eliezer. He believed that natural eunuchs could be cured. Rabbi Eliezer said,

> ...a eunuch-by-nature submits to *chalitsah*[84] and *chalitsah* is also arranged for his wife, because he may be cured. A man-made eunuch neither submits to *chalitsah* nor is *chalitsah* arranged for his wife, since he cannot be cured.[85]

He goes to great length to detail certain characteristics that describe such a person, but he never mentions testicular integrity. Again, he was concerned with various acts (behaviors) and the performance thereof, not the absence of penis or testicles.

St. Gregory the Theologian was the Christian Bishop of the Church in Constantinople in the 4th century. In his *Oration* 37: 16 and 17 he wrote of Eunuchs,

> Be not proud, you who are eunuchs by **nature**. Your abstinence is practically involuntary...That which is good by nature is spurious: that by deliberate choice is laudable...Since your abstention is not laudable, I ask something else of eunuchs. Do not commit prostitution in divine matters. Having yoked yourself to Christ, do not dishonor Christ...

St. Gregory is speaking of eunuchs by *nature*. What if the Matthew verse dealing with *born eunuchs* encompassed those individuals who were physically intact but felt compelled **not** to have sexual relations with a person of the opposite sex (which was the expected and sanctioned sexual act within the ancient Hebrew community)? Mathew's Biblical notation certainly supports such an assumption. Will the biases of the fundamentalists hinder their acceptance of such a hypothesis?

The Reverend Nancy Wilson has written in her book, *Our Tribe: Queer Folks, God, Jesus and the Bible,* some thoughts which have led to an interesting hypothesis about the Biblical reference to being born eunuch. She proposes that the phrase "eunuch from birth" was actually a reference to a gay male; his status as a eunuch had nothing to do with being castrated.

The designation of eunuch was in reference to a gay man's innate desire not to have sex with women and not to desire becoming a father as was the norm for males in early

---

84   A Jewish ritual rebuke of the brother of a dead man who refuses to have sex with the dead brother's wife to insure an heir (hopefully a son) for the dead man.

85   <http://www.well.com/user/aquarius/cardiff.htm> September 2, 2007

Jewish culture. We need remember Jews believed they were instructed by God "to be fruitful and multiply." Heterosexuality was not the innate orientation or drive of these non-physical eunuchs. They were to be fruitless by drive / desire, orientation, and by "programming" they obtained, from God, prior to birth.

These men (eunuchs) had no desire to marry women. They were considered to be "dry" and "cutoff" from the Jewish community in which they lived. Both words, "dry" and "cutoff," are a reference to having no children and hence no way of passing on a part of themselves as a way of becoming immortal. Being cutoff may have also been a reference to them being cast out of normative Jewish culture.

Jesus makes it clear that heterosexual marriage is not the norm for everyone. Would the religious-right consider single people of marriageable age (eunuchs) to be inferior to married people?

Infertile men such as eunuchs or "eunuchs from birth" may never fulfill the obligations of marriage to reproduce but were welcomed into the fellowship of the early church. An Ethiopian eunuch, mentioned in Acts 8, is baptized by the apostle Philip. The eunuch was seen reading a passage from Isaiah about messianic prophecy that described the destiny of the Suffering Servant who would be "cut off" from the land of the living. The eunuch got the message that those who have been "cut off" are to be included among the faithful. Hence his question, "What is to prevent me from being baptized?"

Philip the apostle answered, "Nothing!" Personal biases may lead people to decide in which state of physical being this eunuch was, but the scriptures do not help us beyond saying he was a eunuch.

In Isaiah chapter 56, we are told that there are two groups of people chosen to symbolize a new and future group of God's children. This new group would include eunuchs and gentiles.

Isaiah, 56: 3 & 4,

> Neither let the son of the stranger, that hath joined himself to the LORD, speak, saying, The LORD hath utterly separated me from his people: neither let the eunuch say, Behold, I am a dry tree. For thus saith the LORD unto the eunuchs that keep my Sabbaths, and choose the things that please me, and take hold of my covenant…

Isaiah, 56: 8,

> The Lord GOD, which gathereth the outcasts of Israel saith, Yet will I gather others to him, beside those that are gathered unto him.

As Nancy Wilson (p. 127) points out, if half of this new group included only eunuchs that had been physically castrated there would not be very many new group members among God's children. Why then would Isaiah waste his time to prophecy about such a small group of new members? Surely, gay eunuchs were to be included. We should recall that modern sexology research suggests that 5 - 10 percent of the population is a non-castrated eunuch or gay person.

This fact increases the possible numbers of new members to God's new group. Isaiah is really saying to us that God wants to acknowledge eunuchs (no matter where they are or where they are from). God is changing the rules for admission to the group, known as the people of God, regardless of their sexual orientation or ability to reproduce. Remember, one can be unable to reproduce for physical, mental, psychological, or orientation reasons. Faithful and true believers of God will be rewarded, and this means members of the gay community. The scriptures noted below help to support our beliefs in ourselves.

The book of Acts presents an account of the early Church's attempts to preach and live an "unhindered gospel" (Acts 28:31). Two crucial stories are central to such a gospel: Peter and Cornelius (Acts 10) and Phillip and the Ethiopian eunuch (Acts 8). Both passages have their roots in the prophecies of Isaiah 56. Isaiah proclaims a future day when Gentiles and eunuchs will be included among the people of God, and their sacrifices will be "acceptable." The Greek translation of the Hebrew word for "acceptable" in Isaiah 56:7 also appears in Acts 10:35.

One fact is often overlooked with a conservative reading of the Book of Acts regarding the eunuch mentioned in,

Acts 8: 27,

> And he arose and went; and behold, there was an Ethiopian eunuch, a court official of Candace, queen of the Ethiopians, who was in charge of all her treasure; and he had come to Jerusalem to worship.

The temple in Jerusalem was still intact and functioning at the time of the writing of the Book of Acts. According to Jewish law, **only** physically intact persons should be in the temple to worship God.

Deuteronomy 23: 1,

> He that is wounded in the stones, or hath his privy member cut off, shall not enter into the congregation[86] of the LORD.

---

86   **Congregation** (Heb. kahal), the Hebrew people were collectively known as a holy community. Every circumcised Hebrew from twenty years and upward was a member of the congregation. (Exodus 12:19; Num 9:14; Num 15:15) who met at the door of the tabernacle (Num 10:3]) for the purpose of engaging in solemn religious services (Exodus 12:27; Num 25:6; Joe 2:15) *Easton's Bible Dictionary.* See http://www.sacred- texts.com/bib/ebd/ebd088.htm#004

Nevertheless, Acts records the fact that a "eunuch" had gone to Jerusalem (the temple) to worship God. This can only mean the Ethiopian was not a physical eunuch but a psychological eunuch. Philip would have had to have seen the man's genitals (or have seen signs of feminization which he apparently didn't see) to have known the man was a physical eunuch. This would have been most unusual for two strangers. The foreigner was a gay man. Presumably, Philip knew this and yet he made no attempt to cure the eunuch (either physically, if he was a physical eunuch, or a psychological eunuch) as he had done for people possessed by demons. Philip simply baptized the man.

In the story of Peter and the Roman centurion, Cornelius (a gentile), Peter was given a divine revelation from God:

Acts 10: 34 & 35,

> …God shows no partiality, but in every nation anyone who fears God
> and does what is right is acceptable to God.

The word nation is translated from the Greek word *ethnos* from which we derive our word ethnic. The term refers to a race, culture, or people.[87] Thus Peter learns that every race, culture, or people (Jew or gentile) who fears God, and does what is right, are eligible for baptism (and church membership) as was the above mentioned eunuch.

Is the gay, lesbian, bisexual, and transgender (GLBT) community just a political lobby for advancing homosexual behavior, or is it an ethnos (nation) as seen in Acts? Certainly, there are many homosexuals who engage in various forms of sex, but there are some GLBT people who never have sex at all. The question of orientation versus sexual acts is causing society to consider the question, "Are GLBT people a *kind of behavior*, or a *kind of people* for whom homoerotic attraction is but one characteristic?" We often hear of, or read in the straight media, the phrase "gay culture or gay community." At least some people, and part of the American body politic, recognize the gay community as a separate culture. Whether or not those same groups would consider the gay community as constituting a separate ethnic group or "nation" is yet to be determined.

An ethnos (nation) could be defined by a common history, vocabulary, culture, institutions (schools, libraries, clubs, churches, synagogues, social organizations, businesses), heroes, political leaders, scholars, values, even Christian Saints, and the ability to recognize each other, even when submerged in a more dominant (non-gay) culture. If the preceding descriptive words help constitute an ethnos, I believe GLBT people are included in the word *nation* used in Acts10. The gay community does have its own language, social organizations, clubs, churches, etc., and has a broad enough culture to qualify as a nation. This belief is in keeping with the thoughts of Reverend Nancy Wilson and her book *Our Tribe*.

---

87   http://www.thefreedictionary.com/ethnos

Any American caught speaking out against any Nation of American Indians would be considered as bigoted as any person who speaks hatred against African Americans. While many Native Americans are Christians, many are either exclusively Animistic (Mother Earth, Sky Father, etc.) or some may combine the two religions as do many hills tribe people in Central and South America. Nevertheless, no one openly speaks out against Native Americans or their Nationhood because of their religious beliefs or ancient culture which, in many instances, accepted homosexuality as a special blessing. The culture of Native Americans is simply accepted by most US citizens. Why then cannot the nationhood of the gay community be accepted by heterosexuals and religious conservatives? The answer is religious prejudice.

In closing this section, I would like to point out what I, and others, think is overt discrimination against the gay community. While many in the fundamentalist community use the *King James Version of the Bible* exclusively, some rely on the *New Revised Standard Version* (NRSV). In it, neither the story of Phillip and the Ethiopian eunuch, nor the Ebed-melech story in Jeremiah 38: 7, nor the Isaiah 56 prophecy are crossed referenced with the Matthew 19 story. Of note, there is no cross-reference of these four items in any other Bible.

There is a possible relationship between all these scriptures, and to formally ignore that possibility via a cross-reference is a discrimination against the gay community, by publishers who print other Biblical cross- references, perhaps driven by their or their buyers' and readers' homophobia.

Traditional marriage between one man and one woman cannot co-exist with homosexual marriage. It will destroy the family.

DR. JAMES DOBSON,
FOCUS ON THE FAMILY

Victor P. Furnish, author of *The Bible and Homosexuality* (p 22), writes,

> [that] Genesis 2: 23 - 25 neither commands nor presumes a 'monogamous' relationship between man and woman and...it offers no comment on 'marriage' as such.

Old Testament heroes certainly did not model monogamy *de novo*, but followed cultural patterns of their day, which sanctioned multiple wives and concubines. They even took slaves as sexual partners. This behavior was not only religiously approved, but was Biblically mandated. However, as noted by Furnish, the command to "be fruitful and multiply" cannot be interpreted to mean that everyone must marry and have children. This part of the creation stories leaves no wiggle room whatever for the physically or mentally impaired, the celibate, the impotent, homosexual [or those who simply choose not to have children even though they enjoy sex]. The notion that a monogamous, heterosexual marriage for everyone is somehow contained in Genesis One is fallacious. This belief is another artificial construct manipulated by fundamentalists to deny the civil rights of marriage to the gay community.

The word eunuch is frequently used in the Old and New Testaments. In some instances the word clearly indicates a less than physically intact male who is unable to reproduce. The same may be said of some females. I believe the word eunuch may also be used to refer to people who choose to remain asexual (celibate) for religious purposes and still others may be called eunuch because they are so mentally oriented as to be disinterested in male-female sexual relationships. In today's parlance, we call these people gay or lesbian. I believe they have been with us forever.

Just as gay and lesbian people are contributing members of today's society, so too did they contribute mightily in the times of ancient peoples and the early Christian Church. An enlightened reading of the Bible reveals that some of these Biblical gay people were valued community members, loved and accepted by Christ, the Centurion being an example. For various reasons, Christian love or charity, once extended to gay Christians, has morphed into something very un-Christian. What was once love has become hate. Unfortunately, religious fundamentalists have championed this negative change. Their hate, often hidden behind soft words and fake smiles cannot go unchallenged. Neither can their rhetoric of "love the sinner, hate the sin."

Even though the word eunuch was not used to describe Christine Jorgensen who underwent such surgery in 1952, he was a eunuch. He and the press often referred to him as a woman who was among the first of mid-20th century people to undergo "eunuch" surgery because he emotionally and psychologically felt like a woman and believed he was a woman trapped in a man's body. Jorgensen's actions helped pave the way for Renee Richards to confront his discomfort in being a woman trapped in a man's body and his subsequent surgery in1976. Richards' ensuing legal battles about not being permitted to compete in a woman's tennis match dashed legal barriers which had denied transsexuals full recognition of their new sexual identity after sexual reassignment.

Few churches or religions have formally debated the issue of whether or not a person can have the soul of the opposite sex or whether or not the soul has any sexual orientation. Nevertheless, The Church of Jesus Christ of Latter-day Saints (Mormons) did have such a debate in 1980 about Kristi Independence Kelly who was facing excommunication from the Church. The Church held that, though the pre-born souls did have gender before birth, God did not make mistakes. The Church decided, "There is no such thing as a man in a woman's body or a woman in a man's body" and declared this decision to be, "ex-cathedra" by the leader for the Mormon faith. This pronouncement was the strongest such statement the Mormon Church could make. This decision led some people to ask whether or not intersexed people must have intersexed souls? [88]

---

88   http://www.jenellerose.com/htmlpostings/20tfi_century_transgaider.htm

The emotional and psychological drive to change one's physical body to match that of one's "id" can be quite strong. Between 1930 and 1931 a "Lili" Elbe underwent surgeries in Berlin to become a woman. The usual "eunuch" surgery was performed by a Doctor Magnus Hirschfeld who is alleged to have tried the same surgery on his unnamed housekeeper in 1908. The Doctor went on to perform several other surgeries on Lili to include a uterine transplant. Unfortunately, the organ was rejected taking Lili's life in the process.[89]

At this moment there are thousands of men and women in the process of becoming a person of the opposite sex. Hundreds of sexual reassignment surgeries are performed every year in America and other countries. In most countries, these individuals are permitted to change legal documents to denote their new sexual identity. Rarely are they referred to as eunuchs, but they are. Some are permitted to marry a member of their former sex. Why not extend this civil and sacred right to those who desire to be married without undergoing such surgery. Only prejudices and religious biases prevent such actions.

In this chapter, we have seen how the word *eunuch* can pertain to one's physical state as well as an emotional / orientational state of being and that either is acceptable to God. Men and women have for millennia sought to be something other than the sexual image the public sees before them. The desire comes from a place deep within and planted by God. These people are born eunuchs as mentioned in the Bible. As children of God, they deserve respect and all the civil rights of every other American.

---

89   http://en.wikipedia.org/wiki/Sex_reassignment_surgery

CHAPTER XIII

Alternate lifestyles in the Bible

The Bible contains six admonishments to homosexuals and 362 admonishments to heterosexuals. That doesn't mean that God doesn't love heterosexuals. It's just that they need more supervision.

LYNN LAVNER, *COMEDIAN*

*I*n the last chapter, certain Biblical passages were explored in regard to God given sexual desires and what is often called lifestyle choices by fundamentalists. It is they who misquote scripture to buttress their arguments against homosexuals.

We will now explore several possible homoerotic Biblical relationships. These have long been overlooked or ignored because of fundamentalists' homophobic biases. These overtly chosen biases deny the eye to see what the brain refuses to acknowledge. To better understand homoerotic Biblical relationships, one has to approach the Bible with gay insight, which very few people outside the gay community are willing to do.

Secondly, we need to examine the one word that is so often bantered about in the Bible without having any clear understanding of what it means. That word is *love*. In modern English, we can speak of the word *lovers* which can and often indicates both parties in the love affair. These lovers may be male and female, male and male, or female and female. This connotation of the word *lover* was not so denoted in the ancient world. The ancients reserved the word *lover* for the male while the female was the *beloved*. In ancient Greece and Rome, if the parties were involved in a same-sex relationship, the older person was considered to be the *lover* (active partner or wooer) while the younger person was the *beloved* (and usually passive partner).

If there was some kind of acknowledged reciprocity of love in the relationship, it would be labeled *philia* in Greek (a type of tender love). In his *Rhetoric* (1380b36–1381a2), Aristotle defines the activity involved in *philia* (τ ò φ ι λ ε ῖ n) as,

> …wanting for someone what one thinks good, for his sake and not for one's own, and being inclined, so far as one can, to do such things for him.

Philia (φ ι λ ί α) was an ancient Greek word for love, which broadly referred to brotherly love, friendship, and affection. This was in contrast to the ancient Greek terms *eros* (sexual / romantic love) and *agapē,* or detached, spiritual love. English usage differs in some cases from the etymological use, and may refer to sexual attraction.

I like to think that the "love" words can be used in a kind of equation:

$$\text{lover} + \text{lover} = philia$$
$$\text{lover} + \text{beloved} = philia$$

If the love was one sided, it was defined as *eros*, sometimes referred to as sexual desire, erotic love, or simply lust.

$$\text{lover} + \text{non-lover} = eros. \text{ [90]}$$

Agape, rarely used outside the Bible, refers to the paternal love of God for man and man for God but is often extended to include a brotherly love for all humanity.

$$\text{God's love} + \text{a person} = agape$$
$$\text{God's love} + \text{humanity} = agape$$

The Hebrew word *ahev* has a slightly wider semantic range than *agape*. *Agape* arguably draws on elements from both *eros* and *philia* in that it seeks a perfect kind of love that is at once a fondness, a transcending of the particular, and a passion without the necessity of reciprocity.

$$\textit{Supreme} \text{ love} + eros = ahev \text{ [91]}$$

Agape was used as a substitute for *eros* in the language of the New Testament according to Theodore W. Jennings (p 57). For example:

Judges 16: 4, Sampson "falls in love" with Delilah. Sexual attraction is clearly at play in this passage.

---

90   <http://en.wikipedia.org/wiki/Greek_words_for_love> June 20, 2007

91   < http://www.iep.utm.edu/l/love.htm> June 20, 2007.

I Samuel 20: 17, David **loved** Jonathan,

I Samuel 18: 1, Jonathan **loved** David,

I Samuel 18: 16, the people **loved** David,

I Samuel 18: 20, Jonathan's sister **loved** David and became David's first wife.

Song of Solomon (*Song of Songs*): *Agape* is used to refer to the erotic love theme found herein.

Other parts of the Scriptures use the word *love* either interchangeably or as compliments.

Gospel of John 21: 15 & 16, Jesus asks twice about *agape* of Peter For Jesus. Peter responds *philia.*

Gospel of John 21: 17, Jesus asks Peter do you *philia* me? Now Peter is upset because Jesus asked three times if Peter *philia* Jesus. Here *agape* and p*hilia* are used as equivalents.

Gospel of John 11: 3, Jesus *philia* Lazarus.

Gospel of John 11: 5, Jesus *agape* Mary, Martha, and Lazarus.

Gospel of John 11: 36, the Jews note how Jesus *philia* Lazarus.

Of the remaining four references in the Gospel of John to the "disciple which Jesus loved" the verb *agape* is used. The fifth concerns the *philia* verb for the disciple running toward the tomb with Peter.

Our modern English unceremoniously equates the word *love* with all three of the Greek words: *philia, eros,* and *agape.* We Americans, just like the ancients, need to know something about the context in which the word *love* is used in order to appreciate its meaning. The use of *agape* in the Bible cannot rule out or exclude the erotic dimension of the above texts. However, a gay-reading of these texts may open the eyes of the reader to a new understanding. This I encourage readers to do.

Mary, Martha, and Lazarus

Jesus' family relationships differ significantly from the contemporary so-called nuclear family. It is written that Jesus *loved* Lazarus, Mary, and Martha. What attracted Jesus to this very non-traditional Jewish family group? It is composed of an apparent bachelor brother living with two (questionably spinster) sisters. Do these two apparently barren women and a eunuch brother constitute Jesus' adult family of choice? Are we to assume all were celibate heterosexuals? What if we examined this "family group" with contemporary, gay eyes? Maybe Mary and Martha were not "blood sisters" but called each other "sister" as have many lesbians throughout recorded history?

During the time of Christ, it was the norm (expectation) for men and women to be married at an early age, live with their spouse, and to bear children. Why was there no mention that any of these three had been married? I believe marriage is not mentioned because these women were probably not married. There is no mention of spouses or children in the household, but there is mention, by one of the "sisters" of a lack of assistance with household duties. If there had been children older than age four, they would have been expected to help with household chores.

We know that the disciples and Christ were followed and supported by an unknown number of women. There is no mention of additional men among the followers. It appears that the women had financial assets to share with the group. Some had possibly left husbands to follow Jesus' group. However, it would have been highly unusual for a woman accepted by Jewish society to follow after an unmarried man—Jesus. We don't know how most of the followers obtained their money, but let's consider whether or not the female followers were so called "sisters." If they had been lesbian, they would have been free to travel without concern for children or husbands. However, their fathers would have been upset given the culture. Secondly, they would not have been as concerned as straight women about their reputations if they had been considered way-ward women or camp followers by the greater Hebrew community.

In Bethany, Mary and Martha share a house where Martha is apparently the head of the household (owner?). Whether or not their brother, Lazarus, lived within the same household is not clear, but at least, he appeared to live in the same city as the sisters. Property ownership by women was rather unusual in Christ's time but was possible. We might assume that Martha's house was owned by the brother who may have been maintaining the sisters. He may have done so because they are (or appear) to be unmarried. Perhaps they don't live with their father because the father is dead. As a brother, it would have become Lazarus' responsibility to get the sisters married. By Jewish tradition, one would have expected the sisters to be married. Marriage would have removed certain financial pressures from the brother as related to his maintenance of the sisters and perhaps two households.

While we do not know the age of the sisters, we can probably safely presume that they are adult or of marriageable age since Martha is said to be in *her* home. While it is possible that these women were married, nothing in the story suggests such.

Jewish property was usually handed down from father to son. If a husband died with no son, the wife would be expected to marry the husband's brother, and they would produce a child (hopefully a son) for the dead husband. This son became the official son of the first (dead) husband (a Levirate marriage) and could then inherit his dead father's property. Since no sons of Mary and Martha are mentioned, we might assume there were no children.

The absence of children can be inferred because the sisters are not married. Another reason for assuming that there are no children in the house is Martha's complaint that Mary isn't helping with household chores. Those chores would probably have been the responsibility of the children in a house without slaves.

Real property was generally considered to be Hebrew tribal land in the control of a specific family within a given tribe. Everything possible was done to assure that land remained within a specific family's control.

Leviticus 25: 13,

> In the year of this jubilee [forty-nine years of temporary land ownership]
> Ye shall return every man unto his possession.

This would preclude intertribal marriage or marriage to a gentile. If no sons were present, daughters might inherit property but this was unusual.

Numbers 26: 4,

> If they [daughters] be married to any of the sons of the o*ther* tribes of the children of Israel, then shall the inheritance be taken from the inheritance of our fathers, and shall be put to the inheritance of the tribe where unto they are received: so shall it be taken from the loti of our inheritance.

In this verse, someone is complaining that a proposed marriage, outside one tribe of Israel, would cause the loss of tribal property to another tribe. The reply upholding the concern and the remedy to the problem is found in,

Numbers 30, 5 - 9,

> The tribe of the sons of Joseph hath spoken well. This is the thing which the Lord doth command, concerning the daughters of Zelophehad, saying: Let them marry to whom they think best: only to the family of the tribe of their father shall they marry. So shall not the inheritance of the children of Israel remove from tribe to tribe: for every one of the

children of Israel shall keep himself to the inheritance of the tribe of his fathers. And every daughter that possesseth an inheritance in any tribe of the children of Israel shall be wife unto one of the family of the tribe of her father, that the children of Israel may enjoy every man the inheritance of his fathers.

To prevent inheritance disputes, Levirate marriages (see above) were allegedly ordained by God and written into Jewish law. For more information on the rules of inheritance among the ancient Jews refer to this website.[92]

Since Martha is said to live in *her* house, there is the possibility that Lazarus may not be her blood brother since we are led to believe he lives somewhere else other than in the home of Martha and Mary. As the son of a common father, Lazarus should have inherited the father's home—not his sisters. There is no mention of Lazarus having a wife, being a widower or of him having children. At the time of Lazarus' first death, there is no mention of children inheriting a home or of sons or daughters being present at the tomb when Christ arrived. We are, therefore, left with the image of two women who may not be blood relatives but did have a close relationship with a male, who might have just been a friend, but is called *brother.* It is conceivable that these individuals are not a heterosexual family group but are really a gay family group. If this is true, Christ must have been accepting of their status since he appeared to be very close to each member of the group. His acceptance of this family group would be just another way in which Christ ignored the traditional mores of his era and one more example of his overturning the accepted gender roles of his time.

Fourth century copies of certain religious documents, found in Egypt in 1945, were known as the Nag Hammadi (Gnostic) scrolls. They are believed to have been originally written (maybe copied) in the second century. The scrolls provide insight into some early Christian beliefs about Jesus' humanity. In these documents, one reads that Mary Magdalene had a very special (and perhaps intimate) relationship with Jesus.

The Gospel of Philip,

There were three who always walked with the Lord: Mary, his mother, and her sister, and Magdalene, the one who was called his companion. His sister and his mother and his companion were each a Mary.

The extent of this relationship is in doubt, but the scrolls mentioned that "Jesus kissed Mary Magdalene often on her (blank)…" Due to partial loss of the document, we do not know what was kissed by Christ, but the word *lips* is often inserted by scholars. Christ is said to have loved Mary Magdalene more than the disciples and led to the discussion we see in,

---

92   http://www.marxists.org/reference/archive/morgan-lewis/ancient-society/ch29.htm

The Gospel of Philip,

And the companion of the […] Mary Magdalene. […] loved her more than all the disciples, and used to kiss her often on her [mouth]. The rest of the disciples […] They said to him "Why do you love her more than all of us?" The Savior answered and said to them, "Why do I not love you like her? When a blind man and one who sees are both together in darkness, they are no different from one another. When the light comes, then he who sees will see the light, and he who is blind will remain in darkness.

While many would argue against a carnal relationship between Jesus and Mary Magdalene, others would say that Jesus may have had his own *alternate* life style. John's gospel refers no less than eight times to John as the "one whom Jesus loved." He was also called the

Beloved disciple. Scholars rarely explore the possible ramifications of the fact that Jesus obviously had a particularly close relationship with this one man. Whether Jesus was gay or not we can't say, but homophobia and fundamentalists have silenced all exploration of this possible relationship until recently. We will explore such an issue later.

There are interesting writings within and without the canon of the Bible about Jesus and possible homoerotic relationships. Those passages are to be found in the Gospel of Mark and the Secret Gospel of Mark. The Gnostics of Alexandria, in the late First Century and the early Second Century, had their own branch and brand of Christianity. To many, this was an errant and heretical form of Christianity. Church leaders of what was to become the orthodox branches of Christianity opposed these so-called mis-guided forms of Christianity. Clement of Alexander (circa 150-250 AD) appeared to acknowledge one book of the Gnostics, the Secret Gospel of Mark, but questioned certain of its passages. Other scholars concluded that the commonly accepted Gospel of Mark may have actually been part of the Secret Gospel of Mark (or vice versa).

Mark 10: 17-22 speaks of a man, "who possessed a fortune," asking Jesus how to attain eternal life. In Mark 10: 21, Jesus looks at the man (questionably Lazarus) and *loves* him. The *Secret Gospel of Mark* makes the point that the Bethany youth is apparently rich because he owns his own home. Lazarus, in the Gospel of St. John, may also be wealthy based upon the same criteria. Some scholars will say this helps to identify Lazarus and the rich young man as being the same person. Miles Fowler has written,

In the following translation of Clement's version of the first chapter of *Secret Mark* (*SGM* 1:1-13), I have borrowed the style and vocabulary of the Scholars Version of Canonical Mark except that I use the more traditional term "the kingdom of God," rather than the Scholars' "God's imperial rule." I have not used the Scholars' Version of Secret Mark because it ignores the way Mark and Secret Mark echo each other in

Greek, as has been shown by several authors, i.e., Morton Smith and John Crossan.

Secret Gospel of Mark: 1 - 13,

They come into Bethany, and there was a woman whose brother had died and [she] approaches and bows down before Jesus and says to him, "Son of David, have mercy on me." But the disciples scolded her. And Jesus got angry and went with her into the garden where the tomb was. Right away there was a loud voice from the tomb. Then Jesus went up and rolled the stone away from the opening of the tomb. He went right in where the youth was, reached out a hand and raised him, taking hold of [his] hand. The youth **loved him at first sight and began to plead with him to stay.**[93] And coming out of the tomb, they go to the young man's home for he was rich. And six days later Jesus called him. And when evening came, **the young man went to him wearing a shroud over his nude body. And he stayed all night**[93] and Jesus taught him the secret of the kingdom of God. From there he gets up and goes back across the Jordan.[94]

The above reference to a cloth and nakedness is repeated in:

St. Mark 14: 48 - 52,

And Jesus answered and said unto them, Are ye come out, as against a thief, with swords and with staves to take me? I was daily with you in the temple teaching and ye took me not; but the scriptures must be fulfilled. And they all forsook him and fled. And there followed him a certain young man [neaniskos, meaning in the prime of his life,] having a **linen cloth cast about h**is **naked body**; and the young men laid hold on him: And he left the linen cloth, And **fled from them naked.**[95]

Based upon these above references, some scholars equate the "disciple loved by Jesus" as being Lazarus and the young rich man. Expressed another way:

"Disciple **loved** by Jesus" = Lazarus = Rich young man.

Whether such reasoning is accurate or not will require more time and study. On the other hand, we may never know the true facts about what, at first glimpse, seems like a Biblical homoerotic relationship.

---

93   Author's emphasis
94   http://depts.drew.edu/jhc/fowler.html
95   Not the same young man seeking eternal life

David and Jonathan

Passages in First and Second Samuel describe an extremely close bond between David and Jonathan, the son of King Saul and next in line for the throne. However, Samuel anointed David to be the next king, which conflicted with Saul's desired inheritance for Jonathan. Religious conservatives generally view the relationship of David and Jonathan as non-sexual. The religious-right cannot believe that God would allow a king of Israel to be a homosexual. Fundamentalists are unwilling to consider a gay person as worthy enough to fulfill such a role because the incumbent would be "_____" (insert any of the derogatory adjective from the list provided earlier). There are, however, religious people and scholars who have no problem believing that David and Jonathan had a consensual homoerotic relationship. The Holy Bible itself suggests this relationship.

Some verses which describe their relationship are:

1 Samuel 18: 1,

> …Jonathan became one in spirit with David and he loved him as himself…the soul of Jonathan was knit with the soul of David, and Jonathan loved him as his own soul.

Most translations use the term *soul*[96] rather than *spirit*[97] to describe the bond. They speak of an *"immediate bond of love,"* their souls being *"in unison,"* their souls being *"knit"* etc. Genesis 2: 7, as written in the original Hebrew, described how God blew the **spirit** into the earthen body of Adam so that he became a living **soul**. This strongly suggested that in ancient Israeli times, the word *soul* represented a combination of body and spirit. Thus David and Jonathan appear to have loved each other both physically (soul) and in essence (spirit).

1 Samuel 18: 2,

> From that day, Saul kept David with him and did not let him return to his father's house.

David left his parent's home and moved into Saul's house, where David could be with Jonathan. This strongly indicated that the relationship was extremely close. Note the words *left* and *moved into*. These are words of volition; nowhere are we led to

---

96   **Old Testament**: Hebrew (*nephesh*) meaning "life" or "possessing life." Occasionally means whole person, inner life, one's self, psychological or spiritual life. *Holman Illustrated Biblical Dictionary*. **New Testament**: Greek (*psuche*), similar to Hebrew word *nephesh*, meaning entire person, emotions, passions, separate from physical existence. *Holman Illustrated Biblical Dictionary*.

97   Hebrew *ruach*, Greek *pneuma*, "wind," "breath," "spirit." May refer to God, nonphysical beings (good or evil) or human beings and their thinking, understanding, emotions, attitudes and intentions. *Holman Illustrated Biblical Dictionary*.

believe that David was a prisoner or kept against his will. Their relationship parallels the marriage passage in,

Genesis 2: 24,

> Therefore shall a man leave his father and his mother, and shall cleave unto his wife: and they shall be one flesh.

1 Samuel 18: 3 - 4,

> And Jonathan made a covenant with David because he loved him as himself. Jonathan took off the robe he was wearing and gave it to David, along with his tunic, and even his sword, his bow and his belt [everything].

Underwear was essentially unknown to these ancient people. When Jonathan stripped himself (naked) in front of David, he would have been considered to have acted extremely unusually (then and now) unless their relationship was, and had been, intimate.

1 Samuel 18: 20 - 21,

> Now Saul's daughter Michal was in love with David, and when they told Saul about it, he was pleased. 'I will give her to him', he thought so that she may be a snare to him and so that the hand of the Philistines may be against him. Now you have a **second opportunity to become my son-in-law**.[98] (NIV)

In the *King James Version of the Bible*, the end of verse 21 reads:

> Thou shalt this day be my son-in-law, in [*the one of*] the twain.

Saul first offered his daughter Merab to David, but the offer was rejected, presumably by her. Saul then offered daughter, Michal. Saul wanted David to be so distracted by his new wife, Michal, that he would not be an effective fighter and would be killed in battle while fighting the Philistines.

There is an interesting phrase used at the end of verse 21 stating that David would become Saul's son-in-law through "one of the twain [two]." The verse seems to refer to one of Saul's two daughters but this is a mistranslation. The King James, the phrase "the one of" does not exist in the Hebrew original. These words are shown in [ ] and in italics in the King James Version. This means the translators inserted the words on their

---

98 Author's emphasis

own volition (perhaps to make the passage read better or to reflect their own biases) but if the translators had been forthright, they would have written,

> Thou shalt this day be my son-in-law, in the **twain**[99]

In modern English, this might read,

> Today, you are son-in-law by marriage to **two** of my children.

The phrase would refer to Saul's son, Jonathan, and his daughter Michal. The Hebrew original would appear to bestow on David's and Jonathan's homosexual relationship an equivalency to David and Michal's marriage. We don't know if Saul approved of his son's homosexual relationship with Jonathan, but he apparently recognized it. The *King James Version of the Bible* acknowledges the rewriting of the original Hebrew by placing the three words, *the one of*, in italics and within [ ]. *The New International Version of the Bible* (NIV) translation is not so honest. Someone's bias against the gay community may be showing in the NIV version.

Jonathan constantly frustrates Saul's efforts to rid himself of David, the young rebellious pretender as seen in:

I Samuel 20: 30 - 31,

> Do I not know that you have chosen the son of Jesse to your own shame, and to the shame of your mother's nakedness? For as long as the son of Jesse lives upon the earth, neither you nor your kingdom shall be established.

This is the exasperation of a man not understanding how friendship (love) can be placed above family loyalty. The angry king casts aspersions upon David's parentage while linking the shame of Jonathan's behavior to the 'shame of your mother's nakedness.' Nakedness is a phrase used with regard to illicit sexual relationships. The word *shame* is often associated with sexual activity in Hebrew scripture. A precise meaning here is unclear, but it is obvious Saul found his son's relationship with David deeply disturbing. It could be that Saul felt the relationship violated a father's (or king's) right to his son's loyalty or perhaps the king is offended by some unstated sexual transgression.

1 Samuel 20: 41,

> After the boy had gone, David got up from the south side of the stone and bowed down before Jonathan three times, with his face to the ground.

---

99   Author's emphasis

Then they kissed each other and wept together—but David wept the
most. (NIV)

Other translations have a different ending to this verse:

…and they kissed one another and wept with one another, until David
exceeded. (KJV)

…and they sadly shook hands, tears running down their cheeks until
David could weep no more.(Living Bible)

They kissed each other and wept aloud together.(New American Bible)

Then David and Jonathan kissed each other. They cried together, but
David cried the most. (New Century Version)

Then they kissed one another and shed tears together, until David's grief
was even greater than Jonathan's. (Revised English Bible)

The Living Bible translators could not handle the image of two men kissing, so they
innocuously translated the passage as the two men shook hands. This is clearly a biased
position of fearful, homophobic heterosexuals, which has led some scholars to say that
the *Living Bible* is no more than a paraphrase of scripture—not a translation.

The original Hebrew text says they kissed each other and wept together until David
became "*gadal*" which means "great" in the original Hebrew. The word is found else-
where in the Hebrew Scriptures and refers to King Solomon being greater than other
kings. Clearly, David had not become a king. Some theologians interpret "*gadal*" in
this verse as indicating that David had an erection. The thought of David getting an
erection after kissing Jonathan was too threatening for many Bible translators. They
chose to omit the verse's ending or make up one more in keeping with their biases
against homosexually.

In the story, the men separate and Jonathan hides from Saul in the woods of Ziph.
Reconciliation occurs in,

I Samuel 23: 16 & 17,

And Jonathan Saul's son arose, and went to David in the wood and
strengthened his hand in God. And he said unto him, Fear not: for the
hand of Saul my father shall not find thee; and thou shall be king over

Israel, and I shall be next [second] unto thee; and that also Saul my father knoweth.

These verses don't dogmatically tell us very much, but when taken in context, they raise the spector of something more than a close relationship. In ancient times, the person who is most often "next" to or second to a king is "A" spouse, if not more than one. We are left with wondering why Jonathan would expect to be second and why would Saul expect Jonathan to be second. Some authorities would argue that the meaning is quite clear. Jonathan knew quite well that his relationship to David was special and different, and Saul knew it as well. We are left with making an intelligent guess about their relationship—the men were lovers. Much Later in

I Samuel 30: 5, we are told that David had two wives, but this does not preclude him from holding Jonathan in his heart. Then as now, some men took wives to cover their interests in gay relationships. Unfortunately Jonathan is slain. He is then lamented by David as seen in,

2 Samuel 1: 26,

I grieve for you, Jonathan my brother; you were very dear to me. Your love for me was wonderful, more wonderful than that of women.

In ancient Israel, unmarried men and women did not normally speak to each other in public. Societal morés would not permit David to have any social relationships with women, except family members. He may, however, have had sex with prostitutes or Saul may be referencing wives of some arranged marriage. David must be referring to physical sexual love in verse 26. It makes no sense here to compare non-sexual love for a man with sexual love for a woman. The comparison is like apples and oranges. I believe that David is referring to his sexual love for Jonathan. Context is everything.

Ruth and Naomi

The Book of Ruth describes the closest relationship to be found between two Biblical women. The Reverend Mona West writes in *The Queer Bible Commentary*,

It is important to realize that the artistry and message of Ruth are dependent on the interplay of law and narrative within the book. This artistry is lost if the book is approached as a legal treatise or test case for the laws it contains. Instead, the legal material should be viewed as a creative matrix for plot movement and character development. The laws are intentionally ambiguous in order to provide possibilities for the characters to act above and beyond what society requires of them…
(p. 190)

Ruth and her two daughters-in-law are widowed and without sons. Without husbands or sons, the women are socially worthless. They had limited resources and few chances for improving their living situation. They wondered if they should marry Moabites or seek *legal* Hebrew reprieve through Levirate marriages?

Other Jewish laws that impact the story are: the gleaning of wheat and "spreading the skirt or cloak." In Chapter 2, Ruth "happens" onto the field of Boaz where she decides to take advantage of the Israeli gleaning law that provided for the poor and the foreigner (Lev. 19: 9-10; 23: 22; Deut. 24: 19-22). Ruth makes known to Boaz the relationship between her and Naomi. Boaz, a gentleman, offers Ruth his protection from violence that could befall a lone woman gleaning in the fields. Boaz and Ruth make arrangements so that she and Naomi have food. This plan makes it possible for the two women to continue to live together. In chapter 3, Ruth "proposes" to Boaz by uttering the phrase "spread your cloak over your servant." This phrase is a traditional Israeli symbol of marriage (Deut. 22: 30). It is difficult to know how the Ruth and Boaz marriage was structured, but there is no doubt that it permitted Ruth and Naomi to remain together.

Perhaps the best known passage in Ruth is one that is often read during heterosexual and homosexual marriage ceremonies. Some readers of this passage see it as a kind of "coming out" of Ruth to Naomi. That passage is,

Ruth 1: 16 &17,

> …were you go I will go, and where you stay I will stay.
> Your people will be my people and your God my God.
> Where you die I will die, and there I will be buried.
> May the Lord deal with me, be it ever so severely, if anything but death
> separates you and me. (NIV)

Ruth 1:14, refers to the relationship between Ruth and Naomi and mention that "Ruth **clave** onto her" (KJV). The Hebrew word, *davka*, translated in the *King James Version of the Bible* as *clave* is almost identical to that used in the alleged first heterosexual marriage (Adam and Eve).

Genesis 2: 24,

> Therefore shall a man leave his father and his mother, and shall **cleave**
> unto his wife: and they shall be one flesh.

Mona West (p 191) has this to say about the relationship of these two Biblical women.

> …Ruth names her relationship to Naomi using words that depict a relationship that crossed the boundaries of age, nationality, and religion. Ruth chooses against all the odds to stay with Naomi—one worthless woman joining herself to another, and, in her choosing, she refuses to accept the status quo of a society that limits and defines their existence as worthless, empty, and marginally based on marital status or reproductive ability.

The Book of Ruth was probably included in the Hebrew Scriptures because King David was one of the descendants of Ruth. Although the relationship between Ruth and Naomi appears to have been very close, there is no proof that it was a sexually active relationship. Nevertheless, the story of these two Biblical women has served as a kind of role model for modern women who call themselves (sisters) lesbian.

Daniel and Ashpenaz

Ashpenaz was a court official (eunuch) for Nebuchadnezzar, the King of Babylon. The Biblical verses which point the way to the relationship between Daniel and Ashpenaz begin in Daniel. English translations of the verse differ greatly:

Daniel 1: 9,

> Now God had brought Daniel into favor and tender love with the prince of the *eunuchs*. (KJV)

> God made Ashpenaz want to be kind and merciful to Daniel. (New Century Version)

> Now God made Daniel to find favor, compassion, and loving-kindness with the chief of the *eunuchs*. (Amplified Bible)

> Now, as it happens, God had given the superintendent a special appreciation for Daniel and sympathy for his predicament. (Living Bible)

> God caused the master to look on Daniel with kindness and goodwill. (Revised English Version)

Religious conservatives view the relationship of Daniel and Ashpenaz as totally nonsexual. They find it unbelievable that God would permit an Israeli prophet to be a homosexual. Why, one might ask, is the fundamentalists' bias any better or more correct than those who disagree?

Some religious liberals acknowledge the possibility of a homosexual relationship between these two men. The Hebrew words describing the relationship are *chesed v'rachamim*. The most common translation of *chesed* is mercy (It may also mean love or kindness).[100] *V'rachamim* is a plural form which emphasizes its relative importance. The word has many meanings: among them are mercy and physical love. I believe it is unreasonable to believe that the original Hebrew would read Ashpenaz "showed mercy **and** mercy." I believe a more realistic interpretation would be Ashpenaz showed mercy and engaged in physical love with Daniel. This would be absolutely unacceptable to later translators, so they gave into their personal biases and provided a more conservative interpretation. Below is a side-by-side comparison of the various translations:

> Now God had brought Daniel into favor and tender love with the prince of the eunuchs. (KJV)

> God caused the master to look on Daniel with kindness and good-will. (Revised English Version)

> Though God had given Daniel the favor and sympathy of the chief chamberlain. (New American Bible)

> Now God had caused the official to show favor and sympathy to Daniel. (NIV)

> Now, as it happens, God had given the superintendent a special appreciation for Daniel and sympathy for his predicament. (Living Bible)

> Then God granted Daniel favor and sympathy from the chief of the eunuchs. (Modern Language)

> God made Ashpenaz want to be kind and merciful to Daniel. (New Century Version)

> And God gave Daniel favor and compassion in the sight of the chief of the eunuchs. (Revised Standard Version)

---

100   http://www.babylon.com/define/106/Hebrew-Dictionary.html

The KJV reference to "tender love" appears to come closest to the truth.

One might question whether Daniel and Ashpenaz could sexually consummate their relationship. They were both eunuchs. The use of the word eunuch does not always mean that any or all of the male genitalia had been removed. The word may have meant they were physically intact or sterile.

Males, castrated after puberty, may still retain some sexual drive due to androgens (sex hormones) produced in body parts other than the genitals. Another explanation of their "coming together" might be that they were perfectly normal males in terms of their anatomy and physiology, but they were eunuchs in that they choose NOT to engage in heterosexual acts. In short, the men may have been gay. B.A. Robinson, a consultant to the Ontario, Canada, Consultants on Religious Tolerance has written widely on this relationship.[101]

The Centurion

More about this Roman officer can be seen in,

Matthew 8: 5 - 13,

> And when Jesus was entered into Capernaum, there came unto him a centurion, beseeching him, And saying, Lord, my servant lieth at home sick of the palsy, grievously tormented. And Jesus saith unto him, I will come and heal him. The centurion answered and said, Lord, I am not worthy that thou shouldest come under my roof: but speak the word only, and my servant shall be healed. For I am a man under authority, having soldiers under me: and I say to this man, Go, and he goeth; and to another, Come, and he cometh; and to my servant, Do this, and he doeth it. When Jesus heard it, he marveled, and said to them that followed, Verily I say unto you, I have not found so great faith, no, not in Israel. And I say unto you, That many shall come from the east and west, and shall sit down with Abraham, and Isaac, and Jacob, in the kingdom of heaven. But the children of the kingdom shall be cast out into outer darkness: there shall be weeping and gnashing of teeth. And Jesus said unto the centurion, Go thy way; and as thou hast believed, so be it done unto thee. And his servant was healed in the selfsame hour.

This is an often overlooked Biblical story of love. First, the story is about two males. One is a high ranking Roman soldier. The other is a servant, which meant that he was most likely a slave under the control of the Centurion.

---

101   http://www.religioustolerance.org

Roman citizens (peers) were almost never held as slaves, unless they sold themselves into slavery. For the Romans, slaves were somewhat disposable, especially if they were captured slaves. They were at the bottom of the social hierarchy when it came to personal respect from Roman owners. Slaves could be sold, beaten, starved, raped, or killed at the whim of the owner.

The servant in the Matthew story is referred to as *pais*, in the original Greek. The word *pais* is usually interpreted as boy, while a slave is usually indicated by the Greek word *doulos*. Luke says this *pais* was the centurion's *entimos doulos*—a special or honored slave. (See Mader) The use of the word *pais* carries a strong suggestion that the slave / servant was a young male lover. (Dover p. 16, Sergent p. 10)

Nevertheless, the story presents us with a powerful Roman officer who had feelings for a slave who is said to be at home. Ordinary slaves did not have "homes." The emotional feelings of this officer are so strong for the "boy" at home, that the officer went in search of Christ to heal his "boy" servant.

Christ agreed to go to the home, but the officer declined the offer stating that he was unworthy to have Christ in his house. It is conceivable that the officer was a gay man with a special (gay) servant who was, perhaps, a male lover. If Christ had come into their house, such a relationship might have become obvious to Christ. I believe that knowledge was something the officer did not want Jesus to know, because a Jew (Christ) would be expected to reject men engaged in male-male sexual activities, even though Romans would not have cared. Christ surely knew of the Centurion's situation. Regardless of the relationship, Christ healed the servant. In helping the soldier, Christ went against the social-political norms of the day. Readers should remember that at the time of Christ, the Roman invaders / conquerors and the Jews despised and distrusted each another.

Secondly, the officer most assuredly was a pagan who offered the required sacrifices to his god-emperor. Neither fact bothered Jesus.

I would like to think Christ knew the centurion had an ill, male lover, but we will never know. Christ was amazed by the faith the soldier had in him, the Jewish healer, and had to know of the love the Centurion had for the male servant (lover), yet the Centurion was not chastised for either his pagan religion or love for his servant, as today's conservative Christians most assuredly would have done. A Centurion could have commanded any Jew to do so-and-so, and the officer would expect the request to be fulfilled. In this story, a simple request, based on faith produced the desired results.

Saul, Saul...

Saul was a Jew and very dedicated to his Jewish faith. He allegedly lived in Tarsus, an area known today as Turkey, which borders today's Lebanon. We know Tarsus had a sizeable Jewish community because there was a synagogue there. Greek culture had a great influence on this region and the Jews who lived there. They probably used the Greek version of the Torah known as the *Septuagint*. This was an area of learned men and scholars who spoke several languages. Saul spoke and wrote Hebrew and Greek. The name Paul is Greek for Saul.

His family had considerable financial standing and his father was a Roman citizen, by which means (birth, military service, etc.) we are unsure. However, to be a Roman citizen gave him stature in his community. We are told that Saul was a tent maker, but as a young Jewish man from a family of means, he would have spent time in formal Jewish training in Jerusalem with the rabbis of the Temple. The book of Second Acts 22: 3 implies that Saul trained with *Gamaliel* the *Sanhedrin*, a noted Jewish scholar. As a student, Saul became familiar with and adhered to all the rules and regulations of his orthodox faith. Regarding his knowledge of the Jewish faith, he has this to say in,

Galatians 1: 14,

> I advanced in Judaism beyond many of my own age among my people,
> so extremely zealous was I for the tradition of my fathers.

The Holiness Code of Leviticus 17 - 26 played a great role in Paul's youth and post conversion life. This code dwelt on uncleanness of the body and bodily functions. Jewish men came to obsess about bodily functions during and after the Babylonian exile. This may have been a way of keeping themselves apart and different from their pagan captors. By 100 BCE, Jews were making a distinction between the sacred sphere, spiritual realm, the profane world of the bodily and a person's spirit. It was Greek philosophy, particularly Platonism (ideas are ultimately real, and different from non-ideal things), which helped to create a dualistic understanding of the person (body) as having a separate spirit. This dualism would become a cornerstone of western, Greek-influenced, Christianity.

For the ancient Jews, the body was finite, fallen, and sinful, while the spirit was eternal and of God. The spirit was believed to continually battle the body in which it is held captive and from which it will ultimately be freed (by death) to return to God. Bodies were thought to be associated with un-controllable passion, desire, and emotion. The spirit was associated with the rational, the will, and self-control. Women were perceived as being less spiritual than men and unable to transcend their bodilyness and therefore subject to passion and irrationality. Due to this weakness, the female body needed to be tamed for the good of its spirit and the good of men who might be tempted by its feminine wiles. Nature (and natural law) was associated with the body and had to be tamed and transcended by all persons. The earthly body was what all people needed redeeming from by a God who is spirit only and therefore good. As author Luce Irigaray wrote in *Marine Lover of Friedrich Nietzsche* (p.174), "…the earth becomes a great deportation camp, where men await celestial redemption."

Paul became a staunch defender of his Jewish faith against the fledgling Christian Church and its early leaders. While on the road to Damascus to "do in" some Christians whose teachings threatened his Jewish faith, Saul had a vision of God who asked why Saul was persecuting him (God and his Church).

Acts 9: 4 - 9,

> And he fell to the earth, and heard a voice saying unto him, Saul, Saul, why persecutes thou me? And he said Who art thou, Lord? And the Lord said, I am Jesus whom thou persecutes: it is hard for thee to kick against the pricks. And he trembling and astonished said Lord, what wilt thou have me to do? And the Lord said unto him arise and go into the city…And the men which journeyed with him stood speechless hearing a voice but seeing no man. And Saul arose from the earth; and when his eyes were opened he saw no man but they led him by the hand, and brought him into Damascus…And he was three days without sight…

On the spot, Saul was converted to the Christian faith and gave up his fight against the Christians. He was baptized, preached his new faith, and became a pillar of the Christian Church. He wrote much of the New Testament under the name of Paul. His temporary blindness was only one of many hardships to be endured during his lifetime. We read in,

II Corinthians: 24 - 28 (*King James Version*),

> Of the Jews five times received I forty stripes save one. Thrice was I beaten with rods, once was I stoned, thrice I suffered shipwreck, a night and a day I have been in the deep; in journeyings often, in perils of waters, in perils of robbers, in perils by mine own countrymen, in perils by the heathen, in perils in the city, in perils in the wilderness, in perils in the sea, in perils among false brethren; In weariness and painfulness, in watchings often, in hunger and thirst, in fastings often, in cold and nakedness. Beside those things that are without, that which cometh upon me daily, the care of all the churches.

This passage was written about seventeen years after Paul's conversion. His sufferings were quite burdensome for a man described as being small and physically weak. As one reads Paul's writings, one is impressed by the zeal with which he writes. Some of his prose is almost like poetry. However, some passages remind me of Shakespeare's, Hamlet, Act 3 scene 2, "The lady doth protest too much, methinks." Paul is often too defensive about what might be considered his lifestyle.

His writings can be quite negative and at other times convey a sense of "I am better than you." At times, his words seem like listening to one side of a telephone conversation. Devotion to his Jewish-Christian faith is so strong he appears to be overly defensive of it, so much so, one is left wondering what is being shared or hidden in his writings. If one spends any time reading Paul, one cannot but wonder why Saul was as anti-Christian as he had been prior to his conversion. What did he fear from Christians and their faith? What was Paul defending, or may I suggest asking, what was he running from, covering up, or hiding from? What caused so much angst in Paul's pre-Christian life? To try and answer these questions, I propose we examine more closely Paul's writings, keeping in mind that a person does not persecute that which is not fearsome and at the same time contains some kernel of attraction. I would like to refer readers to a book, *Rescuing the Bible from Fundamentalism,* (written by John Shelby Spong now retired Bishop of the Newark Diocese of the Episcopal Church) for another view of Paul's work and possible alternate lifestyle. Paul's writings reveal him to have had one foot firmly planted in his former Jewish faith and the other in his newly acquired Christian faith. He seemed torn between adhering to Jewish laws regarding sex within marriage and suggested avoiding "things of the flesh" that are allowed by Christianity. He was never far from discussing sex and the (his) need for self-control. His focus on sex has led some readers to question if he was making sub-rosa remarks about himself or the illicit, ritual sex conducted in pagan temples all around him. Some of these forbidden acts can be seen in:

Galatians 5: 19,

Now the works of the flesh are manifest, which are these; Adultery, fornication, **uncleanness**, lasciviousness.

I Corinthians, 7: 25,

Now concerning virgins I have no commandment of the Lord: yet I give my judgment, as one that hath obtained mercy of the Lord to be faithful.

I Corinthians 7: 1,

Now concerning the things whereof ye wrote unto me: It is good for a man not to touch a woman.

Galatians 5: 23,

...the fruit of the Spirit was self-control.

In the preceding verses, we see that Paul was not a marrying man. He may actually have feared women or at least feared something about them. He appeared not to want to touch them, much less have sex with them. Perhaps this fear was a carryover from his Jewish background where menstruating women were "unclean." A man would not know if a woman was or was not menstruating, so they should avoid touching all women. Saul, the Jew, was not known to have married. Greek / Roman / Jewish cultures, of his time, would have expected him to take a wife and procreate. As far as we know, he did not. He does, however, appear to have an attraction to the subject of hair. Samson (Judges 16) and Absalom (II Samuel 14) are the most famous men with long hair who are mentioned in the Old Testament (or Torah). In both cases, the men's hair caused their downfall. Saul admonishes men about their hair length.

1 Corinthians 11: 14 - 16,

> Doth not even nature itself teach you, that, if a man have long hair, it is a shame unto him? But if a woman have long hair, it is a glory to her: for her hair is given her for a covering. But if any man seem to be contentious, we have no such custom, neither the churches of God.

Paul herein suggests the hold of his Jewish customs may have been giving way to Christianity. He seems to revert to some "natural law" issue with his discussion of men having long hair. Men and women's hair will grow unless nature is interrupted and it is cut. However, Jewish "custom" expected men to keep short hair (an unnatural act). Jewish men covered their head and short hair while in the Temple, out of respect to God, but women had long hair as their cover (presumably wound on top of their head). Paul finds long hair appealing (bringing honor) to women but not men. Jewish custom expected men to keep their hair short. However, the
hairstyles of men in his ear were a mixture of long and short. Could he have meant that long hair on a male was effeminate? If so, why should he care? Could he be equating men wearing long hair with pagan worship, castrated males, and ritual homosexual acts? If so, long hair might have been "contentious" within Paul's Christianity.

1 Corinthians 14: 34 - 35,

> Let your hai [102] [those][103] women keep silence in the churches: for it is not permitted unto them to speak; but they are commanded to be under obedience as also saith the law. And if they will learn anything, let them

---

102   Hai in Greek is the feminine form of those. In New King James scriptures the same word in the masculine form—"hoi" is translated "those": John 6:14, "those men" ; John 8:29, KJV, "those things"; Romans 8:5 "For those who"; Romans 8:8, "those who are in the flesh" NKJ; 1 Cor 10:18, "those who eat"; 1 Cor. 15:18, "those who have fallen asleep"; and 1 Cor. 15:23, "those who are Christ's"; Gal. 3:9, "those who are of faith"; Gal. 5:24, "those who are Christ's"; Gal. 6:13, "those who are"; 1Thes. 5:7, "Those who sleep"; 1 Tim 3:13 "For those who have served well; 2Tim. 1:15, "all those in Asia"; 2 Tim 3:6,"those who creep." In using the feminine "hai," Paul is saying, "Let those wives keep silent..." Not ALL women, just those causing confusion!

103   Author's addition

ask their husbands at home: for it is a shame for women to speak in the church.

These verses reveal Christian women to be subservient to husbands and are to be silent in Christian places of worship as was the Jewish custom. Contemporary commentators knew that this passage conflicted with 1 Corinthians 11: 2-16. In antiquity, one prayed and prophesied aloud, not silently. How could women pray and prophesy in assembly if they were forbidden to speak there? It has been said that ancient Jewish women should not speak in the temple to prevent them from being seen as solicitors of men (whores). Secondly, women need not attend or participate in temple services. While Paul may have had difficulty in casting off Jewish customs, he tried to embrace his new religion, a work always in progress, and his new congregation. Another glimpse into Paul's psyche can be seen in:

II Corinthians 6: 8 - 10,

By honour and dishonour, by evil report and good report: as **deceivers**, and yet true; As unknown, and yet well known; as d**ying,** and, behold, we live; as chastened, and **not killed**; As s**orrowful,** yet always rejoicing; as **poor**, yet making many rich; as **having nothing,** and yet possessing all things.

II Corinthians 12: 7 - 9,

…a thorn was given me in the flesh, a message of Satan, to harass me, to keep me from being too elated. Three times I sought The Lord about this, that it should leave me…

Galatians 4: 13,

Ye know how through infirmity of the flesh I preached the gospel unto you at the first. To you at first; and though my condition was a trial to you, you did not scorn or despise me but received me as an angel of God…

Paul spoke of some "thing" that bothered him like a "thorn in the flesh" and as something that he believed was known (a trial) to his friends. When taken in toto, one could read into Paul's verses that he may have had what we know today as a gay orientation. For Paul, the flesh was a place for evil to hide and possess him. Certainly, such a lifestyle was not unknown to the ancient peoples living in the Greek and Roman communities of the Middle East. While Paul's Jewish peers would find such a lifestyle as being very "gentile," the gentiles were not so scandalized by what was or had been a significant and acceptable part of their pagan communities. Paul` could have been gay and not just pagan.

Romans 7: 14 - 15,

> For we know that the law is spiritual: but I am **carnal**, sold under sin. For that which I do I allow not: for what I would, that do I not; but **what I hate, that do I.**

What more can one say after saying, I AM CARNAL? Paul is not a married or a divorced man, as far as we know. If he doesn't want marriage or any kind of close relationship with a female, the only "person" left with whom to be carnal is one's self or another man. One could be led to believe that the erotic part of Paul's life was homoerotic. We cannot say, with 100% assurance, that Paul acted on this inclination, but a reading between the lines certainly suggests the temptation.

Romans 7: 18,

> For I know that **in me** (that is, in my flesh,) dwelleth n**o good** thing: for to will is present with me; but how to perform that which is good **I find not.**

Read from a homoerotic standpoint, it appeared that Paul was aware of his homoerotic feelings and knows that his Jewishness precluded such acts and thoughts. His newly acquired Christian faith compelled him to want to abolish evil thoughts, but he found it difficult to will what is good, and for him, proper.

Romans 6: 12,

> Let not sin therefore reign in your mortal body, that ye should obey it in the **lusts thereof**.

Romans 7: 13,

> Was then that **which is good** made death unto me? God forbid. But sin, that it might appear sin, working death in me by that which is good; **that sin** by the commandment might become exceeding sinful.

In the two preceding verses, one can read lust as desire, thoughts and leanings far and away from what Paul considered to be morally good and away from sin. In this time period, no one knew of, or considered, a same-sex orientation. Paul's historical peers spoke only of the act or behavior of same-sex coupling. We are generally led to believe that adult same-sex *love* did not exist between men in this era (a "fact" I doubt), even though man-boy "love" was acceptable in Greek culture. We often read of same gender sexual acts as if it was void of the emotion of love but apparently filled with raw passion, lust, or is connected with pagan worship.

Romans 7: 21 - 24,

> I find then a law, that, when I would do good, **evil is present** with me. For I delight in the law of God after the inward man: But I see another law **in my members**, warring against the **law of my mind**, and bringing me into **captivity** to the law of sin which is in my **members. O wretched man that I am**! who shall **deliver me from** the body of this death?

The above verses lead one to ask about what Paul was speaking. Did he have everything; yet, he felt as though he was empty (hollow) and in need or want of something else? Was he leading a secret inner life? He is feeling "**carnal**" and simultaneously feeling the love of Christ. He tells himself that he should do "x" yet his body (not his mind or spirit) compels him to do "y" and that "y" is not of his liking. He seems to be approaching a schizophrenic state of mind regarding something. His **member** is against him. He feels wretched. Why? Perhaps he is fighting self-recognition that he **is** a person with same-sex interests. He is fighting to stay in the closet.

Romans 6: 21,

> What fruit had ye then in those **things** whereof ye are **now ashamed** for the end of those things is death.

Some "**thing**" in the past had been fruitful or giving of something desirable to Paul, but here he was feeling ashamed and deserving of death because of those "**things**." What is Paul saying about himself?

Romans 6: 19,

> I speak after the manner of men because of the infirmity of your flesh: for as ye have yielded your **members [as]**[104] servants to uncleanness

---

104   Author's addition

and to iniquity unto iniquity; even so now yield your **members [as]**[104] servants to righteousness unto holiness.

I Corinthians 12: 21 - 25,

And the eye cannot say unto the hand, I have no need of thee: nor again the head to the feet, I have no need of you. Nay, much more those **members** of the body, which seem to be more feeble, are necessary: And those **members** of the body, which we think to be less h**onourable,** upon these we bestow more abundant honour; and our **uncomely parts** have more abundant comeliness. For our **comely parts have no need**: but God hath tempered the body together, having given more abundant honour to that part which lacked. That there should be no schism in the body; but that the members should the same care one for another.

Could it be that Paul is speaking homoerotically of his penis as "member," or a type of sexual arousal or even of impotence? Does it not sound as though there is some sexual drive being referred to in these passages? Paul wrote, "There is no good in me. I can't change in me what I want to change in me."

Romans 7: 25,

I thank God through Jesus Christ our Lord. So then with the mind I myself serve the law of God; but with the flesh the law of sin.

1 Corinthians 6: 18,

Flee fornication. Every sin that a man doeth is without the body; but he that committeth fornication sinneth against his own body.

1 Corinthians 9: 27,

But I keep under [discipline] my body, and bring it into subjection: lest that by any means, when I have preached to others, I myself should be a castaway.

Paul laments that his body is sinful and in need of self-mortification, saying that sexual immorality punishes the body (maybe his body). Fornication may not always be a reference to a male-female sexual relationship. There is certainly the suggestion here that Paul's body deserves punishment.

II Corinthians 7: 5,

> For, when we were come into Macedonia, our **flesh had no rest**, but we were troubled on every side; without were fightings, **within were fears**.

What is this fear within? Could it have been an innate homoerotic personality fearing a loss of self-control or an unwanted acting out of some homoerotic drive awakened by the city's activities?

Galatians 4: 8 - 9,

> Howbeit then, when ye knew not God, ye did service unto them [men][105] which by nature are no gods. But now, after that ye have known God, or rather are known of God, how turn ye again to the **weak and beggarly elements**, where- unto ye desire again to be in bondage?

How does one attach a statement of ownership to "them?" I believe the "them" could be a reference to pagan gods and temple prostitutes, or other men who might have overtly repressed their homoerotic orientation or as heterosexuals who involved themselves in homosexual pagan rituals even if these men did not have what we today consider a "proper" name for the relationship.

Romans 1: 24 - 25,

> Wherefore God also gave them up to uncleanness through The **Lusts of their own hearts,** to dishonor their own bodies between themselves: Who changed the **truth of God into a lie**, and worshipped and served the creature more than the Creator, who I blessed forever. Amen.

Aramaic Bible, Romans I: 24 - 25,

> Because of this, God handed them over to the vile desires of their heart to disgrace their bodies among themselves. And they exchanged the truth of God for lies, and they revered and served created things [pagan idols] more than their Creator, to whom belong praises and blessings to the eternity of eternities, amen.[106]

---

105   Author's addition

106   http://aramaic-plain-english_scripturetext.com/1htm

Galatians 5: 13,

For, brethren, ye have been called unto liberty; only use not liberty for an **occasion to the flesh**, but by love serve one another.

Galatians 5: 16,

This I say then, Walk in the Spirit, and ye shall not fulfill the lust of the flesh.

Paul is telling us that he and others were under some compulsion that is demonic in spirit. Paul had difficulty in controlling it but he did and admonished others to do the same.

This Paulian theme was echoed many years later by,

St. Augustine,

De Nuptiis et Concupiscentia, 1.6.

When the first man transgressed the law of God, he began to have another law in his **members** which was repugnant to his mind, and he felt the evil of his dis- obedience when he discovered himself most justly punished by the disobedience of his flesh…For how is it that the eyes, lips, tongue, hands, feet, and the bending of back, and neck, and sides, are all placed in his power to be moved in ways suitable to perform their work but when it comes to children being generated, the **members** created for this purpose do not obey the will, but lust has to be waited for to set these **members** in motion, as having rights over them, and sometimes it will not act when the mind is willing, while sometimes it even acts against the mind's will! Does the freedom of the human will not blush at this, and through despising God when he commanded, it has lost all proper command even over its own **members**?

Galatians 5: 24,

And **they** that are Christ's have **crucified the flesh** with the **affections and lusts.**

Apparently some members of the Church at Corinth thought they had to observe certain Jewish laws in order to be good Christians. Some had apparently undergone circumcision to better define their Jewish-Christian observance of certain Laws. In Galatians, we find Paul preaching against observing laws as a way to salvation.

Galatians 5: 3 & 4,

> For I testify again to every man that is circumcised, that he is a debtor to do the whole law. Christ is become of no effect until you, whosoever of you are justified by the law; ye are fallen from grace.

Paul is telling his flock that observing (Jewish ritual) laws, e.g., circumcision is not the way to salvation. Paul implies that Jewish ritual laws need not be observed. Does this mean that men may touch menstruating women and still be clean? The ancient Hebrews had a dualistic approach to life. They had a system of taxonomy by which they separated thing into categories. Things in one class were not to be mixed with another class. This helped Jews to be seen as different and separate from their pagan neighbors. Some examples are:

- Don't wear garments made of different materials, e.g. linen and silk, as did the Romans and ancient Persians.
- Don't mix various foods such as meat and dairy products, keep Kosher.
- Two kinds of things swim in the waters. Eat only those that have scales, don't eat shrimp or lobster.
- There are two kinds of animals. Eat only those with cloven hoofs.
- There is a man's and a woman's style of clothing. Men should wear men's clothes not women's clothes (women should not wear slacks. They are not men).
- Men's and women's genitalia are complimentary. Men should have sex with (complimentary) women not (uncomplimentary) men. Man-man sex was what pagans did, not Jews.

These laws or rules had a purpose, but they were more ritual than anything else. Observing Jewish law would not bring salvation to early Christians. In I Corinthians, Paul taught us that love was the most important guiding factor in the lives of early church members.

I Corinthians, 13: 13,

> And now abideth faith, hope, charity*, these three; but the greatest of these [is] charity.[107]

---

107   often translated as love

Paul does promote one "law" as found in the book of Leviticus.

Leviticus 19: 18,

> Thou shalt not avenge, nor bear any grudge against the children of thy
> people, but thou shalt love thy neighbor as thyself: I [am] the LORD.

This melds so well with I Corinthians, 13: 13 and no doubt reflects the constant
mental images Paul carried with him as he moved toward Christianity and away from
his Jewish roots. Does Paul imply that restrictions are removed in cases of homosexual
behavior emanating from homosexual orientation? Is this particular law no longer one
that needs to be observed by Christians? That is difficult to say, but at least such things
should be questioned. While ritual laws may be ignored, Paul is dogmatic that ethical
laws, such as don't kill, etc., are to be observed.

I believe Paul is sharing his desire, and need, for self-control as well as offering
advice on such matters to others. Make no doubt about Paul's writings. His words
reveal another side of a torn man that many Christians refuse to see or read. To ignore
a possibly gay side of Paul's personality and his plight is to do a disservice to religion
and Paul.

The Beloved Disciple

One of the most interesting books in modern, religious literature is *The Man Jesus
Loved* by Theodore w. Jennings, Jr. Doctor Jennings has dared to reread the Bible from
a gay viewpoint. He strips away the real from the artificially possible and probable
interpretations of the scriptures. His work warrants great accolades even if one cannot
identify with all his conclusions.

Prior to the late 19th century, no one spoke of homosexuals or "gay" people. Persons
or groups currently so classified were spoken of only in terms of their behavior. There
were several ancient terms used in reference to this behavior and none had anything to
do with either sexual orientation or emotional love. All references were about behavior.

During ancient times, in order to be a "man" one had to be dominating. He had to
fulfill a male dominant social, psychological, and sexual role. This often meant women
were expected to be subservient and the property of their father or husband.

Male-to-male (note I did not say man-to-man sex) sex was a cultural taboo for
ancient Middle Eastern peoples as well as certain modern peoples. Christian fundamentalists are the major player in this arena. Many ancient, as well as modern, peoples
believe a male who engaged in such sexual activities was denying his manhood, even
his personhood since a *true* "man" did not have sex with another "man." To do so
caused him to be less than a full or complete person. His acts were believed to threaten
his culture and society, as well as lead to his being religiously and physically cut off
from his culture, country, and family. A passive male sexual partner was viewed as a

threat, for he was seen as someone who willingly gave up his dominant male role and therefore socially and culturally more at risk than the person who was the dominant actor in this male-male sexual scenario.

The conservative Christian will quote you scripture to defend their conservative position against such behavior, but we have previously refuted their biased choice and desire to impose their opinions and beliefs on all of America.

The so called "gay reading" of the Bible is similar to that of American people and jurists who decided the institution of slavery had to be abolished even though certain Biblical passages spoke positively about owning slaves. The battle against slavery hinged on an "appropriate" way of reading and interpreting the Bible—not a biased position of the believers who might have owned slaves. Jennings, through his research, said, "…the preponderance of Biblical texts, relevant to the discussion, affirms and celebrates same-sex relationships and practice."

Doctor Jennings goes on to say,

> …if Christianity were to suppose that sexuality is not incompatible with sinlessness, then no reason in principle can be supplied for rejecting erotic attachments for Jesus.

Jesus is said to have loved many people, his disciples as well as all his followers. However, five times we are told in Scripture that there was one "disciple whom Jesus loved." It is this subject which I would like to explore.

In the Passover story, the disciples are in need of a place to conduct the Passover celebration. Christ tells some of the disciples to go into Jerusalem and look for a **man** carrying a water jug. This man will lead them to a place where the celebratory meal can be held (Mark 14: 13 and Luke 22: 10). The verse dealing with the **water bearer** is most often read with no thought as to what was happening in this part of the story. Any reader of the Bible will know that Jesus had a history of overturning or ignoring many laws and cultural taboos. In the Passover story, he has once again reacted against cultural norms. In Christ's day, **men** often translated as love did not carry water. This was woman's work.

Christ's directive was the modern equivalent of asking a friend to go into town and look for a man wearing a pink dress and bright red lipstick. For supporting evidence one is referred to Morton Smith's, *The Secret Gospel: The Discovery and Interpretation of the Secret Gospel According to Mark.* In this case, the disciples were to follow a person who was obviously not a **MAN** in the Biblical sense. As Governor Schwarzenegger might have said, "this was a 'girlie-man.'" The disciples were to find and follow a "girlie-man." This girlie-man led the disciples to the place with the so called upper room. Of interest to me was the fact that this place had space for a group dinner, without reservations, and at the last minute.

This Passover celebration was conducted at a time of the year when thousands of Israelite tourists would have crowded into all available spaces—"commercial" and private. As far as we know, there were no disciple family members living in Jerusalem and none were mentioned as being present at this special Passover celebration. Historically, family members were always present for Passover celebrations. Could this "upper room" have been a place for clandestine meetings—a gay bar of its day?

The Biblical story reminds me of a gay man who was visiting Spain prior to the age of computers. He had forgotten to take his gay guidebook with him and did not know where the local "fun" bars were located. He decided to walk around and look for a girlie-man and once spotted, the tourist would follow the girlie-man to the desired destination. The tourist soon spotted such a person and followed the girlie-man to a gay bar.

Were the disciples, looking for the man with the water jug, on a similar trip?

In the story of the Last Supper, there is no mention of anyone being present except Christ and the disciples. If there had been other of Christ's followers or families coming to Jerusalem with the disciples, one would have expected the Passover meal to have included these men, women and children and be mentioned in the story. Since none are mentioned, we might assume that no such people were present. Only 13 men participated in the ritual.

There are some historians who believe that the Last Supper was not conducted on the same night as the regular Passover celebration, because there was no mention of any family members of the disciples being present for the celebration. A second reason being that during a "regular" Passover meal, the wine is first presented and drunk and then the unleavened bread is presented and eaten. At the Last Supper, according to Scripture, the bread was presented first and then the wine.

I Corinthians 11: 24 & 25,

> And when he had given thanks, he brake it and said, take, eat this is my body, which is broken for you: this do in remembrance of me. After the same manner also he took the cup when he had supped saying, This cup is the new testament in my blood: this do ye, as oft as ye drink it, in remembrance of me.

Luke 22: 17,

> And he took the cup, and gave thanks and said, Take this, And divide it among yourselves. For I say unto you, I will not drink of the fruit of the vine, until the kingdom of God shall come. And he took bread, and gave thanks and brake it, and gave unto them saying, This is my body which is given for you: this do in remembrance of me. Likewise also the cup after supper, saying, This cup is the new testament in my blood which is shed for you.

Here the wine is blessed and divided, but there is no mention of it being drunk at this stage of the meal. Similarly, there is no mention of anyone actually drinking wine or actually eating bread. This reverse order of the Last Supper in contrast to a regular Passover meal sets it apart from a normal Passover celebration. The Last Supper was, indeed, quite different in several ways from the typical Passover meal.

During this unusual Passover, Jesus again presents us with another suppression of gender roles—Christ engaged in foot washing. The Scriptures are filled with notations of foot washings as in,

I Samuel 25: 41,

> **...she** rose and bowed down with her face to the ground and said, your servant is a slave to wash the feet of the servants of the lord.

In Genesis 18: 4, 19:2, 24: 32, 43: 24; Judges 19: 21 & 22, and II Samuel 11: 8 foot washing references are in regard to a host providing water for a guest to wash their own feet.

Luke 7: 38,

> **...she**...began to wash his feet with her tears and to dry them with her hair.

John 12: 3,

> Mary took a pound of costly perfume made of pure nard, Anointed Jesus feet, and wiped them with **her** hair.

This Johnian story is similar to that found in Mark 14: 3 - 9 and Matthew 26: 6 - 13.

I Timothy 5: 10,

> **she** must be well attested for her good works, as one who has brought up children, shown hospitality, washed the saints', helped the afflicted and devoted herself to doing good in every way.

Note that in each case, it is a **woman** who is washing feet. This had clearly been woman's work in the time of Christ. Yet, in another act of overturning the gender role of men in the ancient Middle East, we find that Christ performed foot washing and extolling his disciples to do likewise. Christ asked his disciples to forgo the usual role of men, who would not normally wash anyone's feet except their own. The disciples are asked to assume the subservient role of a woman and wash the feet of other Christians.

Author Theodore Jennings said,

> Jesus divine identity is thus expressed in his disregard for the most intimately enforced institutions of worldly society: gender role expectations.

The Scriptures, however, revealed an even more shocking affront as to how Jesus performed his act of foot washing. Despite how later translations of the verses deal with Jesus' washing the disciple's feet, the earliest text translated this section as saying "Jesus took off his clothes." Other early translations read "he laid aside his garments then tied a towel around his waist." More prudish translations state that "he removed his outer robe."

This removing of clothes may have been another overturning of Jewish law in which one is not to reveal one's nakedness. Likewise nakedness at the Last Supper may be intertwined with the fact that victims of crucifixion were crucified naked, as was to happen to Jesus only hours after the Last Supper. This state of undress is in contrast to modern crucifixes showing the crucified Christ wearing a loin cloth. It is generally believed that Jewish men wore nothing (no underwear) under tunics [outer garments], except Essene men who wore a loin cloth.[108], [109]

In the Gospel of John, we have a glimpse into the intimate life of Christ. This is not to say that we know Christ to be a carnal person, but we do have evidence of same-sex attractions. Nowhere is that better seen than in John's Gospel where Christ's relationship with "the disciple that Jesus loved" is so poignant. At the Last Supper, the 13 men were seated around a sofa and low table common to Jewish, Roman, and Greek custom. At such a meal, diners rested on their left side and elbow; the right hand was free to take food and drink from the low table. We can assume that Christ, as host, was in the center of the seating arrangements. We are told that a favorite disciple is seated (lying) at Christ's right hand. This connotes the most favored position in relationship to a Jewish host. This favorite disciple may have been the disciple called John but that identity is uncertain. Some scholars believe Lazarus was the person in question. He will be discussed later.

Jesus had great affection for all the disciples with whom he had a shared history spanning three years. However, the singling out of just one disciple who is "beloved by Jesus" connotes a relationship quite different from that shared between Jesus and other disciples. In fact, Jesus' relationship is referred to as *love*. This was an intimate and perhaps an erotic love.

---

108   http://www.archaeological.org/pdfs/papers/Comments_on_The_Passion.pdf
109   http://www.earlham.edu/~rel/dick-davis/davis-chas3.html

John 13: 23,

Now there was leaning on Jesus' bosom one of his disciples, whom Jesus **loved.**

This beloved disciple appears to be "snuggled" next to Jesus. During the discussions among the disciples about who is to betray Jesus, the beloved disciple raises himself up from Jesus' bosom and leans toward Peter to better hear Peter's question. Having heard the question, the beloved disciple falls back against Jesus' chest and relays Peter's question to Jesus. Here, it appears that love has assumed the form of physical intimacy through bodily contact, an unusual act for common Jewish men. The kind of intimacy between Jesus and the beloved disciple is unusual enough to be used as a means of later describing the beloved disciple in,

The Gospel of St. John 21: 20,

Then Peter, turning about, seeth the disciple whom Jesus loved following; which also leaned on his breast at supper, and said, Lord, which is he that betrayeth thee?

Here Peter identifies the disciple (who is following the fisherman and Jesus) as "[he]…which leaned on his breast at supper."

Eight translations of this Johnian verse have the beloved disciple against Jesus' bosom. Other translations have the disciple simply sitting next to Jesus. I believe some these translations may reflect homophobia.

It appears Peter is aware of a difference in the relationship between Jesus and the beloved disciple and the other disciples. As one (Peter) might expect, a special friend (the beloved one) might have knowledge about certain things not known to others. Peter (perhaps softly) asked the disciple loved by Jesus, "Who is going to betray Jesus?" The beloved raised himself from Jesus' to better hear the question and then, falling back against Jesus' chest, repeats Peter's question to Jesus in a more private way. Peter's use of an intermediary is acknowledging that the beloved disciple is a special intermediary. Peter could have asked the question directly but obviously thought he would get a better answer or quicker answer if he could enlist the assistance of the beloved disciple. Having heard the question, Christ says to his beloved in,

St. John 13: 26,

…he it is to whom I shall give a sop when I have dipped it…

The Scriptures do not tell us if the message was loud enough for Peter to hear, or did the beloved-disciple actually repeated the message to Peter? We know that Peter sought information through a source thought to be authoritative. That source was the disciple loved by Jesus. At the time of the crucifixion, we gain additional insight into the relationship of Jesus and his beloved disciple.

John 19: 26 - 27,

> When Jesus therefore saw his mother, and the disciple standing by, whom he loved, he saith unto his mother, Woman, behold thy son! Then saith he to the disciple, Behold thy mother! And from that hour that disciple took her unto his own home.

This act of caring for each other is somewhat unusual in ancient Israel, for women were usually taken care of by other women—not other men and certainly not by non-family males. I believe Jesus' desire for Mary to be cared for by the beloved disciple, as her son, suggested a relationship greater than simple friendship between the two men. During Jesus' post resurrection appearances, we read of Peter consoling the beloved disciple and not the other disciples. Was Peter aware of a special relationship between Jesus and the beloved disciple that was different and hence required more consolatory attention than the loss of just a regular friend?

After Christ's resurrection, he revealed himself to his disciples several times. One occasion was at the Sea of Tiberias (Sea of Galiliee). From the shore, Christ called to Peter and the other fishermen to recast their nets. They did and were rewarded with a large catch of fish. The men finally realized that it was Christ who was commanding them so they headed for shore to greet him. Peter, who fished naked, put on his clothes before swimming to shore. What follows is the "if you love me feed my sheep" scenario.

At some point, Peter noticed the beloved disciple and asks of Jesus,

> What shall this man do? Jesus saith unto him, If I will that he tarry till I come, what is that to thee? Follow thou me.

In the next verse we read the phrase,

> If I will that he tarry till I come, what is that to thee…

The beloved disciple is not to be spared death as we read in St. John 21: 23. In this scene, Jesus informed Peter that he had his own destiny. Jesus had a different destiny for the beloved one, which would have no bearing on Peter's mission. At the same time, I believe Peter was acknowledging again that there was a special relationship with this beloved disciple, and Jesus said, "So what." Jesus had clearly become responsible for the fate of the beloved-disciple and in so doing set this man apart from the other disciples who are to be in the care of Peter, as the head of the Church and its apostles. We can see that the disciple whom Jesus loved had a personal and intimate relationship with Jesus while Peter had an official relationship with Jesus and his Church.

What we have seen is a public display of affection between Jesus and his beloved disciple. We have no way of discerning what, if any, carnal relationship existed between the two. Such ignorance is no different than what, if any, carnal relationship existed between Peter and his wife or that of the parents of Jesus. We can only assume that in a close, loving, intimate relationship a sexual relationship is possible.

The unnamed disciple whom Jesus loved is not the only male that Jesus is said to have loved. The named person loved by Jesus was Lazarus. We read about Lazarus in St. John 11. Lazarus was ill and his sisters Mary and Martha send for Christ to come see Lazarus saying,

> Lord behold he whom thou lovest is sick.

Jesus waited two days before he set out for Lazarus' grave and once there, Christ wept. Fellow mourners said,

> …behold how he [Jesus] loved him.

There are some scholars who believe the disciple whom Jesus loved and Lazarus are the same person, but there is no conclusive proof for such suppositions.

To this point, we have examined portions of the scriptures that make reference to what we would call alternate lifestyles. The reading of these verses is made with a bias no worse than those of traditional interpreters who are married to Victorian and controlling western ideologies adopted and promoted by many in the fundamentalists' community to generate hate toward the gay community. These people of ill will selectively choose scripture to support their misbegotten battle because they fear truth. Most refuse to move beyond the concept of inerrancy, refuse to consider context, or self-debate of their beliefs.

In the next Chapter, we will examine the so called "sacred" union of one man and one woman debate.

CHAPTER XIV

Types of Marriage Mentioned in the Bible

Each individual's journey through life is unique. Some will make this journey alone, others in loving relationships—maybe in marriage or other forms of commitment. We need to ponder our own choices and try to understand the choices of others. Love has many shapes and colors and is not finite. It cannot be measured or defined in terms of sexual orientation.

THE QUAKER MEETING *IN AOTEAROA, NEW ZEALAND*
STATEMENT OF AFFIRMATION AND RECONCILIATION

The word marriage is so bantered about in today's parlance that it has assumed a rather homogenized meaning for most Americans. Many assume that marriage is and always has been a thoroughly wholesome thing. However, even in America, we occasionally hear of "honor killings" because a woman has "sinned" against her family's honor and has, among other things, become unfit for marriage. For these families, marriages are usually arranged and dowries are exchanged as a business deal as well as a social or cultural matter. The woman is her father's (brother's) property.

Doctor Barrie Wilson, Professor of Religion at York University, Toronto, Canada, lectures on marriage and its place in the Bible. He publicly challenges his students to find a truly healthy endorsement of marriage in the New Testament. If they can convince him of such, he offers a free trip to Florida in the winter. So far he has not had to pay for a single trip.

For most people, the word marriage conjures up what is described as the standard nuclear family described below. However, this has legally changed in New Jersey (Civil Unions) and marriage in Iowa, Massachusetts, Connecticut, New Hampshire, New York, Maryland, Washington, Washington, DC, and for a few couples in California where gay marriages were once legal.

We need to examine the types of marriage known in the western world but rarely considered when the religious-right speaks of marriage being "a sacred thing between one man and one woman.

- **Standard nuclear family:** Genesis 2: 24 describes a man leaving his birth family, joins (legally marries) a woman, consummates the marriage and lives as a couple. There are, however, differences between customs and laws of contemporary North Americans and ancient Israelites. In ancient Israel certain arrangements and beliefs existed.

- Interfaith marriages were theoretically forbidden. They rarely occurred.

- Children of interfaith marriages were considered illegitimate (many had no inheritance).

- Marriages were generally arranged. They did not result from a gradually evolving relationship during a period of courtship.

- The bride was expected to be a virgin. Brides presented as a virgin and later discovered not to be a virgin could be stoned to death (Deuteronomy 22: 13 - 21). There appears to have been no similar penalty for men who were not virgin but how would one know?).

- **Polygamous marriage:** A man takes a first wife. If finances allow, he could marry additional women. The new wives would join the man and his other wives in his established household. Polygamy had been practiced by members of the Church of Jesus Christ of Latter Day Saints (the Mormons). The practice has been suspended by the ruling body of the Church; however, polygamy is still practiced by some separate fundamentalist Mormons living primarily in the American Southwest. This group has one legal wife and several religiously married wives.

There are many references to polygamous marriages in the Bible:

- Lamech, in Genesis 4:19, became the first polygamist with two wives
- Subsequent men in polygamous relationships included:

- Esau with 3 wives
- Jacob: 2
- Ashur: 2
- Gideon: unknown numbers
- Elkanah: 2
- David: unknown numbers
- Solomon had 700 wives of royal birth
- Rehaboam: 3
- Abijah: 14
- Jehoram: multiple wives
- Joash: multiple wives
- Ahab: multiple wives
- Jeholachin: multiple wives
- Belshazzar: multiple wives
- Herod the Great: nine wives (From historical records)

It is doubtful that unions involving a woman and multiple men existed. It is unlikely such unions existed because of the distinctly inferior status given to women who were often considered man's property in Hebrew Scriptures and culture.

- **Levirate Marriage**: The name of this marriage is derived from the Latin word "levir," which means "brother-in-law." This involved a widow who had no son. She would be required to leave her home, marry her brother-in-law, live with him, and engage in sexual relations. This arrangement might have been acceptable to the widow. If not, the woman would have to endure what could have been essentially serial rape.

The first-born son of this new relationship was considered to have been sired by the dead husband. In Genesis 38: 6 - 10, Tamar's husband Er was killed by God for an unspecified sinful act. Er's brother, Onan, was required to marry Tamar according to Hebrew tradition. Not wanting to have a child who would not be considered his, Onan engaged in coitus interruptus (with drawl) resulting in his seed not being deposited intravaginally where it may have led to conception. Being displeased with Onan's behavior, God killed him. Ruth 4 reveals that a man would be required to enter into a levirate marriage not only with his late brother's widow, but with a widow to whom he was the closest living relative.

- A woman as property—a female slave: In Genesis 16, Sarah (half-sister and) wife to Abram (Abraham) were infertile. How- ever, Sarah owned Hagar, a purchased female slave. Hagar was Sarah's property and was presented to Abram as a substitute- wife so that Abram might have an heir. The "gifting" was done without Hagar's consent (and probably no concern for Hagar's wishes). Abram and the slave woman had sex causing Hagar to conceive and give birth to a son, Ishmael.

- **Wives and concubines:** A Hebrew man could legally and religiously keep numerous concubines **and** one or more wives. Concubines held an even lower status than wives. As implied in Genesis 21:10, a concubine could be dismissed at will. According to Smith's Bible Dictionary, a concubine would generally be either:

  [1]   a Hebrew girl bought…[from] her father;
  [2]   a Gentile captive taken in war;
  [3]   a foreign slave bought; or
  [4]   a Canaanite woman, bonded or free.

Whom do we know to have had concubines?

Abraham had 2
Gideon at least 1
Nahor: 1
Jacob: 1
Eliphaz: 1
Gideon: 1
Caleb: 2
Manassah: 1
Saul: 1
David: at least 10
Rehoboam: 60
Solomon: 300
An unidentified Levite: 1
Belshazzar: more than 1

- **Soldiers and a female prisoner of war:** Numbers 31: 1-18 described the ancient Israelite army killing every adult Midianite man in battle. Moses then ordered the killing of the captives, including some 32,000 male children. About 32,000 virgin women were spared; some of which were given to the priests as slaves. Most were taken by the Israeli soldiers as captives of war. Deuteronomy 21: 11 - 14 describes how each captive woman would shave her head, cut her nails and be left unbothered to mourn her losses for a month. Then the women would be required to submit to their owners, sexually, as a wife. In most cases, we can assume that these women would be raped. They became a breeder of new Israelites.

- A rapist and his female victim: Deuteronomy 22: 28 - 29 requires that a raped female virgin, who is not engaged to be married, must marry her attacker. Her feelings towards the rapist were of no concern to her community. A man could actually become married to a woman he desired by simply sexually attacking the woman and paying his father-in-law to be, 50 shekels of silver as a kind of payment for "damaged goods." One disadvantage of this approach was that he was married for life. He was not allowed to divorce a wife so garnered. Was this also a sacred marriage?

- **Male and female slaves:** Exodus 21: 4 reveals that a slave owner could assign one of his female slaves, as a wife, to one of his male slaves. These women were probably not consulted about the arrangement that would probably involve rape.

In the time of ancient Hebrew Scriptures, Israelite women could be sold into slavery by their fathers where they could remain a slave forever. When a slave changed ownership or left his owner as a free person, the "arranged marriage" between the slaves would usually be terminated. The wife could remain behind, or go to another owner, with any children she may have had. The "husband" could remain a slave, if he wished so for family reasons, but he was under no legal obligation to do so.

All of the above forms of marriage were seen as valid in the context in which they existed. Some may have been blessed by God. However, if God can bless a Levirate marriage with its potential for repeated episodes of rape and abuse, surely God could bless a marriage between two loving individuals in a same-sex-marriage. I am referring to God's will since the Bible makes no mention for or against a same-sex marriage. Although same-sex behavior was known during ancient times, we have little information from that era about their knowledge of same sex *orientation*. However, I believe that some ancient same-sex relationships did evolve into committed relationships whether or not the parties lived overtly as a "married" couple. I would like to point out that just because the Bible says nothing about males or females bonding or same-sex marriage is not a reason to deny same-sex relationships existed. The Bible says nothing about the internet, automobiles, television, I pods or psychological studies. Does that mean they should not or do not exist without the authority of the Bible?

Situated in Colorado is an influential fundamentalist Christian group known as the Focus on the Family Organization. They are vehemently opposed to gay marriage rights. The group argues that only men and women are made to fit emotionally, spiritually and physically. As such, a heterosexual couple's main function is to raise children. One could argue that if this is true, heterosexual families without children are not true families and such units should be abolished. This would include families where the absence of children is by choice or by nature. The argument is a bit fallacious in that we all know marriage is not required for people to have and to raise children. Some people actually accomplish this role quite successfully without "the benefit of clergy" or city hall.

Many modern families produce children out of love for each other and the joy they receive from having children in their lives. Marriage adds a measure of safety to the lives of children because it provides a framework for multiple types of training and role playing which can be helpful in the future lives of each child. We also know that most disturbed children are in trouble because of failures within their family unit as well as failed interpersonal relationships between the father, mother, and the children. This is not to say that a single parent cannot perform a successful job of raising children. In fact, they can as witnessed by many successful Americans in the work-a-day world of politics, science, and the professions as well as blue collar families.

The Focus on the Family Organization would like us to believe that without marriage, children will suffer, and suffer gravely, if they are raised in a homosexual family unit. What the organization fails to realize is that most gay individuals were once children within a heterosexual family structure. There is little discussion as to what, if anything, this type of highly praised family structure has done (or failed to do) to "make" children gay. Likewise, if the organization truly believed that being gay is a sin should the heterosexual family, who has a gay child, be punished legally or by their church(if the belong to one). Would the Focus organization consider straight parents producing a gay child worth of a special admonition for failing to raise a straight child or "blame" the child in question? Would be Focus group provide a rule book or *Guide to Raising a Straight Child*?

The Focus on The Family group believes that allowing gay marriage would lead to unsavory excesses. Incest and bestiality have been mentioned as a consequence to such "aberrant" marriages. However, this group lacks any authentic verification of such threats or happenings in any state or county where legalized gay marriages are legal. Perhaps fear prevents such a study because it would lead to nothing but a nullification of the group's argument against gay marriage and its alleged ills for society. The undermining of heterosexual marriage is said to be a goal of the gay community. One has only to look around to see that heterosexuals have undermined marriage by seeking and obtaining divorce with the help of mostly Christian legislative leaders on the local, State, and National levels of government. Heterosexuals seem to be doing a pretty good job of destroying marriage by themselves. They don't need the help or assistance of the gay community.

Another fundamentalist organization, the Christian Coalition has campaigned against gay rights, and through its legal arm, the American Center for Law and Justice, has filed many church-state lawsuits over their desire to deny the gay community equal civil rights such as marriage. This righteous appearing organization is led by Ralph E. Reed, Jr. who was involved with the convicted former G.O.P. lobbyist Jack Abramoff. Reed used his espoused conservative values to get conservative Christians to vote against allowing an Indian owned casino to be built. In exchange for his lobbying, millions of dollars passed hands.

According to *Time Magazine*, February 19, 2007, p. 56, Americans still love marriage. The article stated that 90 percent of women who are eligible to marry do so. This percentage has held true in since the mid 1880's. Research has revealed that 52 percent of American households are composed of married couples or a widow / widower. The author of the articles points out that

being a widow / widower does not equate to divorce. Americans now wait longer to get married than previous generations. The surprising finding of marriage research is that it is freedom that makes us the most happy and not the bonds of marriage. It is healthier and more satisfying to be single or divorced than trapped in an unhappy marriage.

Bella De Paulo, in her 2006 book, *Singled Out: How Singles are Stereotyped, Stigmatized and Ignored and Still Live Happily Ever After*, believed that marriage made us only a fraction of a point more satisfied than unmarried persons. The question is, "which comes first the marriage or happiness." Marriage may be the victory of hope over real life experience in our modern world.

Once, the Christian community thought it was acceptable to deny marriage rights to interracial couples. However, such discriminatory laws were finally overthrown toward the end of the 20th century. Roadblocks to changing in this law were those pundits who espoused their biased belief that `interracial marriage would forever undermine the status quo of the sacrament of all-white marriages. We know all too well, that nothing has happened to confirm that early and erroneously held belief.

Most, if not all, of the arguments made by the Focus on the Family group, are based on their religious biases. This is generally true of other religious organizations. These groups have the right to restrict what is believed within their own organization but such groups do **not** have the right to impose their religious biases on me. the gay community, or my country where civil rights equality is assured by the Constitution.

The Focus on the Family group believes that the Bible condemns all forms of homosexual behavior. Arguments previously presented in this book should help clear the air about the absurdity of such mistaken beliefs. The eyes of bigotry and bias can only be opened through objective attempts at the truth—traits in short supply within the fundamentalists' community.

Marriage is the institution from which gays and lesbians are distinctly excluded. The blockage of gays and lesbians from the estate of marriage constitutes a legal disenfranchisement that points to the social dishonor in which gay and lesbian love is held. By establishing the right to marry, gays and lesbians can gain public recognition of the moral equivalent of gay and heterosexual love.

RONALD E. RONALD E. LONG, PH.D., *AUTHOR*

The Focus on the Family group believes that (heterosexual) marriage is good for individuals and society. The gay community believes that same-sex marriage can be good for its members as well as for society. The movie, *Shall We Dance,* was released in 2004 and starred Susan Sarandon. She played the role of Beverly Clark. In the movie, Beverly discussed marriage and had this to say about the subject,

> …in a marriage, you're promising to care about everything. The good things, the bad things, the terrible things, the mundane things…all of it, all of the time, every day. You're saying, 'Your life will not go unnoticed because I will notice it. Your life will not go un-witnessed because I will be your witness.

There are some who would say that such sentiments are the essence of what marriage is all about. The fundamentalists would give such a statement a round of one-hand applause, primarily because gay-marriage seeks the same outcome. "What is missing," according to fundamentalists is "the blessings of God." I personally find the movie quote filled with the "love of God" even though the word God is never uttered. The essence of the statement is love and love for another person who is tantamount in one's life. This is what God wants us to do, love one another in all possible ways and in so doing, mirror his love for all of us.

Ernest T. Thompson, in *Presbyterians in the South*, p. 218, reports there was a time (1867) when Christian leaders such as Robert Lewis Dabney said, "If blacks were allowed to vote, it would be the end of civilization itself." In1838, Charles Hodge, a leading theologian, was reported by Rondald W. Hogeland[110] to have said,

> If women were not kept subordinate to men, we would soon have a country from which all order and all virtue would speedily be banished.

These arguments were echoed well into the 20th century until our legal system, with the support of many citizens and church groups, changed the rules to overturn this injustice and inequality of ideology. Having done so, the world has not come to an end. This precedent can and should be repeated in the 21st century by allowing members of the gay community access to the same set of rights and freedom as the so-called straight community. Gay people want to marry whom they choose, not a person some disassociated religious leader would have them marry.

The gay community wants for themselves, and their children, access to the same rights enjoyed by married heterosexuals. The Government Accounting Office, in a letter to a Congressional Committee on January 31, 1997, reported that there were 1,049 federal rights and approximately 400 state's rights for straight, married couples not available to gay couples and their children. This is a measure of gross inequality in our system of individual rights whose cornerstone, long ago laid by religious fundamentalists, needs to be extracted so the walls of religious bigotry and biases may crumble

---

110   Charles Hodge, *The Association of Gentlemen and Ornamental Womanhood*, p. 248,

and the civil rights of the gay community may rise from the ashes and dust of civil inequality.

* * *

We near the end of a journey of understanding about the Biblical "bullets" used in fundamentalists' battle against the gay community. I hope it is clear that there is room for alternate interpretations of scripture, interpretations other than those dictated by the conservative religious-right. A liberal Christian interpretation of the Bible is no less valuable than that of our conservative oppressors.

Ten Ways in Which Fundamentalists Say Gay Marriage Will Ruin Society

Being gay is **not** natural. Real Americans always reject unnatural things like eyeglasses, polyester clothing, hybrid fruits, antibiotics, and air conditioning.

Gay marriage will encourage (young) people to be gay, in the same way that hanging around tall people will make you tall.

Legalizing gay marriage will open the door to all kinds of crazy behavior. People may wish to marry their pets because a dog has legal standing and can sign a marriage contract.

Straight marriage has been around a long time and hasn't changed at all; women are **still property**, blacks still can't **marry whites**, and divorce is **still illegal**.

Straight marriage will be less meaningful if gay marriages were allowed; the sanctity of Britany Spears' 55-hour just-for-fun marriage would be destroyed.

Straight marriages are valid because they produce children. Gay couples, infertile couples and old people shouldn't be allowed to marry because our orphanages aren't full yet, and the world needs more children.

Obviously gay parents will raise gay children, since straight parents only raise straight children.

Gay marriage is not supported by religion. In a theocracy like ours, the values of one religion are imposed on the entire country. That's why we have only **one** religion in America.

Children can never succeed in life without a male and a female role model at home. That's why we as a society expressly forbid single parents to raise children.

Gay marriage will change the foundation of society; we could **never** adapt to new social norms. Just like we haven't adapted to cars, the service-sector economy, or longer lifespans.

Epilog ????????

"City air makes free," was a favorite medieval quote used by urban studies pioneer, Jane Jacobs. The quote was applicable to hundreds of thousands of young gay men and women who "fled the farm" for the anonymity of the big city in the latter part of the 20th century. There, gay people found an underground community of kindred souls. A common meeting place was the gay bar, often in remote sections of the city and behind unmarked doors to avoid harassment by homophobes, police seeking "hush money" and black- mailers. Once inside, the customer could feel relatively safe both physically and psychologically. Everyone there was a kindred spirit and each person could be who they were, warts and all. It was a safe place, a community resource center, a place where politics and health matters were frequent topics of discussion, a sex education center, a newcomers welcome center, a center for fundraisers, a theater for budding comics and aging drag queens, a place to laugh and to cry, an endless source of cheap beer, a dating scene…and for many men and women it was another home.

The gay bar and gay restaurant has slowly become a thing of the past. The gay mystique is lost. Insider knowledge is now open knowledge; everyone now knows the meaning of the word gay, drag queen, Mary, friend of Dorothy, member of the royal family, etc., and it seems like gay culture is disappearing. There are some members of the gay community who lament this fact; yet, others applaud the trend for it means that the gay community is gaining acceptance in the heterosexual world. The so called gay "third places" of meeting have become obsolete because they are no longer as socially necessary as 30 or 40 years ago. The *Boston Globe* felt it necessary to chronicle these changes in a recent article, "Last Call, Why the Gay Bars of Boston are Disappearing, and What It Says About the Future of the City."[111] The demise of the gay bar is

---

attributed to economic pressures such as high inner city rents, demands for new office spaces and the internet where meeting new friends and dating, in general, is so much easier and convenient than going downtown. [Having] fewer gay bars has negatively impacted such things as the gay pride parades conducted all over the county. "In these parades were outrageous parade floats, featuring drag queens and go-go boys, sponsored by local gay bars. Now those delightfully pointless displays are outnumbered by contingents of waving employees from banks and utility companies in matching T-shirts…the parade has become a lot less fun for gay and straight spectators alike."

While the gay community maybe losing its 20th century culture, the gay community has discovered that they can hold onto their Christian religion as churches of all flavors have awakened to God's command to love one another.

Too bad there are believers who cling to hate for God's gay community because of fundamentalist's refusal to consider that they might be wrong about being "right."

Time

Ecclesiastes 3: 1 - 8

To everything there is a season, and a time to every purpose under the heaven:

A time to be born, and a time to die; a time to plant, and a time to pluck up *that which is* planted;

A time to kill, and a time to heal; a time to break down, and a time to build up;

A time to weep, and a time to laugh; a time to mourn, and a time to dance;

A time to cast away stones, and a time to gather stones together; a time to embrace, and a time to refrain from embracing;

A time to get, and a time to lose; a time to keep, and a time to cast away;

A time to rend, and a time to sew; a time to keep silence, and a time to speak;

A time to love, and a time to hate; a time of war, and a time of peace.

* * *

"To everything there is a season…" Our time, the gay communities' time, has come!

A Manifesto! The Time Has Come!

Bishop John Shelby Spong[112]

"*I* have made a decision. I will no longer debate the issue of homo- sexuality in the church with anyone. I will no longer engage the biblical ignorance that emanates from so many right-wing Christians about how the Bible condemns homosexuality, as if that point of view still has any credibility. I will no longer discuss with them or listen to them tell me how homosexuality is "an abomination to God," about how homosexuality is a "chosen lifestyle," or about how through prayer and "spiritual counseling" homosexual persons can be "cured." Those arguments are no longer worthy of my time or energy. I will no longer dignify them by listening to the thoughts of those who advocate "reparative therapy," as if homosexual persons are somehow broken and need to be repaired. I will no longer talk to those who believe that the unity of the church can or should be achieved by rejecting the presence of, or at least at the expense of, gay and lesbian people. I will no longer take the time to refute the unlearned and document-able claims of certain world religious leaders who call homosexuality "deviant." I will no longer listen to that pious sentimentality that certain Christian leaders continue to employ, which suggests some version of that strange and overtly dishonest phrase that "we love the sinner but hate the sin."

That statement is, I have concluded, nothing more than a self-serving *lie* designed to cover the fact that these people hate homosexual persons and fear homosexuality itself, but somehow know that hatred is incompatible with the Christ they claim to profess, so they adopt this face-saving and absolutely false statement. I will no longer temper my understanding of truth in order to pretend that I have even a tiny smidgen of respect for the appalling negativity that continues to emanate from religious circles where the church has for centuries conveniently perfumed its ongoing prejudices against blacks, Jews, women, and homosexual persons with what it assume is "high-sounding, pious rhetoric." The day for that mentality has quite simply come to an end for me. I will

112   Used by permission of Waterfront Media, Bishop Spong's online publisher.

personally neither tolerate it nor listen to it any longer. The world has moved on, leaving these elements of the Christian Church that cannot adjust to new knowledge or a new consciousness lost in a sea of their own irrelevance. They no longer talk to anyone but themselves.

I will no longer seek to slow down the witness to inclusiveness by pretending that there is some middle ground between prejudice and oppression. There isn't. Justice postponed is justice denied. That can be a resting place no longer for anyone. An old civil rights song proclaimed that the only choice awaiting those who cannot adjust to a new understanding was to "Roll on over or we'll roll on over you!" Time waits for no one. I will particularly ignore those members of my own Episcopal Church who seek to break away from this body to form a "new church," claiming that this new and bigoted instrument alone now represents the Anglican Communion. Such a new ecclesiastical body is designed to allow these pathetic human beings, who are so deeply locked into a world that no longer exists, to form a community in which they can continue to hate gay people, distort gay people with their hopeless rhetoric and to be part of a religious fellowship in which they can continue to feel justified in their homo- phobic prejudices for the rest of their tortured lives. Church unity can never be a virtue that is preserved by allowing injustice, oppression and psychological tyranny to go unchallenged. In my personal life, I will no longer listen to televised debates conducted by "fair-minded" channels that seek to give "both sides" of this issue "equal time."

I am aware that these stations no longer give equal time to the advocates of treating women as if they are the property of men or to the advocates of reinstating either segregation or slavery, despite the fact that when these evil institutions were coming to an end the Bible was still being quoted frequently on each of these subjects. It is time for the media to announce that there are no longer two sides to the issue of full humanity for gay and lesbian people. There is no way that justice for homosexual people can be compromised any longer. I will no longer act as if the Papal office is to be respected if the present occupant of that office is either not willing or not able to inform and educate himself on public issues on which he dares to speak with embarrassing ineptitude. I will no longer be respectful of the leadership of the Archbishop of Canterbury, who seems to believe that rude behavior, intolerance and even killing prejudice is somehow acceptable, so long as it comes from third-world religious leaders, who more than anything else reveal in themselves the price that colonial oppression has required of the minds and hearts of so many of our world's population. I see no way for ignorance and truth to be placed side by side, nor do I believe that evil is somehow less evil if the Bible is quoted to justify it. I will dismiss as unworthy of any more of my attention the wild, false and uninformed opinions of such would-be religious leaders as Pat Robertson, James Dobson, Jerry Falwell, Jimmy Swaggart, Albert Mohler, and Robert Duncan. My country and my church have both already spent too much time, energy and money trying to accommodate these backward points of view when they are no longer even tolerable.

I make these statements because it is time to move on. The battle is over. The victory has been won. There is no reasonable doubt as to what the final outcome of this struggle will be. Homosexual people will be accepted as equal, full human beings, who have a legitimate claim on every right that both church and society have to offer any of us. Homosexual marriages will become legal, recognized by the state and pronounced holy by the church. "Don't ask, don't tell" will be dis- mantled as the policy of our armed forces. We will and we must learn that equality of citizenship is not something that should ever be submitted to a referendum. Equality under and before the law is a solemn promise conveyed to all our citizens in the Constitution itself. Can any of us imagine having a public referendum on whether slavery should continue, whether seg- regation should be dismantled, whether voting privileges should be offered to women? The time has come for politicians to stop hiding behind unjust laws that they them- selves helped to enact, and to abandon that convenient shield of demanding a vote on the rights of full citizenship because they do not understand the difference between a constitutional democracy, which this nation has, and a "mobocracy," which this nation rejected when it adopted its constitution. We do not put the civil rights of a minority to the vote of a plebiscite. I will also no longer act as if I need a majority vote of some ecclesiastical body in order to bless, ordain, recognize and celebrate the lives and gifts of gay and lesbian people in the life of the church. No one should ever again be forced to submit the privilege of citizenship in this nation or membership in the Christian Church to the will of a majority vote.

The battle in both our culture and our church to rid our souls of this dying prejudice is finished. A new consciousness has arisen. A decision has quite clearly been made. Inequality for gay and lesbian people is no longer a debatable issue in either church or state. Therefore, I will from this moment on refuse to dignify the continued public expression of ignorant prejudice by engaging it. I do not tolerate racism or sexism any longer. From this moment on, I will no longer tolerate our culture's various forms of homophobia. I do not care who articulates these attitudes or who tries to make them sound holy with religious jargon.

I have been part of this debate for years, but things do get settled and this issue is now settled for me. I do not debate any longer with members of the "Flat Earth Society" either. I do not debate with people who think we should treat epilepsy by casting demons out of the epileptic person; I do not waste time engaging those medi- cal opinions that suggest that bleeding the patient might release the infection. I do not converse with people who think that Hurricane Katrina hit New Orleans as punish- ment for the sin of being the birthplace of Ellen DeGeneres or that the terrorists hit the United States on 9/11 because we tolerated homosexual people, abortions, feminism or the American Civil Liberties Union. I am tired of being embarrassed by so much of my church's participation in causes that are quite un- worthy of the Christ I serve or the God whose mystery and wonder I appreciate more each day. Indeed I feel the Christian Church should not only apologize, but do public penance for the way we have treated people of color, women, adherents of other religions and those we designated heretics, as well as gay and lesbian people.

Life moves on. As the poet James Russell Lowell once put it, more than a century ago, "New occasions teach new duties, time makes ancient good uncouth."

I am ready now to claim the victory. I will from now on assume it and live into it. I am unwilling to argue about it or to discuss it as if there are two equally valid, competing positions any longer. The day for that mentality has simply gone forever.

This is my manifesto and my creed. I proclaim it today. I invite others to join me in this public declaration. I believe that such a public outpouring will help cleanse both the church and this nation of its own distorting past. It will restore integrity and honor to both church and state. It will signal that a new day has dawned and we are ready not just to embrace it, but also to rejoice in it and to celebrate it.

Appendix—Eunuchs

Biblical References to Eunuchs in the Old and New Testament of the Bible in Order of Appearance.

Genesis 37: 36, 39:1
Genesis 41: 8
1 Kings 18:3
1 Kings 22:9
2 Kings 9:38
2 Kings 20: 28
2 Kings 18:17
Ezra 4:5 & 9:91
Nehemiah 1:1 & 7:5
Ester 1:10 & 11, 13& 14
Ester 2:3, 14, 21-23
Ester 4: 4, 5-11
Ester 6: 4
Ester 7:9
Ester 9:3
Jeremiah 36: 11-20
Jeremiah 38: 7-13
Jeremiah 41: 16
Jeremiah 53: 25
Daniel 1:1-21
Daniel 2: 1-11
Daniel 2: 12 (wise men=eunuchs)
Daniel 2: 12-25, 46-49
Matthew 2: 1-8
Matthew 19:10-12
Acts 8:9-24, 26-40

Bibliography

Adorno, et. al., *The Authoritarian Personality*, New York, Harper and Brothers, 1950

Ammerman, Nancy T., "North American Protestant Fundamentalism" in the book *Fundamentalisms Observed*, ed., Martin E Marty and R Scott Appleby, Chicago, University of Chicago Press, 1991

Aristotle, *Generation of Animals*, 727B:34—729A:33, Translated by A.L.Peck, Harvard University Press, 1943

Armstrong, Karen, *A History of God: the Four Thousand Year Quest in Judaism, Christianity and Islam*, Gramercy, London and New York 2004

Armstrong, Karen, *The Battle for God: A History of Fundamentalism*, Ballantine Books, Random House Publishing Group, New York, 2000

Arterburn, Stephen, Felton, Jack, *Toxic Faith: Experiencing Healing from Painful Spiritual Abuse,* Waterbrook Press, Colorado Springs, CO, 1991

Bailey, D. Sherman., *Homosexuality and the Western Christian Tradition*, 1995

Bailey, J. Michael, The Man Who Would be Queen, The Science of Gender Bending and Transexualism, Joseph Henry Press, Wash. DC, 2003

Baltsan, Hayim, *Webster's New World Hebrew Dictionary*, Wiley Publishing, Chicago, Ill, 1992

Bamberger, Bernard, *"Leviticus," in the Torah: A Modern Commentary*, (ed.) W. G. Plant, Urj Press, 1981

Barclay, William, *The Daily Study Bible: The Gospel of Luke; The Gospel of Mark,* The Westminster Press, Philadelphia, 1996

Beard, Mary, John North, , Simon Pierce, *Religions of Rome*, Volume I, Cambridge University Press, Cambridge, England, 1999

Blankenhorn, David, *The Future of Marriage,* Encounter Books, New York City, 2007

Bond, Alan, Hopsell, Mark, *A Sumerian Observation of the Köfels' Impact Event,* Alcuin Academics Publishing, Great Britian, 2008

Booth, Leo, *When God Becomes a Drug: Breaking the Chains of Religion-addiction and Abuse,* Tarcher/Putnam, New York, 1991

Booth, Leo, *The God Game: It's Your Move*, SCP Limited, Long Beach, CA, 1998

Boswell, John. *Christianity, Social Tolerance, and Homosexuality: Gay People in Western Europe From the Beginning of the Christian Era to the Fourteenth Century.* Chicago: University of Chicago Press, 1999.

Bottero, J., Petschow, H., "Homosexuality," in *Reallexikon der Assyriologie*, ed by Erich Ebeling et al., Gruyter, Berlin 1928—2000

Bradshaw, John, *Healing the Shame that Binds You*, Dearfield Beach, Health Communications Inc., 1988

Brand, Chad, Draper, Charles, England, Archie, *Holman Illustrated Bible Dictionary*, Holman Reference, Nashville, Tennessee, 2003

Brentlinger, Rick, *Gay Christian 101*, Salient Press, Pace, Florida, 2007

Brooks, Pat, *The Return of the Puritans*, 2nd. Ed., New Puritan Library, Springfield, Pa., Dist. Whitaker House, 1976

Capps, Donald, *The Childs Song: The Religious Abuse of Children*, Westminster John Knox Press, Louisville, KY, 1995

Clement of Alexander, Paedagogus, III 4.25 in **Wood, Simon P.**, *Christ the Educator* Fathers of the Church series, Catholic University of America Press, New York, 1953

Countryman, Louis William. *Gifted by Otherness: Gay and Lesbians in the Christian Church.* Morehouse Publishing, 2001.

Crossan, John Dominic, *Four Other Gospels*, Polebridge, Sonoma, CA, 1992, p. 73-75, and 82-83).

DePaulo, Bella, *Singled Out: How Singles are Stereotyped, Stigmatized, and Ignored and Still Live Happily Ever After*, St. Martin's Press, New York City, 2006

Dobson, James, C., *Bringing Up Boys*, Tyndale House Publishers, Wheaton, Ill, 2001

Dods, Marcus; Watson, Robert Alexander; Farrar, Frederich William: *An Exposition of the Bible*, vol. 1, S.S. Scranton Co., Hartford, Conn., 1903

Duberman, Martin, *About Time, Exploring the Gay Past*, Penguin Books USA, Inc., New York City, 1991

Dynes, Wayne R., Donaldson, Stephen, *Homosexuality in the Ancient World*, Garland, New York, 1992

Ehrman, Bart D., *The Lost Gospel of Judas Iscariot*, Oxford University Press, New York, 2006

Eidsmore, John, *God and Caesar*, Crossway Books, Westchester, Ill., 1984

Ellens, J. Harold, *Sex in the Bible*, Prager Publishers, Westport, Conn., 2006

Erzen, Tanya, *Straight To Jesus: Sexual and Christian Conversions in the ex-Gay Movement*, University of California Press, Berkley and Los Angeles, CA, 2006

Fee, Gordon D., *The First Epistle To The Corinthians*, Erdmans, Grand Rapids, 1991

Fone, Byrne, R. S., *Homophobia*, Picador, NYC, 2001

Fox, Robin, *Kinship and Marriage: An Anthropological Perspective*, Penguin Books, Baltimore, 1967

Fuller, Robert, *The Watchtower Examiner:* "Naming the Antichrist," July, 1920

Furnish, Victor P., *The Bible and Homosexuality, in Homosexuality in the Church*, J.S. Siker, ed., Westminster John Knox Press, Louisville, Ky, 1994

Gagnon, Robert AJ, *The Bible and Homosexual Practice*, Abingdon, Nashville, 2001

Garner, Bryan, *A Dictionary of Modern American Usage*, Oxford University Press, 1998

Goss, Robert E and Mona West, ed., *Take Back the Word*. Pilgrim Press, 2000

Grahn, Judy, *Another Mother Tongue*, Boston, Beacon Press, 1984.

Greenberg, D.F., *The Construction of Homosexuality*, University of Chicago Press, 1988

Grossman, Cathy Lynn, "Young Adults Aren't Sticking With Church." *USA Today*, Tuesday, 6D, August 7, 2007

Hadley, Judith M., *The Cult of Asherah in Ancient Israel and Judah*, Cambridge University Press, 2000.

Harding, Susan, "Contesting Rhetorics in the PTL Scandal," in Silberstein (ed.) *Jewish Fundamentalism in Comparative Perspective*, New York, 1993

Helminiak, Daniel A. *What the Bible Really Says About Homosexuality*. San Francisco: Alamo Square Press, 2000.

Herdt, G., (ed.), *Third Sex, Third Gender: Beyond Sexual Dimorphism in Culture and History*, Zone Books, New York City, 1996

Heyward, Carter. *Touching Our Strength: The Erotic as Power and the Love of God.* Harper Collins, 1989.

Hogeland, Ronald W., "Charles Hodge, the Association of Gentlemen and Ornamental Womanhood: 1825-1855" *Journal of Presbyterian History* 53, No.3, Fall 1975

Holden, Constance, *Science* 2 November 2001: Vol. 294. no. 5544, pp. 980—982

Horner, Tom, Jonathan Loved David*: Homosexuality in Biblical Times*, Philadelphia, Westminster Press, 1978.

Iigaray, Luce, *Marine Lover of Friedrich Nietzsche*, Columbia University Press, New York, 1991

Jackson, Charles, *Faith of Our Fathers: A Popular Study of the Nicene Cree*d, Canon Press, Moscow, Idaho, 2007

Javors, Irene, and Reimann, Renate, "Building Common Ground: Strategies for Grassroots Organizing on Same-Sex Marriage," in *Queer Families, Queer Politics*, ed. Bernstein and Reimann, New York University Press, New York City, 2001

Johnston, S. (ed) *Religions of the Ancient World: A Guide,* Harvard Univ. Press., 2004

Jordan, Mark D., *The Invention of Sodomy in Christian Theology*, University of Chicago Press, Chicago, Il, 1997

Khouri, Ramj G., *Antiquities of the Jordan Rift Valley*, Solipsist Press, 1988

LaHaye, Tim, *The Battle for the Family*, F.H. Revell Co., Old Tappan, NJ, 1982

LaHaye, Tim and Beverly, *The Act of Marriage*, Zondervan Publishing House, Grand Rapids, Mich., 1998

Leach, E. R., "Polyandry, Inheritance and the Definition of Marriage," in *Rethinking Anthropology*, Athlone Press, London, 1961

Leuba, James H., *The Belief in God and Immorality*, Boston, Sherman, French and Company, 1916

Lindsley, Hal, *The 1980s: The Countdown to Armageddon*, Bantam Books, New York, 1980

Long, Ronald E., *Men, Homosexuality, and the Gods: An Exploration into the Religious Significance of Male Homosexuality in World Perspective*, Harrington Park Press, New York, 2004

Lutzer, Erwin W., *The Truth About Same-Sex Marriage*, Moody Publishers, Chicago, 2004

Machen, J. Gresham, *Christianity and Liberalism*, Wm. B. Eerdman Pub. Co. Grand Rapids, Mich., 1923

Marius, Richard, *Martin Luther, the Christian Between God and Death*, Belknap Press, Cambridge, Mass., and London, 2000

Marsden, George M., *Fundamentalism in American Culture*, Oxford University Press, 1981.

Martens, Elmer A., *Theological Wordbook of the Old Testament*, Vol. 1, Moody Press, Chicago, 1980

McGrath, Alister, *A Life of John Calvin: A study in the Shaping of Western Culture*, Blackwell Publishing Inc., Oxford and New York, 1988

Meyers, Robin, *Why the Religious-right is Wrong*, Jossey-Bass (A Wiley Imprint), San Francisco, 2006

Milgrom, Jacob, *The Anchor Bible*, Leviticus 17-22, Vol. 3A, Doubleday, 2000

Minor, Robert N., *When Religion Becomes an Addiction*, Humanity Works Publishing, St. Louis, MO, 2007

Moyer, Richard D., *Gays/Justice: A study of Ethics*, Society, and law, Columbia University Press, New York, 1988

Moyers, Bill, *Armageddon & the Environment*, CommonDreams.org, December 6, 2004

North, Douglass C., "Economic Performance Through Time," *American Economic Review*, 84, no. 3, June 1994

Norton, Rick, "Queen James and His Courtiers," *The Great Queens of History*, <http://www.infopt.demon.co.uk/james.html>

Otto, Ekart, *Das Eherecht im mittelassyrischen Kodex und im Deuterononium*, Ed. Dietrich and Loretz, 1993

Penzer NM. *The Harem*: Harrap, London: 1936

Pritchard, James B., ed, *Ancient Near Eastern Texts*, (Trans. S. N. Kramer), Princeton University Press, Princeton, NJ, 1950

Pro-Family Forum, *Is Humanism Molesting Your Child*, Ft. Worth, Texas, 1983

Radcliffe-Brown, A. R., *Structure and Function in Primitive* Society, Free Press, Glencoe, Ill, 1952

Raphael, Simcha Paul, *Jewish Views of the Afterlife,* Jason Aronson, Inc., Northvale, NJ, 1994

Remondino, P.C., "History of Circumcision," the *Physician's and Student's Ready Reference Series*, F.A. Davis Publishers, Philadelphia and London, 1891

Richards, Jeffrey, *Damnation Sex, Dissidence and: Minority Groups in the Middle Ages,* New York: Routledge, 1994

Ringrose, K., *The Perfect Servant: Eunuchs and the Social Construction of Gender In Byzantium,* Univ. of Chicago Press, Chicago, 2003

Robertson, Pat, *America's Date with Destiny*, Nelson, Nashville, 1986

Roth, Martha T., *Law Collections from Mesopotamia and Asia Minor*, Scholars Press, Atlanta, 1997

St. Augustine, *De Nuptiis et Concupiscentia*, 1.6.

St. Augustine of Hippo, *The Confessions of St. Augustine* (Signet Classics), Penguin Publishing Co., New York City, 1963

Schaef, Anne Wilson, Fassel, Diane, *The Addictive Organization*, Harper and Row, San Francisco, 1980

Scroggs, Robin, *The New Testament and Homosexuality*, sixth printing, Fortress, Philadelphia 1989

Segal, Jerome M., "Teaching the Bible in Public Schools: Reading the Bible as Literature," *Philosophy and Public Policy Quarterly*, Vol. 27, No.3/4 (summer / fall) 2007

Shipley, Maynard, *War on Modern Science*, A.A. Knopf, New York and London 1927

Sider, Ronald J., *The Scandal of the Evangelical Conscience*, Baker Publishing, Grand Rapids, Michigan, 2005

Smith, Morton, *The Secret Gospel: The Discovery and Interpretation of the Secret Gospel According to Mark*, Harper and Row, New York, 1973

Smith, Morton, *Clement of Alexandria and a Secret Gospel of Mark*, p. 152-153, University Press, Cambridge, MA, Harvard, 1973

Spong, John Shelby, *Rescuing the Bible from Fundamentalism*, Harper, San Francisco, 1992

Spong, John Shelby, *Living in Sin: A Bishop Rethinks Human Sexuality*, Harper, San Francisco, 1990

Stol, Marten, "Private Life in Ancient Mesopotamia," in *Civilization of the Ancient Near East*, ed, Jack M. Sasson, Hendrickson Publishers, Peabody, Mass., 2000

Stuart, Elizabeth, *Just Good Friends*, Mowbray, a Cassell Imprint, London/New York, 1995

Thatcher, Adrian, *Liberating Sex*, SPCK Publishing, London, 1993

Thompson, Ernest T., *Presbyterians in the South*,vol.2, 1861-1890, John Knox Press, Richmond, 1973

Twerski, Abraham J., *Addictive Thinking: Understanding Self Deception*, 2nd. ed., Center City, Hazeldn, 1997,

Varnell, Paul, "Gay Marriage Ready Set…," *Windy City Times*, Chicago, March 12, 1998

Wilson, Nancy, *Our Tribe: Queer Folks, God, Jesus and the Bible*, Harper, San Francisco. 1995

Ulpian, "Digest," Book XXIII 3.39.1, in **Scott, Samuel Parson,** *The Civil Law*, AMS Press New York, 1973

Van Den Berghe, *Human Family Systems: An evolutionary View*, Waveland Press, Prospect Heights, Ill., 1979

Watts, James Washington, *Ritual and Rhetoric in Leviticus: from sacrifice to scripture*, Cambridge University Press, NYC, 2007

Weinstein, Netta; Ryan, William S.; DeHaan, Cody R.; Przybylski, Andrew K.; Legate, Nicole; Ryan, Richard M., "Parental autonomy support and discrepancies between implicit and explicit sexual identities: Dynamics of self-acceptance and defense." 2012 Volume 102, Issue 4 (Apr), *p 815-832 Journal of Personality and Social Psychology,*

West, Mona, "Ruth" in *The Queer Bible Commentary*, Ed. Guest, Deryn; Goss, Robert; West, Mona; Bohache, Thomas; SCM Press, London, 2006

Wolfson, Evan, "Crossing the Threshold: Equal Marriage Rights for Lesbians and Gay Men and the Intra-Community Critique," *Review of Law and Social Change* 21, no 3, 1994

Internet sites of interest

http://www.religioustolerance.org
http://www.dictionary.com/
http://freedom2201.tripod.com
http://www.studylight.org/dic/ebd/view.cgi?number=T1376
http://www.watchtower.org
http://www.studylight.org
http://www.christiananswers.net
http://www.pamshouseblend.com
http://www.nytimes.com/2007/03/27/us/27churches.html?ex=1176091200&en=36f28
    a3c4e…
http://www.headcoverings-by-devorah.com http://www.family.org/cforum/research
http://www.secularhumanism.org
http://www.earlychristianwritings.com
http://www.qrd.org/qrd/www/media/print/richard.mohr/
http://foru.ms/t5514362-clement-of-alexander-did-not-condemn-loving-homosexual-
    monogamous-relationships.html&page=3
http://www.infopt.demon.co.uk/jamesi.htm   (a biography of the gay King James)
http://www.cs.cmu.edu/afs/cs/user/scotts/ftp/wpaf2mc/serge.html   The Passion of SS.
    Serge and Bacchus
http://www.perseus.tufts.edu/cgi-bin/lexindex?entry=malako/s   Meaning of Malakoi
http://www.rictornorton.co.uk/homopho1.htm
http://www.well.com/user/aquarius/contents.htm
http://www.JohnShelbySpong.com

Author Information

*D*octor Barham did his undergraduate studies at East Tennessee State University and then earned an M.D. degree from the College of Medicine, University of Tennessee. After practicing medicine for a number of years, he earned a master's degree (MSHA) in health services administration from St. Francis University and worked as a hospital administrator. Late in life, he earned a master's degree (MMH) in medical humanities, majoring in bioethics, at Drew University where he also studied for a doctor of letters degree (D.Lit.) in ethics.

Dr. Barham has also written, *Saving the World One Dog at a Time*. He is currently writing another collection of short stories about dogs called *Puppy Love*. It will be published in late 2013.

Doctor Barham is interested in knowing how this book has been received by readers. If the reader purchased either the paper or electronic version of this book, please share your thoughts about the book by writing a book review on the websites of either: Amazon, Barnes and Noble or Goodreads. Those who do will be eligible for a drawing for a free copy of his next book, *Puppy Love,* to be released in late 2013. Thank you.

Made in the USA
Charleston, SC
12 August 2013